Providence
LOST

PAUL LAY is Editor of *History Today*.
He is a fellow of the Royal Historical Society
and a trustee of the Cromwell Museum, Huntingdon.

Providence LOST

THE RISE & FALL *of* CROMWELL'S PROTECTORATE

PAUL LAY

HEAD *of* ZEUS

An Apollo Book

This is an Apollo Book, first published in the UK in 2020
by Head of Zeus Ltd

9 7 5 3 4 6 8

A catalogue record for this book is available from
the British Library.

ISBN (HB): 9781781852569
ISBN (E): 9781781852576

Typeset by Adrian McLaughlin

Printed and bound in Great Britain by
CPI Group (UK) Ltd, Croydon CR0 4YY

Head of Zeus Ltd
First Floor East
5–8 Hardwick Street
London EC1R 4RG

WWW.HEADOFZEUS.COM

To the two Barrys: Barry Dutton and Barry Coward

Contents

Prologue

A Puritan Peak

PROVIDENCE ISLAND, a volcanic dot 'lying in the heart of the Indies and the mouth of the Spaniards',[1] was, for little more than a decade, the furthest outpost of English puritanism. The settlement, 110 miles off what is now the Caribbean coast of Nicaragua, was founded on Christmas Eve 1629, when Philip Bell, former governor of the Somers Isles – modern Bermuda – disembarked from his ship, the *Robert*, to lead an advance party in prayer on its shores. This 'utterly beautiful' eight square miles of light breezes, palm trees, dense scrub and sheltered coves, is dominated by the volcanic 'Peak', from where steep valleys descend, peppered with boulders of hardened lava, a result of the island's explosive surge to the surface more than 10 million years ago.

Providence was settled just as the cause of puritanism in England suffered a desperate blow in the form of the Personal Rule of Charles I.* The Stuart king had ruled without recourse to Parliament, by royal prerogative, his head turned by the innovations of continental absolutism, an idea of immense and obvious attraction to monarchs, which would deliver its

---

* Traditionally, Whig historians called this period the 'Eleven Years' Tyranny'; the concept is outlined in the late Kevin Sharpe's massive study, *The Personal Rule of Charles I* (Yale, 1992).

apotheosis in the shape of the French Sun King, Louis XIV. Peace between England and Spain, the papacy's supreme defender, was soon to break out after years of conflict and tension, much to the chagrin of a small group of Puritan grandees, for whom the Catholic Habsburg foe – hegemonic 'Black' Spain – was the Antichrist. They would need to look beyond Albion's spiritually barren land to advance their cause.

Known to the Spanish as Catalina, Providence Island was named by Bell for that abiding concept of English Protestantism, attracting the attention of an elite group raised on the high Elizabethan buccaneering tales of Drake, Hawkins and Ralegh. Like their violently illustrious predecessors, they took their militant Protestantism to the Spanish New World – or at least encouraged others to do so. Consisting of a noble, wealthy Puritan clique of twenty 'adventurers', they met at Brooke House in the City of London, home of the wealthiest – and youngest – backer of the scheme, Robert Greville, Lord Brooke, then barely in his twenties, who had been the adopted successor of Fulke Greville, the 1st Lord. There they established the Providence Island Company in the summer of 1630 with a working capital just shy of £4,000. Some of the grandees, including Robert Rich, 2nd Earl of Warwick, who employed Bell, had already been involved in the settlement of Virginia and the Somers Isles. His father, the 1st Earl, had been a guarantor of the last expedition of Walter Ralegh, the hero of Elizabethan imperial Protestantism, who had fallen fatally foul of James, the first of the Stuart monarchs of England and father of Charles, in 1618. The battle lines that would contest the coming Civil War were slowly being drawn.[2]

The Providence Island Company's treasurer was the short and pudgy John Pym, who, despite appearances, became a vigorous and eloquent defender of parliamentary rights in the face of

Charles I's incursions. He had played an important role in the passing, in 1628, of Edward Coke's Petition of Right, lineal descendant of Magna Carta and habeas corpus, which defended a subject's liberties – as long as they weren't Catholic – from an overweening monarch. Such men were determined to resume the battles of their Elizabethan forebears. Representatives of an elect within an elect nation, they were to go out into the world, with their providential God removing all obstacles set before them. Rich harvests of Spanish gold and land, abundant in a virgin New World, would be theirs and would provide the means to fight back against the infringements of the king. Victory abroad would signify divine approval for the coming battle at home, where their triumph would complete God's design for His anointed nation of the New Testament: England, the new Israel.

Divine disapproval of Charles I's misrule was already apparent to his Puritan opponents; the cloth trade, the foundation of England's prosperity for centuries, in which many of the Providence grandees had a major financial stake, had collapsed as the brutalities of the Thirty Years War harrowed central Europe. Charles kept his distance from this bloody sectarian conflict, to the disgust of Puritans, who had urged him to back England's besieged fellow Protestants, not least his sister, Elizabeth, whose husband, Frederick V* of the Palatinate, had lost Bohemia to the forces of the Holy Roman Emperor Ferdinand II and the Catholic League. As a consequence of his inaction – against the will of a Protestant God – plague had swept England in 1625 and 1630 and poor harvests stalked the land. The Lord would not

---

* Frederick V ruled Bohemia from August 1619 to November 1620, when his reign was ended by defeat in the decisive Battle of White Mountain. He and Elizabeth thus earned the derisive epithets 'the Winter King' and 'the Winter Queen'.

provide for those who abandoned the true faith. Many Puritans were driven by necessity from their barren home to seed new worlds, prosperous and free from popery. Oliver Cromwell, an East Anglian farmer with a gentleman's education, had considered such a move.

The Providence Company nonetheless sought a royal charter from the monarch whose rule they so mistrusted. They informed Charles of an island 'convenient to receive a fleet that has any design on any leeward part of the Indies, or Cartagena, Portobello, the Bay of Honduras, Hispaniola, Cuba, or Jamaica'.[3] And they emphasized its strategic value: the winds and currents around Providence Island ensured that ships heading in and out of Cuba, Spain's jewel in the Caribbean, with its magnificent harbour of Havana, would have to pass close to its high cliffs and protective shoals. From there, the English could harass and intercept ships carrying wealth from the New World to the Old. The greatest prize of all was the *flota*, the Spanish plate fleet that once a year shipped the immense wealth of Mexico and the Peruvian silver mines of Potosí back to Europe.

Charles, relieved to get this Puritan faction off his back, issued a patent on 4 December 1630 for the 'Company of Adventurers of the City of Westminster for the Plantation of the Islands of Providence or Catalina, Henrietta or Andrea'. There is a hint of cynical fawning in the final words of the name the company gave itself, renaming the island adjacent to Providence, known to the Spanish as San Andrea, in honour of Charles's French – and Catholic – wife, Henrietta Maria. In return, Charles demanded one-fifth of the company's future profits.

Providence, however, was to be no Bermuda or Barbados – semi-removed and clement in the eastern Caribbean – though the scheme's backers were convinced of the island's innate prosperity, which would bloom when watered by the godly. The grandees had little practical experience of the Caribbean. They were armchair adventurers and the project was to be blighted by their insistence, until too late in the day, that it was they who would remain sole owners of land on the island, hindering the humbler ambitions of those settlers who put their lives on the line for the Company's good and asked only for a plot to call their own – their skin in the imperial game. 'Give a man the secure possession of a bleak rock and he will turn it into a garden', wrote the agriculturalist Arthur Young. 'Give him a nine years' lease of a garden and he will convert it into a desert.'[4]

Providence would prove more desert than garden. According to 'Relation of the Isle of Providence', a report drawn up in 1638 – by then too late – by the privateer Samuel Axe, the island could sustain a population of about 1,500 people, maintaining pigs and growing corn, cassava, plantain and citrus fruit. It was a natural fortress, but the only way it could truly prosper was through trade with the Spanish-controlled mainland. Those English who had already settled in the West Indies were comfortable with such compromises; they had discovered early on that it did not pay to be squeamish about conducting business with Catholics: religious idealism is no friend of the merchant.

Providence Island could survive economically only if it paid more attention to the fudge of temporal trade than the pursuit of spiritual perfection. Many of the hotter sort of English Protestants – who had often never set foot outside England – believed that Spain 'denied you commerce unless you be of their religion'.[5] This was palpable nonsense. From the beginning of the seventeenth century, Spain's merchant navy had shrunk and, though trade with England remained illegal, such bans were, in practice, impossible to enforce. Much of Spain's trade with and within the New World was carried out by Dutch and English traders, who worshipped gold every bit as much as, if not more than, God.

What aggression there was towards English ships in the Americas was carried out by Spanish officers remote from official policy in Madrid. The Caribbean, even more than early modern Europe, was a place of limited communications and, as a consequence, enjoyed considerable freedom from the strictures of government thousands of miles away. Spain would never officially concede trading rights in its territories to England or any other nation. But, in truth, as the brother-in-law of Cromwell's future spymaster John Thurloe, a veteran trader, pointed out, the local administration was more than happy to trade with Englishmen – and anyone else for that matter. Trade talks an international language. The rigid attitudes and ideologies espoused by the stay-at-home adventurers and their Puritan peers were those of men far from the realities and compromises of life among the merchants of the Americas; prophetic political perfectionists seeking providential signs of God's working, rather than pragmatists seeking a profit.

God and Mammon battled it out on Providence Island. To the frustration of both settlers and investors, tobacco, though 'of base value', remained a staple crop of the settlement throughout its short life. The Puritan adventurers, from their vantage point of the City of London, looked down on tobacco, and loathed the practice of smoking – as had Charles's father, James I, who, as far back as 1604, had condemned it with typically baroque eloquence and vigour in his 'Counterblaste to Tobacco'. Lord Brooke, the Company grandee, had himself described tobacco as 'that killing-saving Indian herb',[6] which the government judged a 'danger to the bodies and manners of the English people'.

But a trade worse than tobacco prospered on Providence. African slaves had been brought to the island since its settlement, despite a reluctance to accept them on the part of the adventurers. Their objections were not based on a belief that slavery was immoral: outside the 'pure air' of England, Africans could be enslaved without moral qualm on account of their 'strangeness from Christianity'.[7] Rather there was a fear that slaves would pollute the godly, self-sustaining society that was the Puritan ideal. Despite such objections, Providence became the first English colony in which more than half the population were slaves.

The Providence Island Company went out of its way to attract committed Puritans to the Caribbean: men such as Henry Halhead, the former mayor of the Puritan bastion of Banbury in Oxfordshire, a place of 'zeal, cakes and ale', who sailed there with family and friends in 1632. The practicalities of settlement in such a challenging environment meant, however, that its early ideals were compromised. The new colony needed men of arms, soldiers and sailors with experience of the hardships of the Caribbean, whose 'private dissensions and secret heartburnings'[8] might not necessarily accord with the moral and spiritual ideals of its founders.

Political and religious tensions back in England had been ratcheted up another notch in 1633 by the appointment of William Laud as Archbishop of Canterbury. A protégé of the king's favourite, George Villiers, the 1st Duke of Buckingham, Laud was an eloquent opponent of puritanism and a radical proponent of High Church ritual. For him, the fortunes of the crown and the Church of England were inextricably linked: 'If the Church be once brought down beneath herself', he warned, 'we cannot but fear what may next be struck.' The ascendancy of Laud, combined with Charles's taste for absolute rule, was further evidence to Puritan eyes of another step towards the idolatry of Catholicism.[9]

That same year, Sir Benjamin Rudyerd, poet, politician and one of those who had invested in the new settlement in 1630, observed the tensions on Providence: 'We well hoped (according to our Intention) That we had planned a Religious Colony in the Isle of Providence, instead whereof we find the root of bitterness plentifully planted amongst you… these are the uncomfortable fruits of Religion.'[10] It was a portent of the divisive challenges that, a decade or so later, would face Cromwell's Protectorate.

One of Providence's governors, Captain Nathaniel Butler, a privateer with an exemplary record running the Somers Islands, was exasperated by the situation: 'I never lived amongst men of more spleen nor of less wit to conceal it.'[11] When he was replaced by the considerably less able Andrew Carter, an already difficult situation became an impossible one; yet still, a bold band of settlers already within the New World were willing to give Providence Island one last go.

The beleaguered population of Providence Island was to be joined, a decade on from its settlement, by those North American brethren who could be persuaded to venture south, away from the austere security of New England. There had long been murmurings among English Puritans about whether their compatriots in Massachusetts Bay were made of the 'right stuff': those heading for Providence Island in 1641 had no doubt that they were and were willing to prove it. They hoped to be a vanguard for others to follow.

One of those who chose to sail south was Captain John Humphrey, who had been appointed, in absentia, governor of Providence Island in 1640. Humphrey was distantly related, through marriage, to Lord Saye and Sele, another of the Puritan grandees behind the Providence Island Company as well as mentor to Oliver Cromwell in his early political career. The circle who met at Saye and Sele's Broughton Castle north of Oxford were prominent critics of the king. Humphrey, trained as a lawyer, had been treasurer of the Dorchester Company, forerunner of the Massachusetts Bay Company, a joint stock trading company chartered by the crown in 1629 to colonize a vast area of New England. Emigrating to Boston in 1634, he became a prominent member of its community, and was appointed to the senior military position of sergeant major general in 1638.

John Winthrop, a rival to Humphrey and the dominant figure in the Massachusetts Bay Company, was puzzled by those of his fellow New Englanders who had decided to leave the relative tranquillity and security of North America 'to expose themselves, their wives and children, to the danger of a potent enemy'.[12] There had long been a tension between those 'passive' Puritans, such as Winthrop, who had left the persecution of the Old World to settle in northern parts of the New, far from Spanish encroachment, and those such as Humphrey who sought a more active witness, battling either the enemies of puritanism in England or taking the fight to the Spanish in the Caribbean.

Humphrey had recruited around 300 people to accompany him to Providence Island.* The London grandees were impressed by Humphrey's efforts and they offered him and his fellow settlers their own stake on Providence. The lack of property rights for settlers had long been a sticking point in the settlement of the colony, and it would soon become apparent that it had hindered its development fatally. Having flattered Humphrey with the observation that the post of governor was 'below your merit', the grandees promised him the future governance of the entire mainland territories of the Spanish Americas, for which Providence was to be but the stepping stone.

This new wave of migration from New England to Providence

---

* Their numbers may have included Thomas Venner, a future member of the millenarian Fifth Monarchists.

had not escaped the attention of Spain. A second Spanish attack on Providence Island, in 1640, had been repelled, but the idea of an influx of more seasoned settlers with outspoken designs on their American empire concentrated Spanish minds. The Antichrist would not be humiliated a third time.

General Francisco Díaz Pimienta, admiral of the *flota de Indias*, which conveyed the treasures of the Americas to Europe in an annual flotilla, warned Philip IV of Humphrey's intentions. The king gave Pimienta permission to assemble, in Cartagena, chief port of the Spanish Main (Spain's mainland possessions in the New World), a fleet of seven ships carrying 1,400 soldiers.

The Spanish arrived in the waters surrounding the 'peaked hat' of Providence Island on 19 May 1641. Pimienta was determined to learn from previous mistakes. He intended to attack the east of the island, where fortifications were weak, but a storm scuppered his plans and he turned his attention to the harbour of the island's 'capital', New Westminster. At daybreak on 24 May, the Spanish attacked. Despite the efforts of the defenders, English, Irish and free Africans (who may have arrived on the island as crew members), overwhelming force prevailed and the Spanish Habsburg flag was raised above the governor's empty residence. Spanish friars who had been held captive on Providence Island negotiated a peace and the lives of the English settlers were spared. The women and children were sent back to England, while the men would be transported via Cartagena to Cadiz, from where they would be free to pay their way home. Meanwhile, the lost island of Providence awaited one last boatload of the elect.

William Pierce, a New England merchant and 'most expert mariner',[13] was the owner and master of two small ships, carrying thirty men, five women and eight children from New England to a new life on Providence Island. The party stopped off for victuals in May 1641 at St Christopher (St Kitts) in the Lesser Antilles, which had been in English hands since 1622 and was now shared with France. There, Pierce was warned that 'a fleet of Spanish ships was abroad'. His small band of human cargo should, he advised, turn back to their North American home. If the rumours were true, it was likely that the Spanish, after two failed attempts, had finally taken the 'natural fortress' of Providence. Pierce had the cautious nature of the commercial seaman, but his passengers had committed their souls to a providential God, and they insisted on reaching their destination, in this world or the next.

'Then am I a dead man,' judged a resigned and dutiful Pierce, as he submitted to his passengers' wishes.[14] Days later, as Providence Island came into view, he read out to all on board, as he did every morning, a passage from the Bible, this time an excerpt from the Book of Genesis: 'Lo I die, but God will surely visit you and bring you back.'

No Spanish Habsburg flag flew over the island when the two vessels approached on 13 July 1641, but as they closed in on the harbour of tiny New Westminster, a cannonball crashed into the leading ship. Moments later Pierce lay dying, alongside Samuel Wakeman, a cotton merchant from Hartford, Connecticut. More cannonballs rained down, but the second ship, which lagged behind and out of range of the Spanish artillery, seemed to be protected by divine providence. Having fled the scene, the frustrated émigrés pleaded to be abandoned on the perilous Mosquito Coast* in penance. A handful of them got their wishes,

---

* The eastern coast of modern Nicaragua and Honduras, populated by the Miskita people – who maintained friendly contact with the Providence settlement in the 1630s.

but most were returned safely, through skilful seamanship, to New England. Providence Island, it was clear, had been lost to the Spanish at the third time of asking.

John Humphrey never did reach Providence. Soon after the first band of settlers returned to Boston, shaken but safe, he sailed for England. Almost a decade later, he would carry the sword of state for John Bradshaw, lord president of the High Court that tried – and condemned – Charles I.

Providence Island was lost just as the prospect of Civil War in the three Stuart kingdoms – England, Ireland and Scotland – became a reality. Many of those involved in the Providence Island Company assumed prominent roles on the parliamentary side. John Pym became leader of the Commons, while Lord Saye and Sele took up his position in the Lords. Warwick was appointed admiral of the parliamentary fleet in the Civil Wars. Edward Montagua, as 2nd Earl of Manchester, became the (largely ineffective) leader of the Army of the Eastern Association, whose saviour would emerge, after the second battle of Newbury in October 1644, in the figure of Oliver Cromwell. Many others who had settled Providence Island nailed their colours to the parliamentary cause. But once the struggles ahead were over and their victory assured, they would dream once more of a Puritan presence in the Spanish New World: 'Providence seemed to lead us hither,' Cromwell mused.[15]

I

The Path to the Protectorate

What alone gave some stability to all these unsettled
humours, was the great influence, both civil and
military, acquired by Oliver Cromwell.

DAVID HUME

THE STRUGGLE between king, army and Parliament,
which took two civil wars and the deaths of thousands to
decide, concluded with the execution of Charles I, 'that man
of blood', on a wintry morning in Whitehall on 30 January
1649. 'Providence and necessity', so his enemies proclaimed,
had decided his fate. The king took to the scaffold in a pair of
white shirts, concerned that his shivering in the cold air might
be mistaken for fear by the sullen, silent and bewildered crowd
of onlookers that gathered to witness his end. He had risen to
his trial with a majesty that was sometime lacking in his rule and
he accepted his martyrdom with grace and forgiveness, certain
in his belief that monarchy would not perish in perpetuity on
English soil.

Immediately, *Eikon Basilike*, a combination of prayer and justification that purported to be his spiritual biography became
a bestseller among those who cherished hope of a return to

divine-right monarchy.* Symbolic of the shift to a regime of lesser pomp and majesty, the king's statue, which had stood at London's Royal Exchange, was replaced by a plain inscription: *Exit tyrannus, Regum ultimus.* John Owen, Cromwell's religious adviser, preached the day after the execution of Charles I that 'the days approach for the delivery of the decree, so the shaking of Heaven and Earth, and all the powers of the World, to make way for the establishment of that kingdom which shall not be given to another people'.[1] John Canne, a chaplain popular with the army, declared that the death of Charles was 'God's work'. Now was the time for the return of Christ and His Saints, 'overthrowing the Thrones of Kingdoms every where [sic] in Europe'.[2]

Parliament's victory in a war that was, along with the Black Death, perhaps the greatest catastrophe ever to befall Britain and Ireland, had been decisive. The 'Saints' of the New Model Army had proved themselves an elect assigned a solemn mission: to carry out God's purpose on Earth, with England as His great exemplar. Their triumph in the Civil Wars was the outward dispensation of their inward grace. The most considerable figure to emerge from their ranks was Oliver Cromwell, an amateur soldier from the lesser gentry, who, having lived in obscurity for the first two-thirds of his life, was late to a calling born of necessity. He had conquered all before him in a series of victories that were spearheaded by his bold command of cavalry and an abiding faith in divine providence: 'This, as all the rest, is from the Lord's goodness, and not from man.'[3]

This revolution, culminating in the king's death, was a very public, if pyrrhic, triumph for a small faction which glossed the

* *Eikon Basilike* is likely to be largely the work of John Gauden, a former chaplain to the Earl of Warwick, who was loose in his allegiances and became Bishop of Exeter at the Restoration.

illegitimacy of its actions with a sheen of civic respectability. Winning the peace would prove hard in the wake of this decisive decision after which no one knew what to do next. The English would prove a difficult people to move. The vast majority remained committed to the Elizabethan Protestant settlement and the humane moderation of its Prayer Book, a beguiling, pragmatic mix of Calvinist theology and Catholic ritual expressed in language of peerless economy and beauty. A small minority, less than 5 per cent of the population, but a greater portion of the nobility, were 'real' Catholics, accused increasingly of conspiring with the radical dissenting group known as the Levellers (ironically for, after all, the universal male suffrage favoured by the latter would, in the unlikely event of its adoption, assure the return of the king). And then there were those – and they were many – of loose morals, who lived far from God's ideals, frequenting alehouses (often unlicensed), gaming houses and brothels. In one of his most striking and discomfiting phrases, Cromwell declared that the English were 'like the people under circumcision, but raw'.[4] Some of them, at least, bore signs of belonging to God's new Israel. But beyond a godly few who, according to the Calvinistic doctrine of predestination, were already chosen for salvation, the vast majority had yet to prove themselves truly worthy of His name. How could the nation's elect make an elect of the nation?

Cromwell having gained enough respect from the competing factions, even if some of it was begrudging, became the most powerful man in England. Though Fairfax was still his nominal superior, he had become profoundly disturbed by the events leading to the king's death. He melted into the shadows. Yet even together, the army and what was left of Parliament were only ever a minority within a minority. However militarily assured they might be, they were politically uncertain and theologically divided between Presbyterians, who sought a conforming national church, and independents, like Cromwell himself, who sought greater religious liberty. Both sides remained fiercely anti-Catholic. Those politicians who were boldest in their support of the new republic needed the army to ensure its – and their – survival. The army had brought them to power and the army would keep them there, throughout the 1650s. The search for a civilian settlement would unfold as a compelling drama, without resolution.

In the wake of the king's execution, monarchy was formally abolished on 19 May 1649, in Ireland as well as England. It was, according to the Rump Parliament* (which by that time consisted of as few as fifty active members), 'unnecessary, burdensome and dangerous to the liberty, safety and public interest' of the people. The House of Lords, judged to be 'useless' as well as dangerous, was similarly dismissed. A Council of State, elected annually, comprising no fewer than thirteen members and no more than twenty-one (in fact it actually never exceeded eighteen), was to inherit the executive powers of monarchy. Royal rule had been replaced by conciliar government. By May, England and its dominions were declared a 'Commonwealth and Free State'. Almost a year after the king's death, the adult male population was obliged to take 'an Engagement' of loyalty to the Commonwealth as it was then established. Denial of the 'supreme authority' of the Commons was made a treasonable act.

The Rump was quick to act on matters of foreign policy.

---

* The element of the Long Parliament that remained after it was purged of its more radical elements in 1648, and which later voted for Charles I to be tried.

Ireland, devastated by war since 1641, endured the Cromwellian invasion of 1649, and Scotland, a contemptuously tolerated polity in the hands of fellow Calvinists, albeit of even more zealous bent, were to be brought under English control. The Navigation Act, passed in 1651, sought to curb the trading activities of the Dutch, who despite their Protestantism were a naval and mercantile threat. But the Rump was much less united on domestic matters and would remain so. The Toleration Act of September 1650 meant that dissenters were no longer obliged to attend their parish church, though the parish system itself, always a target of the religiously radical, was maintained. Matthew Hale, the barrister who had unsuccessfully defended the king's chief adviser, Thomas Wentworth, Earl of Strafford,* and Archbishop Laud, and who maintained a reputation for neutrality and objectivity, led a non-parliamentary commission on the reform of the legal system. The presence in the Rump of so many lawyers (for whom self-interest was paramount) negated Hale's more radical proposals.

The Rump declined steadily, living 'hand to mouth'. Cromwell grew frustrated with the ineffective Parliament. Bolstered by his providential and conclusive victory over Charles Stuart at Worcester on 3 September 1651 – a 'crowning mercy' – he wrote the following day of his hope that Parliament might now 'do the will of Him who hath done His will for it'. The exact nature of that will would prompt the compelling, increasingly desperate and ultimately frustrated search of Cromwell's remaining years.

The Rump failed to provide an answer and it was forced by Cromwell and Oliver St John, by then a judge who rarely sat

---

* Strafford's execution on 12 May 1641, to which Charles gave his assent, became a source of bitter regret to the king, who remarked before his own execution on 'that unjust sentence which I suffered to take effect'. Laud was executed on 10 January 1645.

in Parliament to set a date, beyond which it would not sit. On 3 November 1651, it agreed that it would abolish itself within three years, and the search for its successor began. The army sought a radical solution, arguing that Parliament should be the preserve of the 'pious and faithful'. Cromwell, not for the last time, became the arbiter between army and Parliament. But with memories of victory receding, it appeared that Cromwell's star was on the wane. A bitterly divided England longed for 'healing and settling', but, by the end of 1651, little had been achieved. In December, Cromwell held a meeting

> With diverse Members of Parliament and some of the chief Officers of the Army at the Speaker's House; and a great many being there, he proposed to them That the old King being dead, and his son being defeated, he held it necessary to come to a Settlement of the Nation.

One faction – let us call it, with some simplification, the civilian faction, dominated by lawyers – favoured a constitutional monarchy. The soldiers – the military faction – wanted a republic. The distinguished lawyer Bulstrode Whitelocke suggested that Charles's youngest son, Henry, Duke of Gloucester, not yet a teenager, might be placed on the throne to govern as a limited, constitutional monarch, a suggestion Cromwell thought would be 'of more than ordinary difficulty' to achieve. Yet a settlement that accepted 'somewhat of Monarchical power' could, he judged, 'be very effectual'. A seed had been planted that would bear bitter fruit.

Eventually, by April 1653, Cromwell believed he had the agreement of both sides to establish a council of army officers and MPs who, the Rump having dissolved itself, would organize new elections from which those ill-disposed to the Commonwealth would be excluded. But, to Cromwell's deep frustration and anger, the Rump pulled out of the agreement and decided to go ahead immediately with elections of its own.

On 20 April 1653 Cromwell, a parliamentarian serially disappointed by Parliaments, headed to Westminster at the head of a group of soldiers and declared, in one of his most famous – albeit contested – utterances, which was to echo in Parliament during the existential crisis of May 1940:* 'You have sat too long here for any good you have been doing lately. Depart, I say; and let us have done with you. In the name of God, go!' The Rump Parliament was abolished, Cromwell claimed, by 'the power God had most providentially put into my hand'.[5] For providence, critics might be inclined to substitute 'convenience'.

By the spring of 1653, with the Rump dissolved, Cromwell had attained a power unequalled thus far by any individual in British history. The Rump had been unable, he argued, 'to answer those ends which God, his people, and the whole nation expected from them'.[6] Cromwell would ultimately and repeatedly put his trust in God (and dry gunpowder) rather than Parliament and the people. Though not a dictator in the modern sense – the early modern state, with its lack of infrastructure and limited communications, was incapable of administering totalitarian government, whatever an individual's ambitions – Cromwell's authoritarian streak was exposed. As early as July 1647, he had observed that it was best for governments to rule 'for the people's

---

* In May 1940, after Britain had suffered a string of military and naval setbacks in the early months of the Second World War, Leo Amery MP attacked Neville Chamberlain's government in a famous speech that quoted Cromwell's words to the Rump Parliament. In fact, the words are not included in the standard collections of Cromwell's letters and speeches, while John Morrill's 'definitive' collection, currently in production, has similarly found no reference to this statement in contemporary sources. It is likely that they are derived from a forged version of Cromwell's words published in 1767.

good, not what pleases them'. And if a Parliament was not doing God's work, it was, of necessity, expendable. The point of Parliament was, ultimately to make the English godly, to elevate an entire nation to the Elect. Cromwell's highest ambitions were, ultimately, more theological than political. He had allies in that regard, more zealous than he.

For the next experiment in governance, Cromwell turned to Major General Thomas Harrison, whom he considered 'an honest man', troubled by 'impatience of his spirit'.[7] A lawyer turned soldier, Harrison was the leader of the Fifth Monarchists, a millenarian sect that espoused radical religious certainties. The Fifth Monarchy Men believed with great sincerity that, following the fall of the four great empires of Babylon, Persia, Greece and Rome (and recognizing a continuity between the Roman Empire and the papacy), the 'fifth' monarchy, that of the thousand-year rule of Christ on earth, would commence and that England would be its seedbed. Harrison was as impatient in peace as he had been when he distinguished himself in several battles of the Civil War. By contrast, Cromwell, militarily decisive, was to prove a prevaricator in politics, a man who would repeatedly shut himself away in prayer, in constant search of guidance in a two-way dialogue with God.* Harrison's certainties knew no such indecision, no such pause for thought.

Cromwell, however, was at his most exultant when, on 4 July 1653, he addressed the Nominated Assembly, or Barebones Parliament. 'Barebones' was the mocking nickname bestowed

---

* The most valuable source for understanding Cromwell would be his dialogues with God, brilliantly imagined by playwright Howard Brenton in his work of 2012, 55 *Days*.

on the parliament by its critics after one of its more religiously ardent members, Praise-God Barebone (full name: Unless-Jesus-Christ-Had-Died-For-Thee-Thou-Hadst-Been-Damned Barebone), a City leather trader. The brainchild of Harrison, the Nominated Assembly was a hagiarchy modelled on the ancient Jewish tribunal known as the Sanhedrin, which Harrison hoped would rule according to Old Testament Mosaic law. 'God hath called you to this work by, I think, as wonderful providences [military victories] as ever passed upon the sons of men in so short a time', Cromwell proclaimed. They were assembled by the 'wise providence of God' and must 'own their call'. The assembly, he said, was 'at the threshold' of something extraordinary.[8]

The 140 men of the Barebones Parliament were supposed to be 'nominated' – hence its official name – by independent church congregations in Britain and Ireland. In reality, the MPs were chosen mainly by the army's Council of Officers, who looked for men with the 'root of the matter' in them: god-fearing and of 'approved fidelity and honesty'. The Barebones Parliament lasted just five months, and became, in Cromwell's admission, 'a tale of my own weakness and folly'. Like the Rump, it foundered upon intractable matters of religion and law.

Barebones attracted ridicule for its perceived ineffectiveness and the supposedly lowly status of its members – a broadsheet of the time dismissed them as 'pettifoggers, innkeepers, millwrights, stockingmongers'.[9] Yet it was not an inactive Parliament: it passed more than thirty Acts on a range of social and economic issues. Nor was it, in practice, a nest of fundamentalists. The Fifth Monarchists, including Harrison, played a relatively minor role in its proceedings, and the Parliament, far from 'Pettifoggers, Innkeepers, Millwrights, Stockingmongers and such a rabble as never had hopes to be of a Grand Jury', was fairly traditional in make-up, with a couple of nobles and plenty of gentlemen, even if most of those were from the gentry's lower ranks. And yet the lawyers among its members, a stabilizing force in all of Cromwell's parliaments, were taken aback when they were outvoted by those who sought the abolition of the Court of Chancery and planned to reduce England's common law into a pocket digest. After a narrow vote in favour of abolishing church tithes, eighty or so moderates – including such notables as Sir Charles Wolseley, William Sydenham, Sir Gilbert Pickering, Edward Montagu, Philip Jones, Sir Anthony Ashley Cooper, Henry Lawrence and John Desborough – held a prayer meeting in which, exasperated by their more radical colleagues, they agreed to 'deliver up unto the Lord General Cromwell the powers which they had received from him'. On 12 December 1653, they presented Cromwell with a signed document, which stated 'Upon a Motion this day made in the House, that the sitting of this Parliament any longer as now constituted, will not be for the good of the Commonwealth'. In the meantime, Colonel Goffe and Lieutenant Colonel White entered Parliament in the company of musketeers and dispersed those MPs who still lingered in the House. Whether Cromwell knew of the plan or not – the historian Blair Worden, in a telling phrase, has described Cromwell as 'practised at not knowing'[10] – he eagerly accepted the Parliament's demise. He and his officers had become concerned by Barebones hostility to the army – still the nation's powerbroker. In particular, the Parliament's unwillingness to confirm the monthly assessment, the source of the troops' financial support, had become a running sore for the regime. The most hostile MPs even proposed that some of the army's more senior officers should serve without pay. The solution to such matters lay in the hands of the army itself and one distinguished figure in particular.

★

Major General John Lambert was then in his thirties. Vain and ambitious, beholden to no one, he was Cromwell's only serious rival for power and perhaps his only viable successor. A brilliant cavalry officer, Lambert's aggressive, almost reckless tactics at Dunbar on 3 September 1650 won the day against all odds: the Scots under David Leslie, fighting for their Charles II in the hope that he would impose a Presbyterian religious settlement throughout Britain, were punished for 'not holding the glory of God's wonderful dispensation in this series of His providences'.[11] The junior officers of the English army – which Cromwell judged a 'simple spirituall one' – pronounced in the Declaration of Musselburgh that they were engaged in a fight for 'the destruction of Antichrist, and the advancement of the Kingdom of Jesus Christ... let not Scotland, not any other Nation say, What dost thou?'

It is hard to overstate the importance of Dunbar in the mythology of the Saints. Reflecting on the battle, Cromwell recalled that 'We knew not what to do. Wherefore it is sealed up in our hearts, that this, as all the rest, is from the Lord's goodness, and not from man.'[12] The Saints were merely 'God's Instruments'. The battle's miraculous outcome, bought at the price of just twenty English dead, confirmed the providential hand of God guiding the Puritan cause. As Cromwell observed, in exultant language:

> Because of their numbers, because of their advantages, because of their confidence, because of our weakness, because of our strait, we were in the Mount, and in the Mount the Lord would be seen... He would find out a way of deliverance and salvation for us – and in deed we had our consolations and our hopes.

At Dunbar, Cromwell was so overwhelmed that, as one eye-witness recounted in the aftermath of victory: 'He did laugh so excessively as if he had been drunk; his eyes sparkled with spirits.'[13]

Even more remarkably, in July 1651 Lambert had led an army into the hitherto untouched Kingdom of Fife and destroyed Sir John Browne's Covenanter army at Inverkeithing: 2,000 Scots were killed and 1,400 captured. At Worcester in September Lambert displayed his bravery when his horse was shot from underneath him – this at the end of a campaign in which he was the dominant military figure, surpassing even Cromwell in his deeds. By now Cromwell, along with Lambert, had been campaigning on and off for almost a decade, during which 'no single operation of war that he ever undertook had failed'.[14]

Dunbar and Inverkeithing were seen by the parliamentarians as the results of divine intervention – they were, literally, moral victories, made possible by the 'chariots and horsemen of Israel'. In a letter to the future speaker of the House, William Lenthall, in the wake of the victory, Cromwell summoned a prophecy with implications for the regime's foreign policy:

> If He that strengthens your servants to fight, pleases to give your hearts to set upon these things, in order to His glory, and the glory of your Commonwealth, besides the benefit of England shall feel thereby, you shall shine forth to other nations, who shall emulate the glory of such a pattern, and through the power of God turn into the like.[15]

In other words, the struggle to establish a Commonwealth that reflected God's glory on earth was a global one.

Cromwell had never lost a battle, and he had usually taken the field with Lambert by his side. Lambert was the only councillor of sufficient status to hold council meetings in Cromwell's Whitehall offices; the only one Cromwell visited at home or who was invited to dine, along with his wife, Frances Lister, at Cromwell's table.

And yet despite his proximity to Cromwell – or perhaps because of it – Lambert was the one who was most likely to challenge him and, ultimately, to succeed him. For there had been hints of Cromwell's mortality. In an intimate note to his wife, Elizabeth, 'dearer to me than any creature', he spoke of how his 'weak faith had been upheld' as his body weakened: 'I grow an old man, and feel infirmities of age marvellously stealing upon me.' When Cromwell had fallen ill during the Scottish campaign, rumours of his death were rife. He had recovered by early March, but, to add to his concerns, a Royalist plot had been uncovered, for which the turncoat Captain Browne Bushell was executed. When Parliament had a medal cast in Cromwell's honour to mark the miracle of Dunbar, he is said to have recoiled in horror at his shaggy, soldierly image. Coins issued by the Protectorate would bear a more imperial profile. Cromwell remained a relatively austere figure, though he had ceased to be, if he ever was, an iconoclast. He was even elected Chancellor of Oxford University. In the words of the historian Wilbur Cortez Abbott: 'Little by little, in his various capacities, he came more and more to be the centre and directing force in the three kingdoms,' with Lambert at his side.[16]

Though he held no formal position after the defeat of Charles Stuart, Lambert was a fixture of the Council of State, where he took a lead in Scottish and Irish affairs. In January 1652, following the death of Henry Ireton, he had been appointed Lord Deputy of Ireland, but he was replaced by Charles Fleetwood, who was married to Ireton's widow, Bridget, Cromwell's eldest daughter. Whether Cromwell was involved in these shenanigans is impossible to judge. The establishment of Barebones had seemed like a defeat to Lambert and a victory for his rival Harrison –'There hath been some late discontents between the General [Lambert] and Harrison', ran a report of 24 November

1653.[17] Lambert was rarely in Parliament, spending most of his time, instead, at his estate in Wimbledon, where he composed the world's first written constitution, the Instrument of Government, which like all new written constitutions, was biased towards the aims and ideologies of the government of the day. With the demise of Barebones came the chance to implement it.

Lambert sought to transform the ancient constitutional trinity of king, Lords and Commons into that of king, Council and Parliament – and give the proposed Protectorate a firm foundation. The Instrument of Government was as astute a document as its author. There was to be no Cromwellian dictatorship: legislative and executive powers were separated, with the Protector and Parliament responsible for the former, while the Protector and his Council embodied the latter. Counsellors were paid stipends of £1,000 a year, a substantial sum that aroused controversy, though hardly inappropriate given the size of the task. The Council would be invested with considerable power; far more than Charles's privy councils. When no Parliament was sitting, the Council became, in effect, its substitute. Cromwell was obliged to follow its advice and could only wage war if a majority of its members consented. The Council ran the government, was responsible for the maintenance of law and order, the administration of tax collection, trade disputes and intelligence. It was also responsible for deciding who would succeed Cromwell, though few had the stomach to consider the implications of such a crisis at that time – an oversight that would prove costly.

And so Lambert, not for the first time, came to Cromwell's rescue with his attempt to place the regime on a sounder footing, and the Instrument of Government was adopted on 16 December 1653. 'The supreme legislative authority', it stated, 'should reside in one person, and the people assembled in Parliament.' The Instrument was modelled on and inspired by previous outlines for governance put forward by the army, such as the Heads of the Proposals of 1647 (in the drafting of which Lambert also took part) and the Officers' Agreement of the People, composed two years later. Cromwell approved the Instrument of Government as a means to promote 'just liberty to the people of God, and the just rights of the people in these nations'. 'What Lambert hath aimed at he has affected,' judged one correspondent in an intercepted letter of December 1653. The liberty of conscience outlined in the Instrument was, for Cromwell, a fundamental. Many of his allies disagreed, as would become increasingly clear as the Protectorate progressed. For most supporters of the regime, especially Presbyterians, who supported a single national church, liberty of conscience came a long way down their list of priorities, which was headed by two issues of overriding importance: national security and the elimination of heresy.

On one issue, the Instrument reverted to a more traditional stance. It proposed that Cromwell take the crown and become king, in order to secure the regime and its succession by traditional means – according to the 'Ancient Constitution'.* But both the substance and title of king were unacceptable to Cromwell and, when he refused, he was offered the novel position of Lord Protector for life. This he accepted and, on 16 December 1653, he ascended to the position in Westminster Hall. From then until his death in September 1658, he would be head of state, his power limited by the need to consult his

---

* The Ancient Constitution was, in John Pym's words, composed of the 'plain footsteps of those laws in the government of the Saxons... which gave bounds and limits' to William I's Conquest, and which 'descended to his successors'. The rights and liberties enshrined in the Ancient Constitution were affirmed in documents such as Magna Carta of 1215. However, Royalists saw Charles I and his heirs as the defenders of liberty, and insisted that an unchecked Parliament posed a greater threat to freedom.

Council, a mix of civilians and soldiers, with Lambert, in the beginning at least, to the fore: it was, said Cromwell, with the 'will of God and the pleasure of the Council' that he had become Protector. Although he was advised by the Council 'in all things', there was no doubting who was *primus inter pares*. Cromwell, as Cardinal Mazarin, the chief minister to Louis XIV, observed, 'had a perfect knowledge of all things'.[18] It was he who appointed the Council's president, he who decided their stipend, he who appointed diplomats, he who called formal meetings of the Council. Cromwell was never averse to acting on a decision made by himself alone; having revealed his will, he would await the Council's consent.

At his inauguration as Protector on 16 December 1653, Cromwell was followed in his carriage by Lambert, who carried the sword of state, and the Lord Mayor of London. The Protector eschewed the trappings of royalty: on this less than splendid occasion, he wore a suit and cloak of plainest Puritan black, 'without any formality of Robes at all'.* Having sworn to uphold the Instrument of Government, he made a speech that was short by his standards, in which he prepared his followers for the long grind ahead: 'These are but entrances and doors of hope, wherein through the blessing of God you may enter into rest and peace. But you are not yet entered.'

Cromwell and his retinue returned to the Banqueting Hall in Whitehall to listen to a sermon by the Puritan theologian Thomas Goodwin on a familiar theme: that they, like the Israelites journeying to Canaan, would spend many years in the wilderness

---

* Ironically, given the expense of the dyeing process, black cloth was never cheap.

before the promised land was revealed to them. This gathering of England's new elite took place beneath the ceiling graced by Peter Paul Rubens's *The Apotheosis of James I*, relic of a monarchical age, looking down upon the vast room through which Charles I had passed to his execution. The austere assembly within was mirrored by the sparse crowds in Whitehall: the lack of fanfare meant that most Londoners were unaware that a ceremony was taking place at all.

Mutterings of opposition to the protectoral regime did not take long to emerge. Two days after his inauguration, on a Sunday, the millenarian preacher Christopher Feake and his Welsh Anabaptist colleague Vavasour Powell, with sulphur on their breath, denounced Cromwell as a 'dissemblingest perjured villain', for which the pair were briefly imprisoned. In May 1654, John Milton, poet, polemicist and pamphleteer, a critical friend of the regime and by far its most eloquent apologist, offered a warning:

> If that man [Cromwell] than whom no one has been considered more just, more holy, more excellent, shall afterwards attack that liberty which he himself has defended, such an act must necessarily be dangerous and well-nigh fatal not only to liberty itself but also to the cause of all virtue and piety.

Milton's fellow radicals, men such as Arthur Hesilrige, Henry Vane and John Bradshaw, were appalled by the creation of the quasi-monarchical position of Lord Protector. The Council to them was not an independent check on the office, but a 'nose of wax, which will wind and turn which way the single person pleases'.[19] It was not a government of council and protector 'but one of protector and council'. Under Charles I, such men had argued that the king had been led astray by councillors. Were they now arguing that the Council was being forced into error by the Protector? It was a betrayal of what would come to be known as the

'Good Old Cause'. But as long as Cromwell commanded the support of the army, there was little they could do.

The Protectorate and its constitution, the Instrument of Government – a 'work of darkness' according to the previously loyal parliamentarian Edmund Ludlow – had been imposed, however peacefully, at the point of a sword. It was the creation of the army and was designed to pursue its ambitions. It emphasized in particular two of the army's fundamental requirements: first, religious liberty – that those who 'profess faith in God by Jesus Christ (though differing in judgement from the doctrine, worship or discipline publicly held forth)' should be allowed to profess their faith – excluding, of course, Anglicans and papists; second, the raising of money, of which the army was always in need, as armies always are. Cromwell's power would, until its end, depend fundamentally on the will of men in uniform and the price of their maintenance and loyalty. Within a year, the government would be running a deficit of almost three-quarters of a million pounds, despite the demands made on the population by revenue-raising schemes such as the excise tax and the direct assessment tax. Reducing the size of the army, the obvious means by which the financial burden could be reduced, was not a realistic option: Cromwell and his closest political and military allies feared enemies within and without. An annual revenue was to be provided in perpetuity for the maintenance of '10,000 horse and dragoons, and 20,000 foot' in all three kingdoms. An additional £200,000 was to be raised annually for the government's administrative duties.

The First Protectorate Parliament was scheduled to meet in September 1654; until that date, Cromwell and his Council of State could issue legal ordinances, albeit dependent on later ratification by Parliament. They did not waste time, passing almost 200 of them, including those that, for the first time, united the Three Kingdoms of England, Ireland and Scotland, and established a High Court of Justice. Closest to Cromwell's heart was the creation of 'Triers' and 'Ejectors', an ambitious attempt to improve the quality of religious instruction. The former was a national body that assessed new ministers to see if they were fit to preach. The latter, organized on a county basis, were empowered to remove, or 'eject' those ministers and schoolmasters deemed 'scandalous, ignorant and insufficient' in their learning and its application. The first proved a more effective scheme than the latter.

Cromwell was never more effusive than when opening Parliaments, his words on each occasion signalling the triumph of hope over experience. Opening the First Protectorate Parliament on 4 September 1654, he swore to uphold the Instrument of Government, and made a speech that was short by his standards, in which he prepared his followers for the heavy weather ahead. Cromwell declared that the purpose of Parliament was 'that this ship of the commonwealth may be brought into a safe harbour; which I assure you it will not well be, without your counsel and advice'.* A week later, Parliament voted that the nature of the government should be 'in a Parliament and single person limited and restrained as the Parliament should think fit'. Within days, members of a traditional parliamentarian cast launched attacks on Lambert's new constitution and on the touchy subject of religious toleration; Parliament sought to emasculate the radical sects, with a plan to establish an Assembly of Divines made up of conservative Presbyterians opposed to liberty of religion.

---

* Anticipating a metaphor employed by the modern conservative philosopher Michael Oakeshott. Contemporaries argued, referring metaphorically to the Ship of State, that sailors being piloted into rocks had a right to mutiny, an insight I owe to Jonathan Healey.

The Protector reacted with a speech, of some length, that outlined four fundamental principles, which, he made clear, were not to be questioned by Parliament or anyone else. A Parliament could not sit permanently and had to be elected frequently; government was to be by 'a single person and a Parliament'; liberty of conscience was a given; control of the army was to be shared by the Protector and Parliament. That was the deal and it must be recognized as such by anyone who sought to sit in Parliament.

Those who disagreed with these fundamentals were 'invited' by troops to withdraw: more than fifty did so, including John Bradshaw who, as Lord President had overseen the King's trial in 1649, and Arthur Heselrige, who continued to argue that Cromwell was guilty of betraying the 'good old cause' in favour of his own self-aggrandizement. The radical religious groups that had emerged in the wake of the revolution, which had strong roots in the army, such as the Quakers, as well as the Fifth Monarchists and Baptists, felt abandoned, too, despite the commitment to religious liberty. The Levellers, who had sought a wider male franchise, were similarly disgruntled. Anyone who wished to remain sitting in the House was ordered to sign a document in support of the regime, which some refused to do. Cromwell's firm action got rid of his more tenacious critics, but the Instrument's clauses continued to be the source of endless, niggardly debate. On 10 November, Major General Desborough* made the kind of tin-eared intervention that was to mark his political career, when he asked why Parliament was so 'reluctant to trust the Lord Protector with the half, that not long had the whole, and might have kept it without any competitor'. Unwittingly, he had reminded the House, if it needed reminding, that Cromwell and

* John Desborough, a member of the Council of State, was married to Cromwell's sister Jane.

the army were the real power in the land, and Parliament sat only at their sufferance. It was hardly prudent of Desborough to be drawing attention to the limits of the power of the Commons, especially since it *did* have the power to cap government finances at little more than a million pounds per annum, barely half the sum needed to maintain the army in its present condition.

Despite Cromwell's harangue, the First Protectorate Parliament continued to act like a constituent assembly, seeking to draft a constitution that would reduce the powers of the Protector and his Council and increase those of Parliament. This constitutional bill insisted that no Parliament could be dissolved without its own consent and that it must have greater control over the army. With its Presbyterian majority, Parliament also wanted to strengthen the national church and rein in 'atheism, blasphemy, damnable heresies' and the usual array of 'popery, prelacy, licentiousness, or profaneness'. Given such provocations, tensions and contradictions, the First Protectorate Parliament was unlikely to last. According to the Instrument of Government, Parliaments were to sit for a minimum of five months. A month was usually interpreted as a calendar month rather than the shorter lunar month. But, given his haste to be rid of it – and against the advice of his Council – Cromwell measured its term by the latter and, on 22 January 1655, the earliest possible moment, he inevitably got his way. He addressed the doomed, divided and discontented assembly with contempt: 'I think it my duty to tell you that it is not for the profit of these nations, nor fit for the common and public good, for you to continue here any longer.'[20] The Protector conveyed his disappointment with considerable force:

> weeds and nettles, briers and thorns, have thriven under your shadow... Dissettlement and division, discontent and dissatisfaction, together with real dangers to the whole, has been more

multiplied within these five months of your sitting, than in some years before.

His opponents were 'without God in the world, and walk not with Him, and know not what it is to pray, or believe, and to receive returns from God, and to be spoken unto by the spirit of God'. Who were they to call 'His revolutions human designs', to see cynicism where there was the spirit? 'I speak for God and not for men.' The regime, he reminded them, had come to power by 'divine providence and dispensation'. It existed by God's indulgence and mercy alone.

With the home front unsettled, hopes ran high among some in the closed circle around Cromwell for a project that would broadcast England's power to the world – a military adventure that would hark back to the days of the blessed Elizabeth and their own victories in the Civil Wars. Such a triumph would reaffirm their election by God. Short-term setbacks and frustrations demanded long-term reassurance, from the highest authority of all.

2

Old and New Worlds

Are we poor? Spain is rich. There are our Indies.

SIR JOHN ELIOT, MARCH 1624

THOMAS GAGE LED one of the most extraordinary lives of any Englishman of his time, during the course of which he executed a 180-degree political and theological turn. Born into a long-established recusant family, both his parents had been condemned to death and then reprieved for harbouring Catholic priests. An uncle of his had been executed for his role in the 1586 Babington Plot, which planned to assassinate Elizabeth I and replace her with Mary, Queen of Scots, the grandmother of Charles I. Robert Southwell, the Jesuit martyr, was a cousin.

Gage had entered the Catholic seminar at St Omer in northern France, the default destination for the brightest sons of English recusants, around the age of twelve. His father intended him to enter the severe, intellectual Society of Jesus – the Jesuits notorious in England since the proselytizing campaigns of the martyr Edmund Campion in the 1580s. But Gage travelled further, to Spain, to the English college in Valladolid, where he joined the Dominicans, an older order, founded in the thirteenth century, and similarly committed to education. It was a move that led his father to disown him.

Though, as an Englishman, he was formally banned from travelling in the imperial possessions of Habsburg Spain, the restless, insatiably curious Gage was smuggled in a barrel of dry biscuit – or so it was claimed – onto a ship in Cadiz harbour (some accounts, fanciful perhaps, suggest he may have over-indulged in the celebrated wines of Jerez). The vessel was bound for Mexico, where he was supposed to begin the next stage of his journey to Manila, capital of the Spanish Philippines, a transfer that never happened. Instead, Gage, now Tomás de Santa María, along with a handful of fellow friars, headed for Guatemala, his 'second patria', where he was to spend the next decade. A gifted linguist, Gage spent lengthy periods of time among the Pokoman Maya, learning their language. Somewhere along the way, he began to question his religious beliefs. His conscience, he admitted, was 'much perplexed and wavering'.

In January 1637, as the English settlement of Providence Island entered its final, troubled phase, Gage began a long and hazardous return to Europe. Robbed by Dutch pirates on the Mosquito Coast, in what is now Belize, he crossed to the Pacific side of the Central American isthmus, from where he sailed to Panama, eventually reaching the major Spanish port of Portobello on the Spanish Main (where Francis Drake was believed to have been buried at sea in 1596, following his death from dysentery). Here, Gage enrolled as chaplain to the captain of the ship that would return him to Spain. Having forgotten most of his native tongue, he arrived incognito in England in 1637, returning to the recusant underground into which he had been born. After travelling to Rome and escaping the clutches of French priva-teers, he returned to England once more in 1640. Within two years he had converted to the Church of England's puritanical wing, inspired, he claimed, by the Long Parliament's promised reforms of religion. He announced his conversion publicly on

28 August 1642 in a sermon later published as *The Tyranny of Satan Discovered in the Tears of a Converted Sinner* – Gage was not one for understatement. A flattered Parliament granted him a parish in Kent, by which time he had married – one of the uncontested blessings bestowed by the reformed religion – before he moved to a more substantial position at the Church of St Leonard's in the Kentish port of Deal.

There he composed his compelling travelogue of self-justification, *The English-American his Travail by Sea and Land, or, A New Survey of the West Indias*.[1] This would eventually be published in England in 1648 and dedicated, with more than one eye on advancement, to Thomas Fairfax, commander-in-chief of the victorious parliamentary forces during the Civil Wars. It was not only the first account of life in the Spanish New World by an Englishman, it was the first to be written by a non-Habsburg subject.

A bestseller in its day, *A New Survey of the West Indias* remains surprisingly readable, despite its long, breathless paragraphs. Food is something of an obsession with Gage, due no doubt to the long periods of privation he endured. He describes, for the first time in English, classic Mexican dishes, such as burritos – which they dip in 'water and salt with a little bruised chilli' – and tamales, and writes movingly and sympathetically of the Indians who prepared them. He appears to have discovered that the Pokoman Maya placed poisonous toads in fermented drinks used for ritual intoxication, thereby increasing their potency. An entire chapter of his book is devoted to chocolate – 'which they minister in great cups as big as will hold above a pint'. He was fascinated by the dark, viscous concoction, though he observed, presciently, that 'those that use this chocolate much grow fat and corpulent by it'. His travelogue is marked by frequent passages of religious satire, including the tale of a Catholic priest who was forced to abandon Mass when a mouse ran off with the communion wafer.

A less attractive aspect of his personality emerged during the Civil Wars, when Gage was active on the parliamentary side. He bore witness in court against three of his former colleagues: Father Thomas Holland, whom he had known at St Omer, and who was executed in 1642; Father Arthur Bell, who was chaplain to one of his cousins and met a traitor's death a year later; and, in 1651, Father Peter Wright, the chaplain of his elder brother, the Royalist cavalry officer Henry (who 'strove to eliminate all memory of Thomas', and who had died in Wright's arms). Arguably worst of all, he testified against his brother George, who was also a priest and who unsurprisingly judged him a 'graceless brother', whose actions 'our whole family doth blush to behold'.[2]

With the unbounded zealotry of the convert, Gage defended the Protectorate's political and religious aspirations in a work published in 1654, *A Full Survey of Sion and Babylon*. Around the same time, encouraged by the regicide Thomas Chaloner, Gage submitted a proposal, *Some brief and True Observations concerning the West Indies*, to Cromwell's spymaster John Thurloe for an English expedition to the heart of the Spanish Caribbean. According to the Venetian ambassador Francesco Giavarina, Gage and the Protector met privately on a number of occasions. It was a fateful coming together, the foundation stone of what the historian David Armitage has called 'the imperial moment of the English Republic'.[3] It would result in the death of one and bring doubt, uncertainty and, ultimately, failure to the other.

In his report, Gage argued, with some reason, that the strength of both the House of Habsburg and, by extension, the papacy, was almost entirely dependent upon the resources of their empire in the New World. Their wealth and their imperial might was to be found in their 'American mines', he declared. Were they to lose them, 'Rome's triple crown would soon fall and decay'.

Gage peddled the old papist stereotypes, marinated in the martyrologies of John Foxe, which found an eager audience among the hotter sort of Protestant and Hispanophobes, including Cromwell. 'The Spaniards cannot oppose much,' Gage asserted, 'being a lazy sinful people, feeding like beasts upon their lusts, and upon the fat of the land, and never trained up to wars.'[4]

This was hubris in excelsis, working cynically on Cromwell's anti-Catholicism, and all the more incredible coming from a man who had seen the might of Spanish imperialism at close quarter. But Gage was partial to rumours and prophecies that spoke of English providence and the fears of Spain: 'It hath been for these many years their own common talk, from some predictions... that a strange people shall conquer them, and take all their riches from them.'

Such prophecies had a pedigree. In 1623, in an ill-fated journey to Madrid, the Duke of Buckingham – the finely calved favourite of James I, who in turn gained the besotted attentions of his heir – accompanied the future Charles I in a crackpot scheme to woo the Spanish Infanta. Charles failed in his amatory pursuit, instead falling in love with European art, which he shipped back to England in bulk. In Madrid, Buckingham had been told by a Spanish bureaucrat, 'Don Fennyn', of an Indian legend, which predicted 'that there shall come a nation unto them, with flaxen hair, white complexion, grey eyes, that shall govern them'.[5] Who were these liberators? They were the heirs of 'Don Francisco Draco' – Francis Drake – who along with Ralegh had nurtured the Hispanophobic 'Black Legend' of Spanish cruelty and exploitation in the New World. According to its tenets, Spain was not only England's natural enemy, but the architect of the *encomienda** under which the indigenous people of the New World were oppressed. This image of a malevolent Spain, there for the taking, had been further bolstered among the English by the publication of translations of the writings of Bartolomé de las Casas, a Dominican friar, whose graphic descriptions of Spanish atrocities against the native peoples of the Americas, published as *A Short Account of the Destruction of the Indies*, found an eager audience in England, not least because it mirrored the accounts of atrocities – almost always exaggerated – against English and Scottish Protestant settlers during the Irish Rebellion of 1641 – similarly the work of papists, Gage pointed out. Having been expelled from 'St Christopher's, St Martin's, from Providence... and from Tortugas, where the English were unhumanly and most barbarously treated by the Spaniards', the time was ripe, argued Gage, for revenge – and for just the kind of overseas victory that could unite a divided nation in celebration of its martial prowess.

At the time of Cromwell's ascendancy, memories of the Providence Island Company, though fading, continued to inspire members of the new ruling class. One reason given for the failure of the Company was its modest size, its limited, private funding and its distance from government. Imagine what could be achieved, urged some, if the full resources of the state were put behind such a project. Who could then stand in England's way?

Cromwell subscribed to the Elizabethan world view of nascent

---

* A grant given by the Spanish crown to colonists in America, which conferred the right to demand tribute and forced labour from the Indian inhabitants.

British imperialism expressed in Ralegh's *History of the World* – possibly the only book, apart from the Bible, that he ever read, and which he impressed upon his son, Richard, because 'history is the working out of the first cause, God's will, divine providence'.[6] The myths were burnished further in *The Life of the Renowned Sir Philip Sidney*, a paean to the 'perfect hero knight of militant Christianity' (whom the poet John Milton, a critical friend of the regime, regarded as a 'greater teacher than Scotus or Aquinas'). Written in the 1610s by the 1st Lord Brooke, Fulke Greville, who had adopted the Providence Company's youngest grandee as his heir, it had been published belatedly in 1652. Its advocacy of an aggressive foreign policy targeting Spain gained approval among supporters of the regime. Publishers peddling safe, comforting, patriotic nostalgia after the bitter divisions of the Civil Wars found profit in reprints of Drake's and Ralegh's exploits.

Cromwell had long sought portents. In his transatlantic correspondence with the Boston-based theologian John Cotton, the biblical scholar would seek to answer the Protector's questions: 'What is the Lord a doing?' 'What prophesies are now fulfilling?' Cotton advised that if Cromwell were to attack the Spaniards in the New World, he would 'dry up Euphrates', referring to a passage from the Book of Revelation: 'And the sixth angel poured out his vial upon the great river Euphrates; and the water thereof was dried up, that the way of the kings of the east might be prepared.' The analogy didn't quite work – Cromwell was more interested in *diverting* the 'Euphrates' of Spain's New World wealth to the benefit of England, leaving Spain high and dry, but the imperfect image stuck nonetheless.

The seizure of the Habsburgs' silver would push Spain towards bankruptcy, weakening it militarily, while enriching the Protectorate and clearing its debts. Beyond that, by cutting off the supplies of the pope's 'under-propper' – as Cromwell described

Spain – English Protestantism's millenarian dreams would be realized. Such beliefs were also evident in Cromwell's desire to readmit the Jews to England in fulfilment of biblical prophecies, and in his fantasizing view of Amerindian peoples as the lost tribes of Israel, whose bearded elders were said to speak Hebrew. They were thought to be in rebellion against the Spanish and therefore to be potential allies against them.

Cromwell's regime was developing a reputation abroad for religious tolerance, at least by seventeenth-century standards, even though the letter of the law placed those who denied the divinity of Christ outside it, as Cromwell was to make evident when he addressed the Second Protectorate Parliament on 17 September 1656: 'I will tell you the truth, that that which hath been our practice since the last Parliament, hath been to let all this nation see that whatever pretensions be to religion, if quiet, peaceable, they may enjoy conscience and liberty to themselves, so long as they do not make religion a pretence for arms and blood.'

While it was Cromwell's personal initiative to readmit the Jews into England, the main Jewish agent for the readmission of his people to England was a Portuguese rabbi and writer, Manasseh ben Israel, whose *Spes Israeli*, translated into English and published as *The Hope of Israel* in 1652, had proved a surprisingly popular work. Ben Israel was especially anxious to find a haven for Jews who were enduring a new round of persecution in Russia. He had met Thurloe in Amsterdam in 1651, just as Cromwell was considering the spiritual and temporal benefits of readmission. The secretary of state pondered the influx of new intelligence on European affairs that might be derived from Jewish networks. A committee was set up to consider Ben Israel's petition for his people to reside in England and on his arrival in England in 1655, Cromwell treated him royally, offering him rooms on the Strand, near to the centre of government in Whitehall. But Ben Israel was asking for more than just residence and trading for Jews. He also requested freedom to worship and the right for Jews to be buried in their own cemeteries. Cromwell's council appointed a subcommittee to consider Ben Israel's request, where it met with a rather frosty reception. A conference of judges, clerics and academics considered the issue further and Cromwell made an eloquent speech in favour of readmission. Despite the obvious commercial attractions, Cromwell's fundamental motive for the readmission of the Jews remained primarily a religious one. Christ's kingdom on earth, it was prophesied, could only be achieved once the Jews had been converted. Here was an opportunity to accelerate history. England, in its efforts to teach the true religion, would be the land most able to reveal the true faith to Jews, because, Cromwell urged, it was the 'only place in the world where religion was taught in its full purity'.[7] Though some still considered the Jews to be Christ killers, cursed for eternity, most of those on the committee did not, though when the debate was opened to the public, it became apparent that popular anti-Semitism ran deep. The real opposition, though, came from merchants – ever worldly – who were fearful of Jewish business skills, experience and networks. Cromwell was not, however, in a position to turn down a new source of money.

The Jews had been expelled under Edward I's royal prerogative in 1290 and so, by precedent, they could be similarly readmitted on the prerogative of the Protector. Two judges present on the committee could find no valid reason to oppose the readmittance, so Cromwell, strongly in favour, made a verbal agreement that the Jews would be welcome, that the recusancy laws, aimed at Catholics, would not apply to them and that a burial ground be bought. Jews worshipped openly, if sometimes precariously, at the synagogue in Creechurch Lane in the shadow of the Tower of London. Though never formally legalized by Cromwell, the readmission of Jews to England is usually dated to 1656.*

Cromwell's foreign policy had a strong moral element to it – rarely an indicator of desirable outcomes. He had sought a Protestant union with the Dutch, to the alarm of his potential allies and co-religionists alike. He had negotiated with the Portuguese, seeking trading rights for English merchants in Lisbon (as well as the right to Protestant worship) and access to the lucrative Brazilian market. But most prominent in considerations of foreign policy were the 'Two Crowns', the great Catholic monarchies of France and Spain. Ironically, 'Black' Spain wanted an alliance with England against France and feared a revival of the Anglo-Dutch naval alliance – the cause of so much grief during the rule of Elizabeth. No one in Madrid wanted to see the 'fleets of the two commonwealths on their way to the Indies', not least because the Dutch were also allied to France.

The diplomacy of France's chief minister, Cardinal Jules Mazarin, was more sophisticated and focused than that of Spain. Mazarin's envoy, Antoine de Bordeaux Neufville, had arrived in London in 1652, when Cromwell was stirring up trouble among the Huguenots of the south-west of France. England had been at war with the United Provinces of the Netherlands since 1652; a cessation of this First Anglo-Dutch War was as worrying to the Spanish as it was to the French, who feared an idle English fleet in the Channel, looking for trouble. Cromwell was closer personally to Alonso de Cárdenas, the Spanish ambassador in London, than he was to Bordeaux, and Mazarin knew that he needed to encourage the view – widely and deeply held among English Puritans – that Spain, not France, was England's natural

---

* British Jews tend to take a very different view of Cromwell from the Irish. Sigmund Freud was not the only Jew to name his son 'Oliver'.

enemy. The French diplomat Jean-Charles de Baas was instructed to make this point to Cromwell: and to suggest, reinforcing Gage's argument, that the Spanish West Indies were an especially vulnerable target for Cromwell's seaborne forces.

England was a tried and tested military force, which could claim increasingly to hold the balance of power in Europe. Cromwell played Spain and France off against one another, telling Cárdenas that he would commit thirty warships and 20,000 troops to fight the French in Flanders for a fee of £1.2 million. Cárdenas could offer no more than £300,000, for which sum Cromwell said he might consider organizing a blockade, but no more. When it became obvious that Cárdenas could not raise even £300,000, the Protector suggested that territory rather than cash might be acceptable. If the less than adequate port of Dunkirk was ceded to England, the Protector would send both naval and land forces to Flanders. Cárdenas accepted.

In a remarkable, if typical, example of duplicity and dissembl-ing, Cromwell proceeded at the same time to make a similar offer to France. He would send support to the French forces in Flanders if Brest, a rather better-appointed port than Dunkirk, was loaned to England in lieu of the permanent gain of an English Dunkirk once that was taken from the Spanish.

The Spanish council rejected Cromwell's offer vis-à-vis Dun-kirk (despite Cárdenas' earlier thumbs-up); the French, who held a stronger hand in their dealings with Cromwell, did not even discuss the option of Brest. Spain was involved in an exchequer-draining conflict in Flanders, in Catalonia and in Italy. France, steered ably by Mazarin, was less vulnerable, its resources less stretched.

Cromwell and his council judged war with France 'difficult and unprofitable'. Weakening the French, whose Gallic church was fiercely independent of the papacy, and 'greatening' the Spaniard would be the 'greatest prejudice to the protestant cause all over Europ [sic]'. Spain was, as it had always been in Cromwell's Elizabethan worldview, 'the greatest enemy to the Protestants in the world… and old enemie to this nation when it prospered best'. There would be 'inconveniencies', not least the inevitable loss of trade with Spain, including the lucrative export of wool, a particular concern to Lambert, whose home county of Yorkshire was a centre for England's cloth industry. But the friendship of the French would outweigh such matters, and a more emollient France would be less inclined to reawaken the Auld Alliance with a relatively pacified Scotland.

The die was cast. Secretary of State Thurloe told the Royalist Edward Hyde, 1st Earl of Clarendon, that Cárdenas had warned him that 'to ask a liberty from the inquisition and free sailing in the West Indies, was to ask his master's two eyes'.[8] His comment was interpreted by the regime, wilfully or not, as an example of Spanish aggression. It would be argued, for public consumption, that the pursuance of the anti-Spanish policy that would come to be known as the Western Design was conceived as the regime's retaliation for such slights, rather than as a pre-emptive strike. Such are the ways that governments persuade themselves into war, especially when they believe they are doing God's work.

3

Some Advantageous Designe

God has not brought us hither where we are but to
consider the work that we may do in the world
as well as at home.

OLIVER CROMWELL

A N 'INDIAN EXPEDITION' was first discussed at a meeting
of Cromwell's Council of State in mid-April 1654, soon
after peace had been agreed with the States General of the
United Netherlands in the Treaty of Westminster. It brought
to an end a conflict – the First Anglo-Dutch War – that had
begun following a dispute about the Dutch 'striking the flag' –
acknowledging England's sovereignty over its coastal waters by
lowering their ensign and dipping the topsail when encountering ships of Cromwell's navy. The treaty had been in gestation
for a while; in 1653 the English had reiterated their troubling
proposal (originally put forward in 1651) for a political union
of the two Protestant powers, but this was again rejected by the
Dutch. They did, however, agree to carry on saluting the flags
of English warships in the Channel, as they had done 'in the
times of Queen Elizabeth'.

Peace having been agreed with the United Provinces, albeit
uneasily, how was England, with '160 sayle of shipps well

appointed swimminge at sea', now to employ its substantial and tested military resources to 'some advantageous designe'? Where, in the vastness of the New World, was the best place to strike at Habsburg power? Gage had pointed out that 'Hispaniola was the Spaniards' first plantation' in the Americas, 'and therefore would bee to them a bad omen to beginne to loose that'. But in addition to Hispaniola,* Cuba, Mexico, Peru and other territories were considered, as was Panama, through which passed the produce of the silver mines of Peruvian Potosí. Guatemala, the region with which Gage was most intimate, was also put on the list. Its garrison was small and lightly defended, but English adventurers would have to pass through the coastal mountains, across which mule trains carried wine every year. The risk might be worth it, however: with the help of indigenous peoples, who would *of course* hail the English as liberators, it might be possible to take the road to the north, and reach as far as Mexico.

As well as Gage's report, the Council had access to another, from Colonel Thomas Modyford, a slightly more rational and reflective figure, though no less convinced of the certainty of his proposed scheme's success. A former Royalist colonel, he and members of his family had emigrated in 1647 to Barbados, an island in a state of rapid and lucrative transformation thanks to the input of Dutch sugar growers and the import of African slaves. Modyford, who had renounced his support for Charles II while in Barbados, had petitioned Cromwell following his dismissal from the island's ruling council, and the Protector now sought his advice on the proposed expedition.

Modyford argued that Barbados, a settled and secure English possession, should be used as a staging post and recruitment

---

* The Caribbean island of Hispaniola is now shared between the modern nation states of the Dominican Republic in the east and Haiti in the west.

centre from where a 6,000-strong invasion of Spanish territory along the River Orinoco on the South American mainland could be staged via Trinidad. The English should ally with indigenous peoples against the Spanish, who, despite English prejudices, were, in his judgement, a formidable foe. They could only be defeated by well-armed, well-resourced and disciplined troops, of which the Protectorate had many. Sickness was the greatest danger, Modyford warned: beef well salted and beer well boiled would be as important as weapons and ships to the success of any such expedition, as would light clothing, suitable for the tropics. Though the mainland was his favoured target, he was willing to consider an attack on Cuba, the Spanish empire's 'back door'. Either way, he stressed, good planning was the key to success. They could not rely on providence alone.

Serious thought was given to Modyford's proposals. One member of the Council, the future Earl of Shaftesbury, Anthony Ashley Cooper, a former Royalist who served on Cromwell's Council of State, had possessions in Barbados, though it is unlikely that he or any of his colleagues had visited them. Two sea captains, Henry Hatsell and John Limberry, who had practical knowledge of the region, were present at the meeting. Hatsell was a member of the Commissioners of the Navy (the Navy Board), based in Plymouth, who aligned ideologically with the more radical members of the regime. A commissioner for 'ejecting' poor quality churchmen, he was an ally of John Desborough, Cromwell's brother-in-law. Limbery was a victualler. Both claimed to have 'lived and traded in Hispaniola'.

Hatsell and Limbery recommended an expedition to capture Hispaniola and Cuba, respectively the first island to belong to the Spanish New World empire and its administrative centre. Hispaniola, they believed, was ripe for settlement and would serve as a base for attacks in the western Caribbean, which would prove 'very feasible'. Once in English hands, the Spanish islands of the Caribbean could be settled by 'our people from New England, Virginia, the Barbadoes, the Summer Islands or from Europe'.[1]

There was another thing that was particularly attractive about Hispaniola. Geographically, it would be the ideal base from which to intercept the Spanish plate fleet, the *flota de Indias*, as it set out on its return to Cadiz. The Dutchman Piet Heyn, in one of the most celebrated acts of state piracy of the time, had captured the treasure fleet in 1628, bringing vast wealth both to himself and to his country. Surely it was not beyond the capabilities of England's powerful and experienced navy, the heirs of Drake and Ralegh, to repeat such a feat?

A second meeting of the Council to explore options for a Design on the New World was held on 20 July 1654. The only record of the meeting is the heavily stylized account by Edward Montagu, the future Earl of Sandwich, of a debate by Cromwell, who was the prime advocate of the project, and John Lambert, the second most powerful figure of the Protectorate and, arguably, its best military strategist, who opposed it.[2]

The arguments over the Design between Cromwell and his second in command revealed a fundamental division in the regime. Cromwell countered Lambert from an imperial stance: 'God has not brought us hither where we are but to consider the work that we may do in the world as well as at home.' There was an inevitability to expansion, he argued, to a new global role, to which 'Providence seemed to lead us hither'. A great navy – with '160 sayle of shipps well appointed swiminge at sea' – was idle,* every major European power bar the Dutch saw

---

* Between 1651 and 1655, the Republic built as much ship's tonnage as was constructed in England between 1588, the year of the Armada, and 1642.

republican England as an enemy or potential one. Cromwell, in an aggressive mood, thought 'our best consideration had to keep up this reputation'. It was good to be bad. In a remarkably sanguine observation, fortified by the optimism of Gage and Modyford, Cromwell stated his belief that 'this design would cost little more than laying by the ships' and realize a 'great profit'.[3]

Lambert, cautious of such providentialism and wary of Spanish power, returned to troubles at home. Domestic matters took precedent, he argued, and 'the charge was not well considered'. How, he asked, was 'this design' to be paid for? 'Our army in Scotland and army and inhabitants in Ireland must quit the country or you must find more treasure.' And there was no evidence that there would be many willing settlers. 'New England and the Barbados will not flock to you in Hispaniola' unless the island was made secure and that was a formidable, perpetual task, eating up time and money, as the Spanish would not give up their lucrative New World possessions without a fight. Cromwell, however, was at his most providential, as he often was in military matters: here was a place to dump Scottish and Irish malcontents, a place where the New Englanders, until now distant from the struggle with Spain, could conquer the tropical climate and prosper. And they had God on their side, as John Cotton's biblical exegesis had made clear. Gage had used similar language in his proposal to Cromwell and his Council, arguing that victory in the Americas would lead to the 'utter fall of Romish Babylon, and to the conversion of those poor and simple Indians'.

Harking back once again to the days of Drake and Ralegh – though omitting to mention that neither Elizabethan hero had conquered substantial Spanish territory – Cromwell outlined his vision of a future where 'Six frigates nimble shall range up and down the bay of Mexico to get prey', rather like the parliamentary fleet that had sailed along the North American coast in the wake of the Battle of Worcester, attacking the six mainland colonies that had declared for Charles. These were the words of a man who had never known military defeat. Cromwell must not miss this world-historical moment, Gage had urged. He should recall the mistake of 'that narrow hearted prince', Henry VII, who had turned down the chance to fund the great voyages of Columbus, missing out on the riches that now accrued to Spain. 'God would not make that prince such an instrument for the advancing glory, as he hath made your highness,' Gage implored, throwing down the gauntlet.

How the project took its final shape is something of a mystery, but as early as 5 June 1654 the Council gave secret orders to the Admiralty and navy to prepare fourteen ships for what was, for the first time, called the Western Design. It was decided that twenty-four ships were to be designated 'for the service of General Blake', the Protectorate's greatest admiral,* who was to launch a blockade of the main Spanish port of Cadiz as soon as the inevitable victory in the West Indies was announced.

By the beginning of July, thirty-six ships had been approved for the assault on the Spanish Americas, with the actual details and target undecided. Its leaders, however, had been appointed. There were to be joint commanders of the expedition: William Penn was to be general at sea, or admiral, while General Robert Venables was to command the land army.

As a parliamentary officer, Venables had distinguished himself at the Siege of Chester, a heavily fortified Royalist stronghold, in

---

* Horatio Nelson was among those who considered themselves inferior in English naval lore to Admiral Blake.

1646. As a colonel, he had taken part in the conquest of Ireland, in particular the defeat of the Marquis of Ormond at Rathmines in August 1649, and he had served alongside Cromwell at the siege of Drogheda in September of that year. In the reconquest of Ulster, a campaign sullied by numerous atrocities, which was not completed until 1653, he had gained a reputation as a ruthless commander for whom Cromwell was full of praise. Yet he returned to England aggrieved. Despite his efforts and ordeals he had 'never received further reward than a letter of thanks'.[4]

It was Cromwell who asked him if he was interested in commanding the land forces for the Western Design, a considerable promotion and, for Venables, long-awaited recognition of his achievements. He was newly married, in curious circumstances, to a widow, Elizabeth Lee, who appears to have been his opposite in temperament, politics and religion. The Western Design was to serve as their 'honeymoon' – she was to travel with the fleet – recognition, too, that Hispaniola was to be settled by men and women, in perpetuity.

Elizabeth was to prove a harsh but perceptive critic of the project. 'A wicked army it was,' she later recalled, 'and sent out without arms or provisions.' She was not wrong. Among numerous elementary mistakes of organization and logistics, for which John Desborough was ultimately responsible, the fleet, though heading for the tropics, ignored Modyford's advice to take enough containers with which to store water, to take ample food, and to dress the men in clothing suitable to the climate.

Penn, in his mid-thirties, was the youngest son of a youngest son – a merchant in the City of London with some knowledge of the sea – whose ambitions would be best realized in the relative meritocracy of the navy. He had risen quickly, and may have taken his first command at the age of twenty-one. Appointed by Parliament to command the *Fellowship* in May 1644, by the end of the year, he was the rear admiral of Parliament's Irish squadron. He played a role in the suppression of a Royalist rising in west Wales, during which doubts as to his allegiance were raised.

He had failed to track down Prince Rupert in the Mediterranean in 1650, but netted a handsome haul of treasure nonetheless. He became Blake's vice admiral in the First Anglo-Dutch War and distinguished himself in the encounter off Portland in February 1653. On Blake's recommendation, he was made an admiral at sea for his 'honesty and ability'. He was appointed to lead the Western Design on 18 August 1654, three months before Venables.

Instructions issued on 9 December spoke only of 'getting ground'. No specific target was identified. While Penn was given licence to wage war on Spanish shipping in the region, Venables had received slightly more detailed orders: 'to gain an interest in that part of the West Indies in the possession of the Spaniard', meaning the Greater Antilles (Hispaniola, Cuba and Puerto Rico), Jamaica, the Main (from the mainland border with Brazil, then Portuguese, to Panama) and 'Mexico' (the area north of Panama).

Venables was offered three possible courses of action. The first was to take Hispaniola in order to stop reinforcements to the Spanish Main. The second, the plan outlined by Modyford, was to land at the mouth of the Orinoco, with the ultimate aim of occupying Cartagena on what is now the northern coast of Colombia and intercept treasure on its way from Potosí and Spain's other mines in Peru and Mexico. The third was a fusion of the first two: take Hispaniola and use it as a base from which to launch an assault on Cartagena. The crew members were not alone in wondering where they might be heading. Royalist intelligencers had noticed that the ships' hulls had been reinforced against the shipworms found in tropical waters and so guessed that the Caribbean might be its destination. In Madrid there was much speculation concerning the destination of the

English fleet: some suggested it might be bound for Madagascar, others the River Plate.

The final decision as to where to attack was left to the commanders, but it was not to be an entirely military operation. A five-man commission, each to receive an annual salary of £1,000, was created by Cromwell to oversee military operations and establish an overall system of government for the new English possessions in the West Indies as they inevitably accrued. Joining Penn and Venables on the commission were Edward Winslow; Daniel Searle, governor of Barbados; and Captain Gregory Butler. Winslow, who grew up in an English Protestant community in Leiden in the Netherlands, was a former governor of Plymouth, Massachusetts, and had sailed on the *Mayflower* in 1620.* As a young man, he played a key role in the tense negotiations with the Wampanoag peoples, on whose land the Plymouth colonists had settled. After the death in Plymouth of his first wife in 1621, Winslow married a widow, Susanna White, mother of the first English child born in New England. Winslow was vastly experienced and reliable; he would be John Thurloe's eyes and ears as the Design progressed.

Searle, a City merchant, had been governor of Barbados since 1651, having travelled with the parliamentary fleet that brought the Royalist possession to heel following the conclusion of the Civil Wars. He would be responsible for dealing with the politics of the fractious island when the Design fleet arrived there and would play little role once it had embarked on its final leg. He was to be aided in the process of recruitment on Barbados by the rather more obscure figure of Butler, whose role would be to make quietly valuable preparation, along with Colonel Richard

---

* Winslow is the only one among that pioneering number for whom a likeness survives.

Holdip and Captain Edward Blagg, in St Christopher. That was before concerns about his drinking arose.

There was to be no looting and plunder in these newly possessed lands and the goods and property of the Spanish settlers was to be held for 'the use of the state'; this would later be interpreted as meaning for those who were willing to settle on Jamaica. Every attempt was to be made to bring the indigenous peoples on side. The 'no plunder' policy did not go down well with the sailors, who were used to being allowed to pilfer as they wished. But this was a state-backed enterprise and, wisely or not, discipline and morality trumped personal enrichment.

Penn set sail from Spithead in the 60-gun *Swiftsure* on Christmas Day 1654, along with thirty-seven other ships, some support vessels and around 2,500 men. Hawkins, the Elizabethan buccaneer, had written that 'Those unfortunate Woods of Hispaniola, like the Gallows under which the Romans once passed, may shame them into such a height of Courage, as will be too great for the Enemy to oppose.' Much was expected, much presumed.

4

Hubris and Hispaniola

We march'd in a most sad and miserable manner
in an unknown Country tormented with
Heat, hunger, and thirst.

GENERAL ROBERT VENABLES

PENN'S 'INVINCIBLE ARMADA' made Barbados on 29 January 1655, where another 5,500 men were recruited, amid considerable local opposition. Barbados came with a history, as Searle knew all too well. In 1650, after years of relative stability under the stewardship of Philip Bell, the former governor of Providence Island, Barbados rejected the authority of Parliament. A number of defeated Royalists, to whom Bell arranged the sale of plantations, made their way there. Humphrey Walrond, a particularly vehement Royalist, led a campaign of harassment against those 'Independents' more sympathetic to Parliament – the 'seven-headed dragon of Westminster' – of whom James Drax was the most prominent. He was one of more than 120 settlers who were arrested by the island's Royalist regime. Drax was fined 80,000 pounds of sugar and banished to England, where he lobbied the Council of State to take action, recommending that they appoint Edward Winslow, the capable former head of the Plymouth Colony, to be the new governor of Barbados.

To complicate matters, the Royalist Francis, Lord Willoughby of Parham had arrived on the island in April 1650 with a commission, from the Earl of Carlisle, appointing him its governor. It was endorsed – so Willoughby claimed – by 'Charles II', whom he unilaterally proclaimed king in May 1650. So many competing factions on so small an island was not a situation likely to endure. In 1650, the Commonwealth sent an invasion force commanded by Sir George Ayscue, whom the government had appointed governor of Barbados, to bring the faction-ridden island to heel. En route to the Caribbean, Ayscue helped Admiral Robert Blake capture the privateer's stronghold of the Scilly Isles for the parliamentarians.[1] Ayscue arrived off Barbados nine months later, on 15 October 1651, in the wake of Cromwell's decisive victory at Worcester, and demanded that the island submit. The Royalists under Willoughby, however, refused to do so, and a standoff ensued. It was Thomas Modyford, adviser to Cromwell and his Council on their Caribbean options, who broke the stalemate, helping Ayscue's men to land and force Willoughby into compliance on 11 January 1652. Liberty of conscience was declared, local tax-raising powers were confirmed, as was the right to trade with countries that were 'in amity with England'. Willoughby chose to move his plantation to Surinam on the South American mainland. Barbados had been pacified.

When Penn's fleet arrived in Barbados on 29 January 1655, it encountered its own problems despite the relatively settled political climate.[2] The sheer scale of the sugar industry, which used every scrap of cultivatable land, meant that most of the island's food now had to be imported, a situation made more precarious by the fact that the population of Barbados had doubled in fifteen years. As for arms, the force could only get their hands on little more than poorly constructed cane half-pikes, which were to prove fatally inadequate when deployed.

Despite parliamentary orders to the contrary, Penn seized a number of Dutch ships, though a jury of resentful locals assembled by Commissioner Searle found for the 'strangers', as the Dutch and other foreign traders were known. Venables became increasingly angered by the delays they were encountering on the island. The inefficiency and disorganization was all a long way, he observed, from the brutally effective Irish campaign that had brought him to prominence. They eventually embarked from Barbados on 31 March, but not before mislaying Colonel Richard Fortescue, for whom a ship had to return.

The largest English fleet ever to sail through the Caribbean headed north to the Lesser Antilles, its final destination, known only to the five commissioners. A minor skirmish took place with the indigenous Kalinago of Dominica: three seamen of the *Tulip* were wounded and one Carib killed in retaliation.[3] But generally progress was smooth. The fleet moored at the Leeward Islands – Antigua and St Christopher (St Kitts) – both in English hands, for provisions. Butler, Cromwell's representative on St Kitts, a territory shared with France, had been there for two months already. He had recruited two invaluable guides to the region. Kempo Sybada, a Frisian based in Antigua, had served in Providence Island and with those residents who had headed for the Mosquito Coast. Captain Christopher Cox had lived among the Spanish for twelve years, serving as a gunner, presumably because they believed him to be an Irish Catholic; he may have been among those Irish residents who fled Barbados when life became difficult following the Irish rebellion of 1641. He was certainly a skilled pilot, whose fortunes would become entwined with those of the Design.[4]

It has long been claimed that Penn and Venables grew to loathe one another. But there is little concrete evidence for a deep rift; the narrative of hatred between the two men appears to stem from Venables' desperate attempt at self-justification when, following his humiliating return to London, he was incarcerated in the Tower and understandably bitter enough to set poisonous thoughts to paper. Yet the duo's working relationship cannot have been helped by the operational confusion that surrounded the hastily and inadequately prepared expedition. Although Penn had command of the navy, he was subordinate to Venables, while both men were overseen by Winslow and Searle, neither of whom had military experience. They, in turn reported directly to Cromwell. Given the limitations of early modern communications, this was an awfully long chain of command. The organization of provisions, the responsibility of a commission headed by Desborough, the Commissioner of the Admiralty and Navy, proved to be inadequate – and there were even claims, albeit unfounded, that the supposedly godly brother-in-law of the Protector was siphoning off materiel for his own benefit. Overall, the logistics of the Design were disastrous, though largely due to Cromwell's haste and the fleet's 'expeditious dispatch'; it seemed that no account had been taken of the conditions the expedition was likely to encounter: gunpowder became useless in the torrential tropical rain; the biscuit rotted. Worst of all, there was never enough water.[5]

The fleet sighted Hispaniola, the second largest island of the Greater Antilles, in April 1655. The target had finally been confirmed at a meeting held in Barbados on 17 March, at which both Penn and Venables as well as Commissioner Searle had been present. But it may not have been until 9 April 1655, four months or so after the fleet's departure from England, that Venables revealed the target to his men.

Covering almost 30,000 square miles but sparsely populated, Hispaniola was thought the easiest option for conquest: had not Francis Drake captured it – albeit temporarily – with a much smaller force in 1586? There could be no better, no gentler springboard for Cromwell's ultimate aim: the conquest of Spanish America.

The fleet would target the same landing point as Drake – Xayna, near the Spanish fort of San Jeronimo – using techniques honed in the Irish campaign. The notably pious and allegedly Anabaptist vice admiral William Goodsonn would be in charge of landing Venables' troops on 14 April. Though he was one of the few commanders to have experience of the Caribbean, he found the coast 'rocky, and a great surf of the sea against it in so much that in many places we saw the beatings of the water appear afar off like the smoke of ordnance, the wind being but indifferent'. It was an inauspicious beginning to the campaign.[6]

Having failed to land at Xayna, Goodsonn sailed 30 miles west to Point Nicayo, where 7,500 men were 'landed very well, and without opposition of the enemy, in a good sandy bay'. The following day, a force under Anthony Buller, former governor of the Scilly Isles, together with some of Holdip's foot soldiers, landed where Goodsonn had tried to disembark the day before. The two forces were now 30 and 12 miles respectively from their ultimate prize – Santo Domingo, capital of Hispaniola. The two forces planned to rendezvous before launching their assault.

The invaders' prospects were not helped by their commanders' ignorance of the local conditions. Believing that access to food and water would be little different from what they were familiar with in Britain and Ireland, where they foraged the land as they advanced, both forces set off with just three days of supplies, including water. To do so at the end of the dry season when waterways were all but dried up was folly indeed.

Venables' force, the furthest from Santo Domingo, passed through a mixture of dense forest and open savannah, completing an impressive 18 miles by the second day. They encountered only minor Spanish resistance. Already short of water, the troops rested overnight at a deserted plantation by the side of a road. Here they ate copious amounts of oranges to slake their thirst, but the excess of citrus merely succeeded in exacerbating the 'flux' that already plagued them. Venables would later recount to Cromwell: 'We march'd in a most sad and miserable manner in an unknown Country tormented with Heat, hunger, and thirst... myself enduring what the meanest suffered.'[7]

Meanwhile Buller's men, having reached the agreed rendezvous point, had camped by a river overnight. The following day, confusion reigned. Members of a party sent by Buller to investigate a nearby fort mistakenly reported that they had caught sight of the colours of the main force. On hearing this, Buller decided to go ahead with the rest of his men to meet it. As a result, when Venables reached the rendezvous point the following day, Monday 16 April, Buller and his men were nowhere to be seen.

Venables' force, used to fording rivers in Britain and Ireland, lost its way in the parched savannah. Their lack of water became critical. A crossing point on the River Hinnum was eventually found and some 2,000 men were positioned there to secure it, while the other troops rested overnight. The following day, they came upon two men of African descent, one of whom claimed to be a former servant of Thomas Warner, the governor of St Kitts. At four o'clock in the afternoon, Venables' and Buller's forces finally achieved their long-delayed rendezvous. No sooner had they done so than they were ambushed.

Headed for their ultimate target of Fort Jeronimo, to the west of Santo Domingo, the English were marching along a wide road, with Venables and the other senior officers leading from the front. As they approached a gateway to what they believed to be an abandoned settlement, one of the English soldiers spotted a prone enemy soldier, and took aim. This prompted the Spanish, at the urging of their Irish cavalryman, Don Juan Morfa (probably a corruption of 'Murphy'), to attack. Up to thirty of the English were killed in the ensuing firefight, including four officers and the invaluable Cox. Although the English regrouped and fought off the Spanish – Goodsonn's regiment of seamen made a particularly strong showing – the firelocks, or musketeers, commanded by Captain Pawlett, had 'shamefully run'. According to Goodsonn, his men came within range of San Domingo, where they awaited the rest of the force, but it never arrived. A rumour circulated that, as the seamen advanced, Venables had walked past them, into a wood, seeking his own regiment. The story, true or not, would be used against him by his enemies in the fallout of failure.[8]

While the army slept that night, the navy bombarded Santo Domingo. The troops were to stay put until the following Monday, enjoying 'some kind of quiet', refreshed, or so they thought, by the waters of the River Hinnum and what victuals the navy could bring ashore in the high surf. Venables rejected a proposal to split the force in two and approach the town in a pincer movement, despite the tactic having widespread support among his officers.

The soldiers faced another Spanish attack on Wednesday 20 April, though the enemy 'were soon put to the run'. The Spanish captain was killed, along with half a dozen of the attackers. The 'negro of Sir Thomas Warners' was praised for his fierce response: 'Give the dogs no quarters', he insisted.

For all these rousing sentiments, the English soldiers became increasingly affected by illness: the river on whose banks they rested was believed to be poisoned by a nearby copper mine. Then, on Thursday, the rains came. It was not until the following Tuesday – eleven days after landing and with their morale low – that they launched their final assault on Santo Domingo, strengthened by light artillery. Moving slowly, on half rations, they approached the fort at San Jeronimo in tight formation.

In the vanguard were the 240 or so troops of Adjutant General Jackson, followed by the Reformados,* Pawlet's somewhat disgraced Firelocks, Captain Carpenter's cavalry and the infantry under the army's second in command, Major General James Heane.† Jackson, it appears, obeying Venables' orders, ignored Heane's advice to establish wings on both sides of the fort and they marched as one. Already under withering fire from the seven heavy guns of the fort, they were ambushed by forces from the neighbouring woods. They fired back – again as one – with a single volley. In the time it took for the English to reload, the Spanish charged and the invaders fled 'like a torrent in a narrow passage'. Pawlet was killed in the rout, while the experienced Reformados stood their ground, paying a heavy price: out of fifty-five men, just eighteen survived.

Major General Heane, too, offered fierce resistance and died a hero, along with his ensign Thomas Boys, his sword 'sheathed in his enemies bowels'. The Spaniards' *vaqueros*, or 'Cowkillers', did most of the damage. Men and women of mainly African descent, their deployment of ferocious lances was athletic and highly skilled. Guns, which took an age to reload, and poorly

---

* Experienced soldiers who, having left the army, later returned to service. Some were former Royalists eager to make peace with a regime whose anti-Spanish sentiments they shared.
† Heane's leading role in the capture of Jersey in 1651 was considered useful experience to take to the islands of the Caribbean.

made Barbadian cane pikes offered little resistance. In total, as many as 1,500 English troops died, a humiliation made worse by the morale-sapping loss of as many as nine colours, a regiment's rallying flag. Only Goodsonn's seamen fought to the city gates of Santo Domingo.

Amid the chaos, Venables called a council of war, which agreed to retreat once the artillery mortar was exhausted. 'The whole armie except the rear guard marched away in all manner of disorder, hasting to get water,' wrote one correspondent. Then the rains came again. Just under a fortnight after the English landing on Hispaniola, the survivors were spotted by the navy. Two days later, the remnants of the English force abandoned their attempt to take Hispaniola. They were in a pitiable and traumatized condition: men were still dying on a daily basis, some of them as a result of friendly fire by fatigued fellow soldiers; disorientated individuals made ham-fisted attempts to shoot cattle for food; few had sufficient energy to fight. The fleet was readied and boarding commenced on the evening of 2 May. The campaign had cost as many as 2,500 lives, many of them lost to the ravages of hunger and thirst. The blessings of divine providence had surely been withdrawn from a blundering campaign – crippled at the outset by egregious omissions, organizational ineptitude and a fatal lack of preparation.

The navy, which despised the army for its incompetence and perceived cowardice,[9] believed that it should be abandoned to its shame. Retribution followed. One lowly soldier, who, in the midst of battle, was said to have shouted 'Gentleman, shift yourselves, we are all lost', was hanged, *pour encourager les autres*, with his crime carved on his chest.

Senior figures were treated more leniently, though their humiliation was complete. Jackson faced a court martial as the fleet prepared to sail – it was said that, unlike the heroic Heane, he had 'sneaked into the bushes, like an old fox'. Venables regarded him with contempt – as a lackey of Cromwell – and Jackson was lucky to be merely cashiered for cowardice. To add to his humiliation, he was ordered to tend to the sick and wounded.[10]

How could Penn and Venables save face after presiding over such a catastrophe? Jamaica, downwind and accessible from the south coast of Hispaniola, offered a redemption of sorts. The island had not featured in any of the discussions held by Cromwell and his Council before the Design was launched, though it had been subject to the occasional English raid, most recently, and ironically, by the now disgraced William Jackson in 1642. It was much smaller than Hispaniola (at 4,200 square miles, it was less than one-sixth of the size). Home to around 2,000 Spanish, Portuguese, Africans and a handful of indigenous people, Jamaica was an afterthought in Spain's conquest of the New World. A minor prize, but arguably better than nothing.

Luckily for Penn and Venables and their men, Jamaica was also the only Spanish possession in the Caribbean without any defensive structures. The Columbus family who owned the island – Jamaica was their last personal possession in the New World – and who claimed rent but little else, argued that Spanish royal law forbade the building of unlicensed fortifications. All that stood between England and its Caribbean consolation prize was a rickety stockade.[11]

Forty English ships entered what became known as the Old Harbour Bay on the south-central coast on 10 May, landing around 7,000 men, who were met by a desultory 'little force of 3 or 4 guns'. The defence offered was chaotic, the Spanish surrendering just a week later, though not before various guerrilla forces had taken to the hills: it would take decades to pacify the island. While attempting to flush them out – Venables had long experience of fighting Tory bandits in Ireland – he became affected by fever. Penn, with the prize of Jamaica secure, abandoned him and set sail on 25 June for England, whose tentative new elite were hoping desperately for good news from abroad.

5

All the King's Men

Thus our punishment sprang from our sins.

CLEMENT SPELMAN, 1660

CHARLES STUART'S DEFEAT at Worcester on 3 September 1651 had marked the end of a chapter in royalism from which its English contingent – unable or unwilling to embrace a life on foreign soil – had been largely absent. Charles had fought the battle as the 'covenanted king' of the Scots' Kirk party, Calvinist fundamentalists backed by a formidable army. It was an unlikely alliance, born of desperation on both sides. The catastrophic defeat of Charles's Scottish Presbyterian forces and his flight to the Continent ushered in a new – and very different – phase of Royalist resistance to Cromwell's regime.

England's Cavaliers were on their own again, a situation that some of the more hot-headed among them welcomed with enthusiasm and exhilaration. Their destiny was, at least, in their own hands. This more militant Royalist opposition, attractive to the maverick, had three principal ambitions: to foment risings and insurrection, ideally on a national scale; to encourage disaffected army radicals to throw in their lot with the Cavalier cause; and to kill Cromwell. The first two would prove difficult when not impossible, despite the bravery and resourcefulness of a few remarkable individuals. The third, dependent though it was on serendipity and chance, was the more likely to succeed. The Gunpowder Plot, half a century ago, had come very close to killing Charles Stuart's grandfather, James I. A similarly desperate project would unveil itself in time.

The King's Council, exiled in Paris, had been dominated by the Louvre group, which gathered around the queen mother, Henrietta Maria. Very much at home in the city of her birth, she gathered a waspish set around her: advisers such as Lord Jermyn, a man of dissolute morals who was rumoured, with no evidence at all, to have secretly married her; and Lord Balcarres, a Scottish covenanter turned engager.* Citizens of anywhere that would have them, they embraced internationalist designs on the lost throne, preferring their diplomats – prominent among whom was the philosopher, Roman Catholic and inventor of the wine bottle Sir Kenelm Digby – to cultivate popes and princes, kings and dukes rather than home-grown conspirators. They looked mistily upon Charles's cousin, the shooting star of romantic royalism, Prince Rupert of the Rhine, a man who had achieved glory as a cavalry commander in the Civil Wars, cared more for canines than commoners and became a pioneer of the Atlantic slave trade. But without substantial foreign aid – financial and military – from a major continental power, a Royalist invasion of England was likely to remain a dangerous fantasy, as the exiled Yorkshire Royalist Sir Marmaduke Langdale had pointed out to Charles Stuart himself:

> Strangers if they can possibly be gotten are the most fit instruments for your Majesty to act in England withal; they are not

---

* 'Engagers' were Scottish Presbyterians who made 'Engagement' with Charles I in December 1647, when the king was imprisoned in Carisbrooke Castle on the Isle of Wight.

interested in the several factions of those that pretend to be for your Majesty, neither have their hands been defiled with the innocent blood shed in England. Those are not your friends, or do not understand England, that will persuade your Majesty that strangers will not be welcome to your friends in England. For God's sake beware of letting your own friends any more appear in arms, unless they have a foreign army to countenance them, or some considerable party of the army to join with them.[1]

Langdale, a lean man, known as the 'ghost', was despised by Edward Hyde, who having set aside his great history of the Civil Wars in 1648, judged him 'a man hard to please, and of a very weak understanding, yet proud, and much in love with his own judgement'.[2] Langdale had been a reluctant Royalist during the civil wars; on the eve of the conflict, he had led the East Riding of Yorkshire in opposition to the king's imposition of the Ship Money. But his experience of the brutalities of continental conflict during the Thirty Years War had made him cautious, and he hoped that civil war, when it seemed inevitable, would be confined to the south of England, 'where the wellspring of our miseries began, and where there is pillage enough to satisfy many armies'.[3] When it did arrive, he fought to preserve the status quo, proving a notable cavalry commander, who got the better of Fairfax at Marston Moor. Following the end of the First Civil War, he was exiled to France but returned to fight again in the second. Following the crushing Royalist defeat at Preston in August 1648, Langdale escaped once more to France. While in exile, he fought for Venice against the Turks and became a zealous convert to Roman Catholicism. Spain was his favoured, if unpopular, choice of ally.

The problem for advocates of foreign intervention was that the king could secure very little support from abroad. Cardinal Mazarin, Louis XIV's Italian-born chief minister, was open to an alliance with Cromwell, whose power, backed by a battle-hardened army and navy, seemed assured. His agents and diplomats in England spoke of the stability and strength of the regime while disparaging the efforts of the Royalists. Spain, unaware as yet of the unfolding campaign to seize its Caribbean assets, was too stretched in its conflicts across Europe to offer any help to the Stuart cause, even were it so inclined. The Dutch were unlikely to join in conspiracy against their fellow Protestants, and the Danes and the Swedes, bitter rivals of one another, were united in their desire to do business with the Protectorate, not least in the trading of the Baltic's raw materials – wood, pitch and tar – that were essential to Cromwell's mighty maritime forces.

The Louvre group's Franco-Scottish policy of *realpolitik*, targeting with some desperation the Scottish Presbyterians as the ally most likely to deliver the throne to Charles, was a call they got catastrophically wrong. Widely mistrusted in England and disparaged by Anglican (and occasionally Catholic) Royalists as the 'chief saints in the Presbyterian calendar', the queen and her coterie would be the targets of much *Schadenfreude* when the Scots were sent homeward by Cromwell to think again.[4] The Louvre group had been belittled, their authority, reliant far more on birth than ability, diminished.

Their failure opened up an opportunity for the 'Old Royalists', focused upon Edward Hyde, the king's erudite and eloquent chancellor, and James Butler, Duke of Ormond, former commander of the Royalist army in Ireland, who had led the resistance to the Catholic rebellion of 1641. Cromwell's devastating invasion of Scotland had called Ormond's nobility and martial ability into question, and he sailed into exile in December 1650. His Irish experience made him wary of unlikely and incompatible alliances, but in his manners he remained a grand

European aristocrat. Both men were more faithful to their principles than the Louvre group and uncomfortable about the alliance with the Presbyterian Scots. Hyde, whose enmity with Jermyn went back to the 1630s, was known to be wary if not contemptuous of the strategy that unravelled on the battlefield at Worcester. On the king's return to Paris – Charles Stuart was, thanks to some remarkable examples of individual bravery and sacrifice, one of the very few senior figures to escape the clutches of Cromwell post-Worcester – the Louvre group was cast out, the Scots abandoned to their fate and the principled, pragmatic and patient strategy of Hyde and Ormond was adopted as 'official' policy.

Just as, in Hyde's words, 'discomposures, jealousies, and disgusts… reigned at Oxford', the Royalist capital during the First Civil War, so faction and fissure continued to preside over those who backed the cause of 'Mr Cross', the Royalist codename for the exiled Charles II.[5] There was no overall intelligencer, no Royalist equivalent of Cromwell's network of spies and agents, run at first by the regicide Thomas Scot and his assistant, the fierce Bristolian Independent, George Bishop. They, aided by the brilliant cryptographer John Wallis, Oxford geometry professor and the man who broke the code to Charles I's damningly duplicitous correspondence captured after Naseby, had access to the considerable resources of the state, which would soon come under the commanding control of John Thurloe. Mr Cross had no such means.[6]

There were other reasons why, after Worcester, Cavalier conspiracy struggled to take root on English soil. The Act of General Pardon and Oblivion, passed by the Rump Parliament on 24 February 1652, pardoned Royalist activity short of treason that took place before the Battle of Worcester. Many former supporters of the king signed the government's Engagement of loyalty to the Commonwealth and verbally renounced the Stuart cause, seeking a quiet life. The typical Royalist, nicely characterized in hindsight by Daniel Defoe, was 'a gentleman of a very plentiful fortune, having an estate of above £5,000 per annum, of a family nearly allied to several of the principal nobility'.[7] Such people had a lot to lose and Cromwell was anxious to win over these 'considerable persons' as part of his project – largely a sincere one – of 'healing and settling'.* The atmosphere in England was changing for Royalists, and for the better. Sequestration of Royalist property, practised since the outbreak of the Civil Wars, had all but ceased. The Anglican liturgy, in which the Prayer Book held sway, was performed almost as frequently as it had ever been, with little interference from the authorities. Legal process slowly became available even to those who had failed to take the Engagement. Many Royalists returned from exile and were, on the whole, 'well received and kindly used'.

The regime's Orders for Securing the Peace classified Royalists according to the threat they posed. Of least concern were those who had been 'delinquent' during the Civil Wars – in other words they had fought on the side of the king – but had been passive since. Most troubling were those hardened subversives, relatively few in number, who actively sought the fall of Cromwell's regime and who were to be imprisoned or banished. By the mid-1650s, most Royalist families in England had come to a pragmatic, if reluctant, accommodation with the government.

This 'passive majority' of Royalists bedded down in England,

* A phrase much invoked by Cromwell; he introduced it in his speech to Parliament on 4 September 1654.

content to live peaceably in a land without a king, though nostalgic for a settled – and by no means vanquished – past of hierarchy, order and holy days. The great political philosopher Thomas Hobbes, a former mathematics tutor to the young Charles Stuart and an advocate of obedience, had himself come to terms with the regime and justified his passivity in the face of the Protector:

> The obligation of subjects to a sovereign is understood to last as long and no longer, than the power lasteth, by which he is able to protect them. For the right men have by nature to protect themselves, when none else can protect them... the end of obedience is protection.*[8]

For the cold-eyed Hobbes, the pedigree of the sovereign was irrelevant. Charles I was defeated, dead, his heir was in exile, with little sign of returning, and his subjects were free to pledge allegiance to whichever power could protect them. Quietist supporters of monarchy spurned exile and the stagnant, dwindling future of the pessimist. Izaak Walton's *The Compleat Angler*, published in 1653, became a kind of manifesto for this Royalist retreat to the rural,[†] creating a humble but divine English arcadia, if only in the prose, which glistens still, like the waters on which he reflected. As a biographer, Walton also recorded for an uncertain posterity the lives of four notable figures in the tradition he sought to preserve: John Donne, Richard Hooker, Henry Wotton and George Herbert. Some Anglicans, as the historian Judith Maltby has pointed out, looked deep into England's past and saw in Cromwell's victory divine

---

* Hobbes had learnt a key lesson from the Civil Wars: that the deciding factor in politics is the need for a state with the power to govern.
† *The Compleat Angler* is the second most frequently reprinted book in the English language.

retribution for the Dissolution of the Monasteries – 'thus our punishment sprang from our sins'.

In his *History of the Rebellion and Civil Wars in England* (revised in the early 1670s and eventually published in 1702–4), Edward Hyde, by then the Earl of Clarendon, described how some disappointed Royalists consoled themselves:

> It was the greatest consolation to miserable men who had in themselves or their friends been undone by their loyalty, to meet together and lament their concision; and this brought on invectives against the person of Cromwell; and wine; and the continuance of the discourse, disposed them to take notice of the universal hatred that the whole nation had of him, and to fancy how easy it would be to destroy him.

The Venetian ambassador, Giovanni Sagredo, painted a more sober picture of both Hyde and his fellow Royalist Edward Nicholas: 'They are so heavily burdened and their fortunes so dilapidated that without money, leaders or support they are better able to grumble than to vindicate themselves.'[9] The historian David Underdown put it more prosaically, though no less accurately: that the talent of most Royalists was 'better suited to the tavern than the battlefield'.[10]

With the chance of foreign intervention remote, those who did seek actively to support the cash-starved cause of the king, his hands far removed from the levers of power, tended to be mavericks: a 'crowd of colonels, majors and captains', the middling sort and minor gentry. The less wealthy and the less grand had, by definition, less to lose. They tended to be connected by ramshackle networks, whose members were reckless, brave and undeniably romantic: in a word, 'cavalier'. The Western Association had emerged, as the name suggests, in one of the strongholds of the Royalist cause, the West Country. The future Charles II's brief stay in Jersey in October 1649 inspired the Association to cook up a number of conspiracies, but to little effect. Its most prominent figure, Henry Seymour, Lord Beauchampe*, along with other members of the group, was a regular at race meetings – the classic conspiratorial gathering for the Cavalier – and the authorities noted his presence at such a meeting in Salisbury in April 1650. But, for all their scheming, the Western Association achieved little, lapsing into inactivity while the king, at the insistence of the Louvre group, had pursued his ill-fated, sub-servient alliance with the Scottish Presbyterians.

Cromwell's intelligence services observed and sometimes exaggerated what opposition there was. But they grew increas-ingly wary, and with good reason. In a speech of 15 February 1655, on the eve of the only Royalist rising of his rule, the Lord Protector warned that resilient, resourceful men, committed to the Royalist cause, were 'restless in their designs'. Among these schemers were the Irishman Daniel O'Neill – whom Hyde would come to nickname 'Infallible Subtle' – and the Royalist spymaster Nicholas Armorer.

At the age of forty, O'Neill – who was related to the earls of Tyrone, 'the shadow of a great name' – stood out among the oppo-sition.[11] His father having recklessly managed the family's estates in Ireland, O'Neill was raised a Protestant in England, where he became an incorrigible plotter in the king's cause. Archbishop Laud had supported the young man in his desire to 'restore to this gentleman that which is lost without his own fault'. The Earl of Strafford, Charles I's lord deputy in Ireland, took a different view: O'Neill was a 'traitor, bred no other, Egg and Bird as they say'.

---

* Third son of the 2nd Duke of Somerset.

His actions suggested otherwise; his devotion to the Stuarts was total, despite the serial difficulties, despair and demoralization he would face as he sought to advance their cause. O'Neill, who had been implicated in the Second Army Plot to protect the king from parliamentary radicals, had escaped the Tower in 1642 in comic-book style. Wearing women's clothing, he had tied his bed sheets together and clambered out of his cell. Quick-witted and charming, according to Hyde he was 'ingenious and reasonable in all things – in subtlety and understanding much superior to the whole nation of the old Irish'. His rapid rise at the exiled court in The Hague was aided no doubt by flattery; Hyde had noticed that O'Neill was 'honest and kind to the Marquis of Ormond and me'. O'Neill had wisely identified the pair of Old Royalists as the most able and hard-headed of the king's supporters – and he had a capable co-conspirator.

'Pretty full and somewhat ruddy faced... with deep brown hair', Nicholas Armorer was the first of the king's agents to explore the practicalities of a solely English Royalist rising against the Cromwellian regime.[12] The younger son of a Northumbrian gentleman, he had played a role in the suppression of the Irish rebellion of 1641, serving with distinction under Ormond. Armorer had fought for the king in the First Civil War, was exiled in Holland following Charles's execution and had returned to England in September 1653, 'upon some particulars of his own'. In a letter dated 24 November, Armorer wrote to Edward Nicholas, the exiled king's secretary of state, seeking authorization to cultivate a group of steadfast Royalists who would 'attend' to the king's affairs, so 'that there may be no clashing' among those who supported the Stuarts. Between November 1653 and February 1654, the Sealed Knot, a sextet of patrician partisans, was assembled and, by the spring, their plans for insurrection, predominantly in the Royalist heartlands of the north and west, took shape. When Armorer returned to the exiled, peripatetic court in August 1654, then in the Rhineland, he bypassed Nicholas, much to his chagrin, and reported to Hyde and Ormond. Nicholas was assured, convincingly or not, that Armorer was simply following the king's orders.

The Sealed Knot is today a group of harmless obsessives dedicated to historical re-enactments of Civil War battles. They thrill tourists and, owing to their rigorous attention to the details of period clothing, kit and weaponry, their activities are of occasional value to historians of early modern warfare. The historical Sealed Knot was the most important Royalist organization to emerge during the Protectorate. Hyde, who at the time was with the king at his court in Paris, was notified of the collective title of this new grouping in a report, dated 2 February 1654, from one of its leaders, Edward Villiers: 'The sealed knot still meet, with an intention to design somewhat.' Charles had been in contact with at least three of its prospective leaders as early as November 1653. In the coded language of business which he adopted in conspiratorial missives, he had written of his longing for the Sealed Knot to 'make another venture in trade'.

The Sealed Knot was a 'conspiracy of younger sons'. All its leaders were second sons or younger, with little land but many years of life to lose. Adventurers and risk-takers in their youth, with solid Civil War records, they tended to be ideologically and intellectually shallow. All but one of them was from the Puritan stronghold of East Anglia, a geographical imbalance that would prove a problem, since they lacked a representative from the Royalist West Country. Beauchampe, the leader of the Western Association, could have played that role, but he was to die in 1654.

John, Lord Belasyse of Worlaby, was the only Catholic among the six (his father had married into a recusant family and converted). He was also the only northerner, and, therefore, a potentially important link to the well-organized recusant Royalist families of the north. Shot in the head during the assault on Bristol in 1643, he had recovered to reorganize the king's forces in Yorkshire, before being decisively defeated by his cousin, the Lord General Thomas Fairfax, commander in chief of the parliamentary forces, at Selby in April 1644. For his services to the king's cause he was raised to the peerage.

Belasyse was in many ways the embodiment of the nation's divisions. He was the second son of the fiercely Royalist Thomas Belasyse, 1st Baron Fauconberg, and yet his nephew, also Thomas, who succeeded to the Fauconberg title in 1653, was to marry Mary Cromwell, the Protector's youngest daughter, in 1657. And he was related not only to Fairfax, but also to John Lambert. Such were the complicated ties and divided loyalties that led to dilemmas and difficult choices – and opportunities – for country families in a fragmented nation. While exiled on the Continent, Belasyse's many adventures included an audience with the pope. On his return to his estate in Yorkshire in 1650, he found himself arrested on the orders of the Council of State. The period of imprisonment he served would have one positive aspect: Belasyse had been Charles Stuart's first choice to lead the northern English forces in the southbound invasion of 1651, but his captivity meant that he played no role in that disastrous campaign.

Henry Hastings, Lord Loughborough, was somewhat grander. The son of the 5th Earl of Huntingdon, scion of a powerful Leicestershire family, he was the only other peer among the Sealed Knot's leadership. Like Belasyse, he was a veteran of both Civil Wars, lauded in particular for his efforts in the relief of the siege of Newark in 1644 and the extraordinarily prolonged defence of his father's house at Ashby de la Zouch, which became a thorn in the side of parliamentary forces in the East Midlands, holding out until February 1646. Loughborough had escaped from Windsor on the very eve of Charles's execution, eventually settling in Rotterdam. He returned to England sometime late in 1652.

William Compton was the militarily precocious son of the 2nd Earl of Northampton, whose devotedly Royalist family, with extensive lands in the south Midlands counties of Warwickshire and Northamptonshire, was unusually unaffected by Civil War divisions. At the age of just eighteen in March 1643 he had accompanied his father into battle and seen him killed. By the time of the Second Civil War, he had become a major general. Beguiling and brilliant, he was said even to have charmed Cromwell, who called him the 'godly cavalier'.

Unlike Compton, John Russell, the third son of the 4th Earl of Bedford, with estates in Devonshire, came from a bitterly divided clan. Before his death in 1641, his father had been a leading parliamentary opponent of Charles I. Russell, however, siding with the Royalists, had commanded Prince Rupert's regiment of foot and been wounded at Naseby in 1645. His intimacy with those on both sides of the struggle gave him some scope for developing contacts with 'neutral' opinion.

Edward Villiers, Hyde's principal contact among the Sealed Knot, was the fourth son of the half-brother of the Duke of Buckingham, Charles I's ill-fated favourite. He was related to the powerful Howard family, the earls of Suffolk, having married Frances, the earl's second sister. Wounded at Newbury in 1643, he, too, had fled to the Continent in 1649 to return three years later. Villiers had served at the Siege of Newark in 1645–6 under Sir Richard Willys, the final member of the Sealed Knot, whose fidelity to the Stuart cause would, in time, be questioned.

Born in Hertfordshire to a Fenland lawyer around 1614, Willys, the only commoner among the group, had abandoned a legal career to become a soldier. He had fought the Dutch at Breda in 1637, had taken part in the Bishops' Wars, the prelude to the First Civil War, and been a member of Charles I's personal guard. He distinguished himself again at Shrewsbury in 1642, this time in the service of Prince Rupert's cavalry. Captured and exchanged, he became governor of Newark in 1645, from where his feud with Lord Belasyse, his fellow member of the Sealed Knot, began. It appears that Willys disobeyed the instructions of Charles I when he welcomed Prince Rupert, who was then in the king's bad books, to Newark. For his actions, Willys was replaced as governor by Belasyse, whom he then challenged to a duel. He was eventually pardoned by the king and created a baronet in 1646, though he did not stay around long, heading instead for a leisurely exile in Italy.

Whatever the state of their personal relationships, the six were judged 'fit and faithful persons', of good breeding, from established county families, 'who had had the most eminent Charges in the war'. As former military men, they were suspicious of reckless schemes. 'Known to none but the marquis of Ormond and to the chancellor', their avowed intent was to wait for the 'first rational opportunity' to strike at the regime. Hyde tried to maintain as much direct control over the Royalists in England as was practical. He and the six members of the Sealed Knot were determined to 'discourage absurd and desperate attempts'. They would wait patiently for the right time for a general, nationwide uprising. The king, with no viable alternative, 'consented to all they proposed'.

The relationship between the canny and elusive Armorer and chancellor Hyde, in whom he had at first aroused suspicion, promised to bear fruit. They were a sober pairing, unlike the reckless Royalist conspirators of the summer of 1654 – the movement's 'lunatic fringe' – who fulfilled all the negative stereotypes of the gaming, drunken Cavalier, demonstrating in two separate plots the liabilities of unfocused, gossipy conspiracy. Principal among them was the 'swordsman' Roger Whitley, an energetic veteran of Worcester, prodigious diarist and compulsive plotter, goaded in his antics by the increasingly erratic Prince Rupert and the aggrieved and marginalized Marmaduke Langdale. Outside the control of the Sealed Knot, Whitley's fellow conspirators had met from early 1653 in the Ship Tavern, near the Old Bailey, and various other London alehouses. From there they hoped to foment a riot among the City's apprentice boys. Their 'grand council' included a number of prominent Cavaliers, including – possibly – the Sealed Knot's Lord Loughborough (though he was later cleared of involvement). Their schemes were known to agents of the regime. John Thurloe, Cromwell's secretary of state, who had recently taken on the responsibilities of spymaster, allowed their activities to smoulder before quietly being snuffed out.

Close family connections were a hallmark of Cromwell's *intimi*. Only twenty men served on the Council during the five years or so of the Protectorate, thirteen of them serving continuously throughout. Among them was John Desborough, the prominent commander of cavalry in the Civil Wars, a former general of the fleet – albeit one who remained on land, which may explain his less than adequate supervision of the victuals for the Western Design. As we have seen, he was married to the Protector's sister, Jane. Charles Fleetwood, a veteran of Naseby and a skilled military administrator, was the husband of Bridget, the Protector's daughter, whom he had married in 1652 (their son was christened 'Cromwell'). Bridget was herself the widow of

Henry Ireton, eloquent champion of the status quo at the Putney Debates of 1647 and Cromwell's second in command during the brutal Irish campaign. The president of the Council, Henry Lawrence, went back to Cromwell's earliest days in East Anglia, when he had been the future Protector's landlord. Philip Jones had been a tenant of Cromwell's in South Wales and was to become comptroller of the Protector's household.

Similarly, John Thurloe, Cromwell's spymaster, was the son of an Essex rector, and had been 'bred from a youth' by Cromwell's cousin, Oliver St John, who trained him as a lawyer. He probably first came into contact with Cromwell as a trustee of the latter's aunt, Lady Joan Barrington, and through his work for St John, who was married to one of Cromwell's cousins. His first service to the state was as secretary to the parliamentary commissioners, who negotiated with Charles I to the point of despair at Uxbridge in 1644. In 1650 he was appointed treasurer for the Company of Adventurers, of which Cromwell was also a member, responsible for draining the Fens around Ely (to the anger of many locals, in whose disputations the future Protector became involved). After leading the diplomatic mission to the United Provinces of the Netherlands in 1651 which proposed a union of the British and Dutch republics, Thurloe was appointed secretary of state in 1652 on a salary of £600. He lived in Whitehall, close to the heart of government, while representing Ely and then Cambridge University as an MP.

Thurloe's control of intelligence, domestic and foreign, was never formally assigned to him. Such nod and wink appointments were typical of the regime, whose secrecy and evasion was symptomatic of its insecurity. The Protectorate rarely declared its hand to a public indifferent to its ideology. 'No government on earth discloses its own acts less… than that of England,' noted the Venetian ambassador in 1654.

They meet in a room approached through others, without number, and countless doors are shut. That which favours their interest best is that very few persons, at most 16, meet to digest the gravest affairs and come to the most serious decisions.[13]

It soon became apparent, however, that, in the words of David Underdown, 'genius' had replaced the 'mere competence' of Thurloe's predecessor, George Bishop. His intimate relationship with Cromwell was recognized at home and abroad. It was through Thurloe that all the Protector's business passed, and Thurloe who protected him from unwelcome representations.[14] It was Thurloe's ear one had to bend if one was to catch that of the Protector, and Thurloe who conspired with Cromwell to catch the Council off guard. However, the historian H. N. Brailsford exaggerated wildly when he wrote that 'the efficient police state' which Thurloe constructed was 'as highly centralised as any of the totalitarian regimes of our own 20th century'.[15] Even if the ambition and talent were there, the means were absent; communications technology, or the lack of it, saw to that. But Thurloe developed what was, for the time, a highly developed system of control, worthy of his Elizabethan predecessor Francis Walsingham. Thomas Carlyle, writing in the nineteenth century, thought him 'one of the expertest secretaries… any state or working king could have'. Few would argue with his judgement, and certainly not those who conspired in the Royalist conspiracy known as the Gerard Plot, which surfaced in the summer of 1654.

The work hatched by maverick individuals on the wilder side of royalism, the Gerard Plot was a serious affair. The clique around Prince Rupert had been contacted in Paris by three rogues: Thomas Henshaw, a former parliamentary spy in the Netherlands who had deserted his mercenary position in the army of le grand Condé, leader of the aristocratic opposition to

Mazarin during the Fronde, one of a series of French civil wars that took place amid the Franco-Spanish war during the 1640s and 1650s; John Wiesmas, his half-brother, also a deserter; and Colonel John Fitzjames, another parliamentary turncoat. The ambition of this unsavoury bunch was simple: to kill Cromwell, by any means available. Of all the strategies employed by Royalist conspirators, this was both the easiest to carry out and – were it to be achieved – the one that would cause most damage to the regime. What would be unleashed into the void was a matter of little concern to the conspirators. Indeed, it might prove fatal to it. Their operating principle was to throw the cards in the air and see where they landed. The Protector was, after all, the fixed point in England's turbulent world of the 1650s; take him out and all bets were off. Killing a single individual, however well protected, would not only provide these hot-headed plotters with a dramatic propaganda coup but would be very much simpler to achieve than coordinating a successful nationwide rising.*

The Gerard Plot had come to the attention of the authorities in February 1654, when a Roger Coates was interrogated by Thurloe. He named a number of conspirators against the life of the Protector, including John Gerard, a cousin of Charles Gerard, 1st Baron Gerard of Brandon, who was similarly compromised. The plot, Coates claimed, involved up to 800 men and, in addition to the Protector, also targeted John Lambert and Thurloe, which gave the search for the conspirators a personal edge.

Henshaw and Gerard had crept into London from Paris; the

---

* Hours after narrowly failing to murder Margaret Thatcher – a Cromwellian figure, it could be argued – and her cabinet in the bombing of Brighton's Grand Hotel in October 1984, the IRA announced: 'Today we were unlucky, but remember we only have to be lucky once – you will have to be lucky always.' Terrorists of the mid-seventeenth century would have shared that view.

wretched Fitzjames drowned on the way. In the capital they circulated a proclamation offering £500 for the assassination of 'a certain mechanic': Cromwell. One potential recruit, a wiser man, warned them 'not to meddle with state matters', and was ignored. On 13 May, a Saturday, the plotters gathered. Henshaw was to lead an unlikely sounding 700-strong troop of men to attack Cromwell's horse guard. Gerard would be at the centre of the action in Whitehall, where the Protector was scheduled to pass on his way to his usual weekend residency at Hampton Court to the west of London. A diversionary manoeuvre would be launched at Southwark, while Francis and Somerset Fox, relatives of Gerard, would put into operation a plan hatched at the Ship's Inn, near the Old Bailey, to incite the City apprentices. Unfortunately for the conspirators, Cromwell decided late in the day to head west via the Thames. The frustrated assassins then improvised a plot to attack him in his chapel in Whitehall the following Sunday, but they were intercepted, and Gerard and five others were detained. The rest of the conspirators were rounded up within days. Willys, luminary of the Sealed Knot, was among them and found himself in the Tower. Inevitably, he believed he had been betrayed by his old rival Belasyse, and petitioned the Protector for his release, declaring: 'I will express my gratitude by obedience.' He even offered Cromwell, in return for his freedom, a desperately hare-brained scheme to lead an army of Irishmen, in the service of Venice, against the Turks. He was to offer much more in the future.

Gerard was examined personally by Thurloe on 5 June. The following day he interrogated Peter Vowell, a schoolmaster from Islington, who had been named by the army agitator John Wildman when the latter was interrogated by John Barkstead, governor of the Tower, zealous regicide and devotee of Cromwell. The involvement of Wildman, the long-time Leveller opponent of the Protectorate, hinted at a nascent alliance of Royalists and Levellers. Thurloe, aware of the targeting of himself and Lambert, was uncharacteristically enraged, describing the plotters as 'the scum and faeces of that party'.[16] Yet the government's response was relatively mild: Gerard and the luckless Vowell were executed on 10 July and three other plotters were transported as indentured labourers to Barbados. Henshaw made it back to the Continent, where he would tell anyone who would listen that the entire scheme was a trap concocted by Cromwellians.

The Royalist cause was probably best served by the elimination of such hotheads. The problem was that, as well as Willys, many more sober Royalists, such as Villiers and Beauchampe, were also collared in the round-ups that followed. This owed much to the efforts of the disaffected Royalist Joseph Bampfield, now Cromwell's agent at the exiled court. Bampfield had authored a secret report for Thurloe, which revealed Charles Stuart's intimate knowledge of the Gerard Plot, identified active Royalist supporters in England and revealed the membership of the Sealed Knot. That organization would now grow even more cautious in the light of the summer's failed conspiracies.

Bampfield's story is a barely believable one, which demonstrates the deep divisions at the exiled court.[17] His career in deception had begun in 1644, when he was asked by Charles I to 'penetrate the designs of the two parties in Parliament'. When the Royalist cause was defeated, he helped organize the escape of the king's younger son, James, Duke of York, to the Continent. Bampfield was arrested in the aftermath of the king's execution, but escaped from Westminster's Gatehouse prison to the Low Countries. In 1652 he had returned to England, was arrested and then 'banished' – a favourite tactic of Thurloe's once a suspect had been 'turned'. Having secretly switched sides, Bampfield spent time in Scotland on supposed service to the king. But suspicions were aroused at the exiled court by the delay – five months or so – in his return to the court in Paris. By December 1652, he was 'looked on as a knave' by some of his former colleagues. But, by 1654, for reasons unclear, he had reappeared at the exiled court, all suspicions of him forgotten, from where he fed Thurloe a constant diet of information in dispatches written in lemon juice. He had also turned another of the king's courtiers, Sir John Henderson, the former Royalist governor of Newark. Both were disliked by Charles and Hyde, who warned the court that Bampfield's 'advertisements from London give us cause to suspect that he is not without correspondence with the most powerful there'.[18] However, enmities within the court-in-exile worked in Bampfield's favour. The very fact that Chancellor Hyde was suspicious of him was enough for the likes of Jermyn and Balcarres to take a more indulgent view of the spy hidden in plain sight.

Charles corresponded with Villiers on 6 July 1654, in his usual jumble of commercial metaphors. 'Mr Westbury [Villiers's codename], I find that the late raising the prices of our wares, from which there was not the least direction from me, hath so disturbed the market, that our commodities may lie too long on our hands.' The letter was carried by John Stephens, the Protestant son of an Irish customs collector, who had also fought alongside Ormond in Ireland and accompanied him into exile. Having failed to obtain a commission in the French army, Stephens had decided to throw in his lot with England's Royalist underground.

Stephens reported back that the leadership of the Knot, spooked by recent events, had become 'shy and wary' and, in his judgement, 'resolved no further, to agitate your [the king's] business'. With the retreat of the Knot, a vacuum had developed and a new group of Royalist agitators emerged. If the Sealed

Knot owed its creation to Armorer, then the roots of this 'New Council' can be attributed to the efforts of Stephens. Appointed to the role of carrying the king's instructions and advice to the Sealed Knot in the summer of 1654, he returned to the court with another plan from an entirely different source.[19]

Stephens's 'Particular Account' sought to unite a wider, more capacious circle of English opposition to the Cromwellian regime. It aimed not just to attract Cavaliers of traditional bent, but to encompass Presbyterians and even those radical soldiers disaffected by the betrayal of the 'Good Old Cause'. It was a taste of things to come. The core of the group included the more belligerent members of the Sealed Knot – Loughborough and Villiers – as well as Lord Willoughby of Parham. An influential Presbyterian and former governor of Barbados, Willoughby, who had played a key role in the Caribbean island's controversies of the early 1650s, was Armorer's contact in the Welsh Marches. The establishment of this group may also owe something to a visit to the king's court in Paris by Charles Davison, a representative of the northern Royalists who had become critical of Hyde's and Ormond's patient pragmatism. Stephens presented a set of proposals to the king in July 1654.

Another note was delivered the following month by Armorer to Charles who, having been forced out of Paris, was residing temporarily in Aachen. It brought promising news of 'Divisions in the Rebels Council about succession'. The Achilles heel of the Cromwellian regime – its ever narrower base – was correctly identified. In response, the king suggested the offer of a general pardon for those former supporters of Parliament who had fallen out with the regime. A particular target were those Presbyterians, such as George Booth, the Cheshire magnate, and, in the capital, Major General Richard Browne, for whom the bitter taste of Pride's Purge and the king's execution lingered still.

Cromwell's high-handed disregard for Parliament had opened the door to a potential alliance between Royalists and supporters of limited monarchy, both of whom opposed revolutionary politics. The traffic ran both ways. Willoughby had made contact with the court towards the end of 1653 and again as the plotting of Stephens's group advanced, in September 1654. He even claimed in a letter to the king that the towering figure of Thomas Fairfax might be persuaded to throw in his lot with them. The lord general, who had strongly opposed the trial and execution of Charles I, had resigned his position in 1650, unwilling to lead Parliament's Scottish campaign. Some rumours suggested he would back a rising in the north, his backyard, while others were wary of Fairfax's continuing, albeit passive, loyalty to the Protector. Some of the more zealous Royalists cried entrapment, despite the fact that Fairfax was widely perceived to be 'an honourable man', incapable of treachery.[20]

The exiled monarch greeted the possibility of Fairfax's backing with considerable enthusiasm. He sent a letter dated 6 July 1654 to Fairfax's brother-in-law, Henry Arlington, which promised that the king had 'forgotten all that hath been done amiss'. Despite the olive branch, Fairfax remained elusive and so, on 26 September, Charles changed tack, writing to Philip Monckton, the Yorkshire Royalist, that perhaps Fairfax could be approached through the Earl of Rochester, who had ambitions to marry the general's daughter, Winifred. It was all becoming a little bit desperate. An anxious Charles lowered his sights, insisting that it was 'absolutely necessary' that an agent make contact with Willoughby. Yet as late as 29 December 1654, Edward Grey reported no sign of the magnate despite 'several appointments', which led O'Neill to conclude that he was simply 'not very forward to meddle'. It is likely that the astute and experienced Willoughby judged the likelihood of such a plot succeeding at the present time to be slim. It may also be that the senior Presbyterians were less than convinced by the offers of toleration proposed by the king's party. Hyde's principled stand echoed in the background, cautious and pragmatic. And yet some Presbyterians kept faith with the conspiracy, at least nominally; they included George Booth, whose son, Colonel John Booth, was close to both Rochester and O'Neill.

What of the more radical opponents of the regime, the Commonwealthmen, who shared Thomas Scot's and Arthur Heselrige's animosity to Cromwell's betrayal of the 'Good Old Cause'? These representatives of a 'mutinous minority' had been fierce in their criticism of the regime since the expulsion of the Rump in April 1653. Thurloe became especially suspicious of Richard Overton, whose *A Remonstrance of many Thousand Citizens*, published in 1646, was recognized as the founding manifesto of the Leveller movement. An ideological republican, with a deep hatred of all things Scottish, Overton had been a critic of both the purge of Parliament and the king's execution. Cromwell was a particular target of his ire, Overton accusing the Protector of replacing old monarchy with a 'new regality'. In the emerging plans for conspiracy cooked up by Heselrige, Bradshaw and Scot, Overton was to be placed at the head of an army numbering more than 3,000, which, having seized General Monck, the commander of the regime's army in Scotland, would march south and join forces with the more radical elements of the army at a number of locations, including the hallowed turf of Marston Moor. It never came to pass. Monck got wind of the plot, arrested Overton and had him sent to London, where, in a lapse of due process, he was to be imprisoned without trial for four years.[21]

Meanwhile, Overton's fellow Leveller, John Wildman, a

persistent thorn in the side of the regime, had written and circulated the *Humble Petition of Several Colonels of the Army*, bearing the signatures of John Okey, Thomas Saunders and Matthew Alured. It was fiercely critical of Cromwell's decision to rule without Parliament and called for the abandonment of the Instrument of Government and the imposition of the Agreement of the People, which had been composed by the radical Council of Officers in 1648. In October 1654, the petition was intercepted and the three officers arrested. They were treated leniently. Okey was court-martialled, found not guilty (though only by two votes) and resigned his commission, as did Saunders who was, as a consequence, spared a trial. Alured was the only one to be sent to prison; not because of his role in the petition but because of his activities as an agitator in Ireland.

Those firebrands of millenarian puritanism, the Fifth Monarchists, had, in Cromwell's biblical phrase, conjured up the 'brimstone of Sodom, and the smoke of the bottomless pit', in a series of violent attacks aimed at the regime.[22] And yet, as intelligence of an imminent Royalist rising gathered, Cromwell held two extraordinary meetings, one with leading supporters of the Fifth Monarchists – Harrison, Rich, Carew, Hugh Courtney, Arthur Squibb and Clement Ireton, younger brother of Henry – at which Carew told Cromwell that, when he dissolved Barebones, he 'took the crown off from the head of Christ, and put it upon his own'. They refused to keep the peace and objected to a Parliament whose power derives from the people when 'all power belongs to Christ', a view with which Cromwell must have been at least partly sympathetic. This may explain why, after discussing the matter with the council, he offered them immunity from prosecution if they retired quietly to their native counties. Predictably, they rejected the generous offer. Major General Harrison, Lambert's great rival, once so close to Cromwell and still a compelling, charismatic focus for opposition, was placed under virtual house arrest in Staffordshire. On his release, he was warned personally by Cromwell 'not to persist in these deceitful ways whose end is destruction'. But persist he did and he was arrested again on 15 February 1655 and sent to Carisbrooke Castle, where the doomed king had been incarcerated; he was to remain in custody for much of the Protectorate.[23]

Just ten days later, Cromwell received an audience with the Quaker leader George Fox. Cromwell, despite being on the end of a tongue lashing, took the irreverent Fox by the hand, saying: 'Come again to my house, for if thou and I were but an hour in a day together we should be nearer one to the other.'[24] It was a remarkable moment, given the widespread suspicion and fear of the religious movement Fox led. Cromwell even invited Fox to dine at the Banqueting House that evening – an offer Fox declined – before releasing him, to the exasperated objections of men such as Colonel Francis Hacker, who had overseen the king's execution and was now in charge of security in Fox's home county of Leicestershire.

Cromwell liked to remind the public of the potential alliance between the Royalists and the radical elements of the army, such as the Levellers. This was not entirely a fantasy on the part of the Protector and his spymaster. The Sussex Royalist Colonel Henry Bishop was a friend of Wildman, and claimed that he had been commissioned by the king to 'treat with the levelling party'. Even the normally sober Hyde had claimed that the army – referred to as 'Mr Archer' among Royalists – might 'begin the business for us'. But, outside a radical minority, the forces of the state were not for turning. With his eye on the bigger picture, from his Olympian heights Thurloe judged that: 'So far from the army falling into the hands of such men as these are, there is no question but they will live and die to maintain the government as it is now settled.' The Instrument of Government, which Parliament had sought constantly to dilute, was too closely aligned with the army's declarations of 1647 and, indeed, the Agreement of the People of 1648. In November 1654 army officers had met with Cromwell in defence of the Instrument, worried by the constant efforts by MPs to amend the constitution. The government's interest was also, by and large, that of the army. The discontent that had arisen in October among Cromwell's powerful navy had been addressed by that most traditional of means – a pay rise – and it, too, was loyal. The regime had near total control of the country, whose population, weary of war, preferred stability to insurrection.

6

Some Great Plot

*We look on the rising of your party but to be
the destroying of themselves.*

THE SEALED KNOT

PLANS FOR A major Royalist insurrection began in earnest early in 1655 and were communicated to the king by Thomas Ross, the author of an epic history of the Punic Wars and tutor to the Duke of Monmouth, Charles Stuart's illegitimate son by his Welsh mistress Lucy Walter. The exiled king liked what he heard. A list of strategic targets believed ripe for insurrection had been drawn up: Hull, Newcastle and Carlisle in the north; Shrewsbury, Ludlow, Warwick and Nottingham in the Midlands; and, in the south, Kent – crucial for the port of Dover – as well as the Royalist stronghold of the West Country. There is no record of any central coordinating committee, but nominal appointments were made of regional commanders: Philip Musgrave in Carlisle; Edward Grey in Newcastle; Richard Scriven in Shrewsbury. Rochester and O'Neill were to liaise with other senior figures, including Thomas Peyton, Humphrey Bennett, Richard Thornhill, John Weston and Thomas Armstrong. Most of these figures were country gentry of relatively modest means. All lacked experience of senior command and were of local rather than national distinction, if they were distinguished at all. None had any close connection to royalism's best strategists, Hyde and Ormond. All had flaws, some more than others. Peyton's sister, Dorothy Osborne, in her waspish but incisive letters to William Temple, described Thornhill as the 'veriest beast that ever was', while Armstrong, a friend of Weston, was a mercenary who, in a largely unaccountable past, had managed to amass a great deal of land in the Irish Pale before returning to England via the mystery that is the Isle of Man.[1]

Soon after Ross departed with the king's message of assent, James Halsall, a Royalist courier who had been held up for six days in his journey to the king owing to bad weather, had delivered a letter from the Sealed Knot. Ominously, it read: 'Now that their own divisions is for the present so allayed as that no rise from the Army is to be hoped, which was the ground of our hope… we look on the rising of your party but to be the destroying of themselves.' It was bleak but sage advice, as was to become apparent. Ormond, in Antwerp, heard from both sides of the royalist divide as the messengers, Ross and Halsall, crossed. He sent Charles an urgent letter, outlining the stark choice: order the Sealed Knot to back the rising in full or abandon the entire scheme. O'Neill carried the king's final message before the rising to the Sealed Knot. 'I cannot look for any great success, if while they [the New Party] stir, you sit still.' The king was unwilling to command the Sealed Knot to take action 'directly contrary to your judgement and inclinations'. One senses that he, too, knew the scheme could end only one way. The king was romantic but wrong, cavalier in every sense. He would not order the Sealed Knot to be involved in a scheme they could enter only half-heartedly at best. Ormond, with a whiff of despair, predicted the 'certain loss of those that should appear'.[2]

★

'Some great plot is intended', wrote one of Thurloe's agents early in March, and the spymaster moved.[3] A letter of restraint was sent to customs officials, allowing any foreigner or person acting suspiciously to be apprehended as they entered the country. A sweep was made of West Country Royalists. Troop numbers in England, which had fallen owing to conflict in the Highlands of Scotland and the demands of the Western Design, were increased. More than 2,000 troops had already been brought over from Ireland, landing in Liverpool on 15 January. The garrison at the Tower was tripled to 1,200 men and London's militias boosted. Shot and gunpowder were seized from private houses and horses were rounded up in Whitehall, where artillery was mounted. In the country, horse racing, strongly associated with gatherings of Royalists, was banned for six months. A plot was revealed in north Wales, with the castles of Denbigh and Beaumaris its target and John Stephens its mastermind, assisted by the Anglesey land-owner Nicholas Bagenal. A convoluted arms-running scheme, headed by the Virginian exile Major Henry Norwood, who passed weapons on to Royalist conspirators under the guise of export-ing them to Barbados and Virginia, was rumbled. Sir Henry Littleton, the High Sheriff of Worcester, was among those dis-covered to be in on the scheme, along with his brother Charles and Sir John Packington. Numerous arrests were made. Richard Thornhill was the most senior figure to be apprehended; inter-rogated by Cromwell, he gave away nothing, unlike two Royalists from north Wales, commissioned to raise cavalry and infantry regiments, who confessed personally to the Protector. They had no connections to national networks, but their loose tongues, along with the arrival of the Irish regiments, put paid to any chance of insurrection in Wales and the north-west of England.

The regime's pursuit of the plotters was updated on a regular basis in the pages of the government mouthpiece, *Mercurius Politicus*, edited by that early blueprint for the Vicar of Bray, Marchamont Needham, throughout the first two months of 1655. There was much to report. On 6 February, Humphrey Bennett, who was accused of being responsible for the attack on Portsmouth, was arrested, along with Grey and Weston as well as the agent Lieutenant James Reid and the army's liaison, Christopher Gardiner. Reid was caught with the king's letter sent the previous July, with all its incriminations. John Grenville, leader of the Devon gentry, was also rounded up. Any chance of the Levellers and other army radicals doing much harm ended when John Wildman was seized at Easton near Marlborough on 10 February, complete with a hand-written declaration 'against the Tyrant Oliver Cromwell'.

On 13 February, the day the insurrection was scheduled to spark, Cromwell summoned the Lord Mayor of London and his common council to Whitehall to update them on the Royalist threat to the City. The Protector read them the letter from Charles that had been carried by Read, as well as Wildman's manifesto. Easily convinced and no doubt alarmed, the City fathers nodded assent to the appointment of Major General Skippon in his task of raising a militia, with the zealous Barkstead as his deputy. Horses were seized, cavalry roamed the City and its hinterland. The capital was secured.

As Cromwell commandeered his capital, the Royalist rising was again postponed. Though the nationwide gatherings planned for 13 February had been cancelled, not everyone involved knew this. A group led by Walter Slingsby had made their way to Salisbury, where they were arrested. One prisoner, John Stradling, squealed to the authorities, identifying the leaders in Somerset: Colonel Francis of Trent, one of the brave souls who engineered Charles's escape after Worcester; and his uncle, Sir Hugh of Pilsdon. It is surprising, however, and perhaps evidence of some collusion between army radicals and Royalists, that some Levellers were also rounded up on the evening of 13 February, at the same meeting places proposed – Marston Moor and Salisbury Plain among them. Perhaps they knew just enough of each other's plans to cause confusion, though not enough to make any impact.

In the company of Ormond and a groom, Charles had left the Rhineland city of Cologne surreptitiously on 14 February, anticipating despite all odds, good news from home. His was a difficult journey: the Dutch had made it clear to Charles's sister, Princess Mary of Orange, that his presence would not be tolerated in their territories. He eventually made it to Middelburg on the banks of the Scheldt, where he waited for news in the house of an English woman and her wealthy husband, with connections to his aunt, Elizabeth of Bohemia, the tragic Winter Queen. Hyde was in nearby Breda. The king, ever hopeful, urged his brother James, Duke of York, then serving in the French army, to be ready for a call that never came. Cromwell, thanks to Thurloe's network of spies, was aware of their every move.

Daniel O'Neill reached Dover on the same day that the king departed for Middelburg. He then spent eight days in custody in its castle before escaping with the aid of Robert Day, a custom's official, who was in on the conspiracy, and heading to London. Ironically, the escape of 'Brian', as O'Neill was known, from the clutches of Dover's authorities convinced the king that the omens for the uprising were promising: 'a very good sign'. Similarly, Armorer, disguised as a Newcastle trader, was apprehended and then freed by the lieutenant governor of Dover Castle, Captain Wilson, again with the connivance of Day. Such penetration of England's porous coastline was to prove the high point of the conspiracy. Getting into England was one thing, claiming it for the Stuarts was quite another.

It dawned on O'Neill, somewhat late in the day, that the scheme was hopeless, such were the forces marshalled against it. In that he was supported by the sound judgement of Armorer. But Thomas Armstrong convinced him otherwise, against all reason and evidence, arguing that O'Neill, ever the Stuart loyalist, must stay true to the task that the king had invested in him. Compton, of the Sealed Knot, suggested that even they, the arch-sceptics, would support him in his task, at least as much as they could. And now the loose-tongued Rochester, father of the libertine and poet, had arrived; as he prepared to sail from Flanders, the man given the king's authority to 'assist and direct' the insurrection had 'communicated his purpose to anybody he did believe would keep him company and run the same hazard with him'. One who agreed to do so was Sir Joseph Wagstaff, a former major general in Charles I's Army of the West, an unreflective man considered fit more for 'execution than counsel'. Rochester met O'Neill in London, where he spent five surreptitious days, before heading to Yorkshire on 27 February. There he would take control of the northern conspiracy. He still believed that, by some miracle, Fairfax would appear, though a vision it was, and a vision it would remain.[4]

Just six weeks after the dissolution of Parliament, the uprising of which Cromwell had warned the nation flickered into light. After a confusion of postponements – 'some mistake in the notice that had been given' – the night of 8 March unfolded as many Royalists had warned that it would. The Knot remained sealed. The Presbyterian faction, including Browne, Waller and Willoughby, failed to show. Those who were to lead the attacks on the southern ports were in custody. Government forces sent south from Scotland secured Hull. Where Cavaliers did gather, it was more farce than show of force. Barely 150 men – 1,500 had been promised – heeded Rochester's call to gather at Marston Moor in preparation for an attack on York. The omens had hardly been good for the Royalists; this was, after all, where they had been forced to abandon the north of England. And the result this time was little different from the events of eleven years before, if somewhat less dramatic.[5]

According to Thurloe's intelligence, the conspirators hoped to 'have surprised York, and they expected for that purpose 4,000 men to have come to them there'. The maniacal delusion that a force under Fairfax was to join them proved just that. When they caught sight of government troops commanded by Colonel Lilburne, they scarpered, leaving behind four carts full to the brim with arms. Lilburne captured a bevy of Royalist notables, including the Royalist son of a regicide, Sir Richard Mauleverer (who later escaped his captors), Sir Henry Slingsby and Sir William Ingram, whose house at Little Cattal, near Harrogate, served as Rochester's Yorkshire HQ. Here the commander had earned no favours, having 'solicited people very strongly, and threatened some'.[6] Rochester escaped in disguise, along with Armorer. One young recusant suffered what may have been a panic attack – or a simple case of cowardice – and on his retreat, he met another band of fifty or so conspirators who, on seeing his condition, themselves turned tail and fled. A local parliamentary officer observed with some glee that the Royalists were 'strangely frightened with their own shadows'.

In Chester, long a Royalist stronghold, the assailants were put off by the mere sight of sentries in the castle's precincts, though they were a greater threat than the force that prepared to take Hull, which failed to turn up. Shrewsbury was lightly defended by its governor, Colonel Mackworth, with about seventy soldiers; on 5 March, Cromwell had warned them with some exaggeration of the 'speedy execution of a very evil design'. A regiment under Colonel William Crowne was ordered in as reinforcements 'for protection of the honest party and securing of Shrewsbury garrison'. In a pre-emptive strike, Mackworth captured Sir Thomas Harries at his residency, Boreatton, 11 miles from the town, where twenty saddled horses were discovered in his stables and gunpowder in his barn. Ralph Kynaston, believed to be an ally of Harries, turned evidence against him.[7]

The biggest group to assemble on the night, around 300 or so, most of whom were veterans of the Civil Wars, was in Nottinghamshire, at Rufford Abbey. But their nominal commanders, Lord Byron and the future Earl of Halifax, George Savile, either couldn't be bothered or were too afraid to leave London, from where Savile had despatched thirty-six horses and some guns for those who had had more of a stomach for a fight. However, baffled by the low turnout and the absence of their leaders and now alarmed by the news from York, the assembly simply broke up and headed home. It was a similar tale in Morpeth, where no more than eighty gathered for the assault on Newcastle and its port of Tynemouth, where they hoped to be joined by rebels from Durham and North Yorkshire. Round about midnight, they too headed home. And so the main thrust of the rebellion was to be confined to the west.

There were no Seymours left in the Western Association, following the death of Beauchampe. The Wyndhams and Grevilles had been arrested, so Somerset, Devon and Cornwall were pretty much out of the picture so far as the conspiracy went. That left Wiltshire and Dorset, where trouble had been anticipated by the government. Disturbances at Bristol towards the end of 1654, caused by a mix of fiery Quaker preaching and a rumour mill of Royalist risings, had prompted the city's garrison commander, Captain Bishop, to write to Thurloe on 14 February 1655 of 'some design of the enemy very near breaking forth… a sad advantage may suddenly be made of such a place as this, even to furnish an army with arms, ammunition, men, money, and other pensions of war'. Two troops of government horse had entered Bristol on 20 February following a gathering of Royalists on the original date for the insurrection a week before, around Salisbury and Bristol, not knowing of the king's postponement. One of those captured, John Stradling, had confessed all he knew. The odds of success were slim. Though 8 March had passed quietly in the west, the region was to see the only shots fired in anger during the entire insurrection.

At the head of the Rising in the West was John Penruddock, a former Royalist soldier in his mid-thirties who had lost his brother Henry in service to the king during the Civil Wars. His was a Cumbrian family that had arrived in the west during the sixteenth century and he had succeeded to his modest estate in 1648. His support for the king cost him dear; he had fallen foul of the Commissioners for Sequestration and 'compounded for his delinquency'. In June 1649 his property was annexed and he was fined £1,000, more than a man of his modest means could afford.

He was joined in conspiracy by his cousin Edward, who had returned from exile, and a former surgeon of the king, Richard Pyle, who was Charles's chief agent in Wiltshire. It was hoped that risings in the north and west, traditional bastions of Royalist support, would draw government troops from the well-defended ports of Kent and allow the exiled Charles Stuart to land there.

But Penruddock had few illusions about the prospects of victory. In November 1654, while the plans for the uprising of March 1655 were being sketched, he settled his accounts with the following statement:

> I have written this partly for my own satisfaction, and withal (in case it should please God to call me away) to satisfy my friends which I shall leave behind me, that the debts which I have contracted may not be laid before my charge. I hope God will so bless me that I shall be able to go through this great trouble; if I happen to die before it be done, I doubt not my wife and children will be so just as to see that no man shall suffer a penny be me.[8]

Penruddock's judgement was closer to the realism of the Sealed Knot than his subsequent actions might imply.

The focus of the uprising in the west was, appropriately, the King's Arms in Salisbury, where the Cavalier Henry Hewitt was the host of an inn noted for its Christmas revels and 'sets of fiddlers'.

Rochester had met with agents of the Western Association, now modestly revived, in London. The Association had appointed Joseph Wagstaffe as its military adviser; despite his limitations, he did have serious experience of soldiering. He had been a lieutenant colonel in John Hampden's parliamentary regiment, but had subsequently changed sides, fighting with considerable courage for the king at the Battle of Langport in Somerset in July 1645. His efforts had been in vain, however: with defeat at Langport, the west was lost to the Royalist cause.

The original plan was for troops to march into Hampshire on 8 March 1655 and head to Winchester, where the judges of assize, the very symbol of the regime's tentacles, were in session. However, a troop of government horse had arrived in

Winchester and so the focus was shifted to Salisbury, where the assizes were due to sit four days later. To cultivate a little chaos, Henry Moore of Fawley was to lead a diversionary attack on nearby Marlborough.

On 11 March, three days after the national insurrection had fizzled out, the 'Rising in the West' began. Wagstaffe and Penruddock managed to collect about sixty horsemen in Clarendon Park, three miles west of Salisbury. Around forty more arrived from the city with Thomas Mompesson, and the combined force marched towards Blandford, where it was joined by another eighty or so recruits, returning to Salisbury in the early hours of 12 March. The marketplace was occupied and guards were put on the doors of every inn. The city's gaol was broken open and eager prisoners, some of them still in irons, were enlisted; the locals, however, proved harder to convince. Two judges, present for the assizes – Lord Chief Justice Rolle and Baron Nicholas along with the high sheriff, Colonel John Dove – were arrested in their beds. Wagstaffe wanted them hanged on the spot. Others among the party continued to assert that Fairfax, with 8,000 men, and the former parliamentary general William Waller, with another 4,000, were on their way to join them. Dove, a regime loyalist who had sat on the court that tried the king and had been involved in the sale of former Royalist lands, refused to proclaim Charles II and was beaten up; according to some accounts his face was cut by a sword, in others he was hit over the head with a pistol. A breakaway group attacked his house, which was successfully defended for half an hour by around thirty men under the command of Major Henry Wansey. Dove was eventually carried off in his nightshirt, but Penruddock, ever the honourable gentleman, 'pretended great friendship for the Sheriff, and sent him a horse and man to wait upon him and sent word he should dine with him that Monday'.

The two judges were released with Penruddock's assurance that they would be spared vengeance when James Duke of York arrived with his 10,000 men to prepare for the return of the king.

Having doubled their numbers in Salisbury, to about 400, Wagstaff left with his troop and the sheriff – still in his night-shirt – at about 8 a.m. The support of William Seymour, Marquis of Hertford failed to materialize, despite the presence of his chaplain, Dr Henchman. The rest of the party, under Penruddock, joined by a gentleman from Surrey, Francis Jones, headed back to Blandford, where Dove was 'permitted to dress'. There they met as cool a response as in Salisbury; the town crier refused to proclaim the king – and was threatened with burning – so Penruddock did it himself.

John Desborough, Cromwell's brother-in-law, appointed 'Major General of the West' in a portent of things to come, was ordered 'to repair with your regiment into the west'. Marching through Maidenhead and Reading, Desborough was hoping to meet up with Butler's force from Bristol. Penruddock and his men, who had received reports that Cromwell's forces were heading their way, might have been wise to wait for reinforcements north-east of Salisbury, as Moore's attack on Marlborough had been abandoned because of the presence of government troopers. The group as it was divided for the evening, quartering at Shaftesbury and Sherborne and then, the following night – in the early hours of Tuesday morning – assembled on Yeovil's Babylon Hill at about 1 a.m. The three or four thousand supporters expected failed to turn up.

The ragtag army wandered through Dorset in the general direction of the Royalist stronghold of Cornwall, one of the darker corners of the realm, with the government forces closing in on them. They may have made it to Dorchester, where, some reports suggest, the prison was again sprung and its bewildered if welcoming jailbirds horsed and recruited. Butler, on 14 March, having marched to Shaftesbury, asked Cromwell's permission to attack. 'They were like men that dreamt', he reported of the rebels, 'to see us so suddenly here... I shall freely adventure myself upon the good providence of the Lord, who I know will own us.' The Lord was little needed. Nor was Colonel James Berry, a former clerk in a Midlands ironworks, who had waited for Desborough's force to join him at Shaftesbury.[9]

Wagstaffe had stopped for the night at South Molton in north Devon, close to the house of the conspirator Sir Hugh Holland. Unfortunately for him, Captain Unton Croke, a member of Berry's regiment based in Exeter and 'resolved to hazard all', arrived at South Molton with just sixty men at about 10 p.m. on 14 March, determined to stop the force from reaching the relative safety of Cornwall. Croke described what then happened:

> By the good providence of God, directing and assisting me, I beat up their quarters about ten of the clock; they disputed it very much with me in the houses for more than two hours, firing very hot out of the windows; they shot 7 or 8 of my men, but none were mortally wounded... some of them yielded to mercy: I promised them, I would use my endeavours to intercede for their lives... my Lord, they are all broken and routed, and I desire the Lord may have the glory.[10]

In the skirmish, Penruddock, who accepted Croke's offer of quarter, Jones and Grove were among those captured – Croke ended up with more prisoners than he had men to guard them. According to local tradition, Wagstaffe managed to evade capture by jumping his horse over the churchyard wall.

The Royalist insurrection was over before it had properly begun. As Clarendon was to put it, 'they did nothing after their first action'. Only in the west was a shot even fired. The parliamentary forces broke into houses of the suspected conspirators, took around fifty prisoners until they were all 'broken and routed' and led them to Exeter jail.

Desborough wrote to Cromwell from Wincanton, where he joined Butler's troop on 17 March: 'The enemy was routed on Wednesday night last', he informed the Protector, 'at Moulton [sic] in the county of Devon.' A week later, Cromwell issued a circular to the militia commissioners and justices around the country announcing the defeat of the rising, imploring them to be watchful for further plots. Desborough sent his forces in pursuit of those that had fled, while he headed to Exeter to interrogate prisoners.

Penruddock had been taken to Exeter from Salisbury, 'no whit daunted by his trial', despite the fact that most people looked upon it 'as the very next step to death'. He knew as much, but remained, in private at least, loyal to the crown and church: 'Be merciful unto me O Lord,' he wrote, 'under the shadow of thy wings will I hide myself till this tyranny be overpassed.'

While the regime's soldiers performed efficiently enough, the customs officials proved less thorough, letting a number of the rising's leaders, including Rochester, flee back to the Continent. This suggested perhaps a certain degree of indifference to the regime among officials, in contrast to the loyal, zealous military. The inefficiency of the Protectorate's policing was in need of iron reform; this would arrive soon enough, with Desborough's deeds in the West Country as its blueprint.

Much of the local population remained quietly loyal to royalism. Wagstaffe's escape, for example, depended, so Hyde claimed, on 'honest houses', where he was 'concealed till opportunity served to transport them into the parts beyond the seas'. Rochester, 'fortunate in disguises', was reluctant to depart from safe houses 'where there was good eating and drinking', and had a number of close shaves. Held by an innkeeper in Aylesbury on the orders of a suspicious county justice, Rochester bribed the publican with a gold chain and fled in the company of Nicholas Armorer, but left his luggage and two servants behind. One agent judged it, 'better that than his head'.

Henry Manning, a government agent deep in the exiled court and a confidant of Rochester, had proffered a number of addresses to keep an eye on and was furious that they had not been acted upon. Although numerous conspirators were apprehended in London raids, Rochester proved elusive; Manning claimed that he could be found at 'Mr Markham's house in the Savoy, the Lord Lumley's, or at those places I know to be their haunts' – by which he meant Covent Garden and a number of taverns in Drury Lane. The principal agents of the king – O'Neill, Rochester and Armorer – had all reached the safety of The Hague by 12 July 1655.[11]

Exeter jail was full; so much so that some prisoners had to be lodged in local inns. The baser sort were generally left alone, but Desborough believed he had enough in captivity 'to make a pattern for all the rest'. Around a third of the prisoners would face trial. Such was the negligible threat exercised by royalism that many of those who took part in the Penruddock Rising were treated with considerable leniency by the state, in the manner of Cromwell's oft invoked, though typically elusive 'healing spirit'. Trial by jury, in Exeter, Salisbury and Chard, was retained for offenders, though the question of what offence they were being charged with was a moot one. The Treason Ordinance issued by

Cromwell at the beginning of his rule had not been passed by Parliament. Edward III's statute defined treason as an offence against a king. But what happened when there was no king to offend against?

Rolle and Nicholas were not allowed to take part in proceedings lest their treatment at the hands of the rebels prejudice their judgement. Penruddock was allowed to challenge as many as twenty-two jurors before the final twelve were selected. Of the thirty-eight sentenced to death, fewer than fifteen, including Penruddock, were actually executed and none were hanged, drawn and quartered, the traditional punishment for treason. Others were transported to Barbados. In the north, where it hadn't already made preventative arrests, the regime made do with fines. Croke was later accused of reneging on a promise he had made to guarantee the life of Penruddock, a claim which appears to be unfounded. Penruddock wrote to his wife on 17 March:

> The best that I can make of this is that it was our fortune to fall into the hands of one Captain Unton Croke, a generous and valiant officer, one that I hope will show something the better, for that we did not basely desert our soldiers as others did.

Most participants in the rising would be released by the following December, having been but gently chastised. Despite its military strength and the weakness of its opponents, the Protectorate remained, throughout its existence, uncertain of itself, its mindset provisional. It could appeal to providence, but not precedent: the checks and balances of the 'ancient constitution', the rock upon which a secure and settled social structure was founded. Until the end, it looked over its shoulder and, throughout its rule, it lacked seasoned legitimacy. Three chief commissioners in the north had cast doubts on whether the actions of the conspirators constituted treason. Questioning the Protector's Treason Ordinance did them no favours; two of the commissioners were dismissed, for effectively querying the legitimacy of the regime. The rebels may not have come anywhere near toppling the Protectorate, but they had at least put a wedge between the regime and its officers of the law.

There were other legal dilemmas and inconsistencies to grapple with, such as the case of George Cony. A London merchant, Cony had appealed to habeas corpus in May after he was imprisoned by the Council for refusing to pay customs duty on the grounds that the particular tax he was liable for had not been approved by Parliament. He had been imprisoned illegally, he argued, citing an Act of 1641 which declared that the Privy Council, as it then was, had no judicial competence. Cony's complaints were met with considerable sympathy by Lord Justice Rolle, who had previously expressed his concern about the Penruddock prosecutions. Judicially competent or not, the Council ordered that Cony's lawyers should be imprisoned and Rolle's retired. The Protector's opinion on such matters was, as so often, ambiguous.

Royalists, the quieter sort at least, found space in such ambiguities. The poet and polymath Abraham Cowley – all but forgotten now but on his death accorded a monument between Chaucer and Spenser in Westminster Abbey – had served as Jermyn's secretary, but had opted for a truce with the regime, returning from exile in 1654. Cowley finally settled into a melancholy contentment, withdrawing, like an early modern Themistocles, into quiet oblivion, self-censoring his more political poems. But in the round-up after Penruddock, he was arrested and interrogated by Cromwell and Thurloe and sent to the Tower before being released on bail. The following year, his collection *Poems* was published and he again reiterated his acceptance of that which had arisen by 'event of battle and the unaccountable will of God'. Both sides embraced divine providence, but Royalists, more certain of the natural order, could be more patient and bide their time. Others took a different view. The uncompromising Daniel O'Neill declared Cowley to be a 'bitter enemy'.[12]

Sir Robert Shirley, nephew of the Earl of Essex and a wealthy Midlands landowner, had been Charles's financial agent and he too was imprisoned in the Tower in 1655 in the wake of Penruddock. The closest the Royalists had to a profound political thinker, Shirley looked on his colleagues and despaired, seeing only a collection of reckless, aimless and thoughtless individuals.

Invoking the guiding spirit of the blessed Laud, Shirley saw the Church of England and the crown as one and indivisible, the source of all potential unity (though he was not above occasional, conspiratorial contact with Anabaptists and former Levellers). The bishops, properly schooled, would return revived to encourage religious discipline among the great mass of the English people, every bit as impressive, though more wide-spread, more deeply rooted – more beautiful – than that of the Presbyterians and Independents. Shirley built the only Anglican church to be constructed during the Interregnum: Staunton Harold, in Leicestershire. Such quietism was to reap rewards at the Restoration, though Shirley did not live to see it; imprisoned in the Tower, he died of smallpox in 1656, aged 27.

The regime, impatient and furtive, had proven its strength. But there was to be a more dramatic consequence of the Penruddock Rising, one that would soon be compounded by the withdrawal in foreign climes of God's providential hand. As a consequence Cromwell and his Council contemplated deeper, wider security measures, unprecedented and unsurpassed in English history.

The Royalist insurrection of early 1655, climaxing in the Penruddock Rising, had concentrated minds on threats to the regime's existence, or – a more cynical take – legitimated public fears that allowed it to tighten its grip. Unpopular regimes often seek legitimacy by exaggerating perils both to themselves and those they govern. The domestic threat, from Royalists, from Levellers, or from a combination of the two, was real but minimal, as recent events had demonstrated. Yet exaggerated or not, they were to prove a catalyst for an ambitious array of security measures – and more – which within six months would be implemented in full.

The regime had four problems to confront. First, Parliament's persistent undermining of the Instrument of Government, which led to the dissolution of the First Protectorate Parliament in January 1655, had convinced Cromwell of a simple undeniable truth: that it was the army more than any Parliament he might call that was the bulwark of his regime. Second, he was concerned for the security of a state which had recently witnessed violent insurrection and the threat of a Royalist–Leveller alliance. Third, crushing financial burdens had badly hindered the nation's defence at home and abroad and threatened to turn the Protector into a less legitimate facsimile of Charles I. And finally, less urgent but most important in the long term – infinitely so – there was the matter of the moral reformation of the English nation.

The means to those ends, what became known as the Rule of the Major Generals, has stained the reputation of the Protectorate ever since.[13] Almost immediately following the introduction of the scheme in October 1655, William Prynne, Puritan politician and polemicist, predicted that such military governance would 'acquire the perpetual infamy of the most detestable perjury, treachery, hypocrisy, fraud, impiety, apostasy, tyranny, atheism that ever any Christian saint-like army and officer were guilty of in the eyes of God'. And so it has proved, not least in the long-standing British aversion to standing armies: no man in uniform has ruled Britain since Cromwell.

★

Where did the idea for the Rule of the Major Generals originate? It has been suggested that John Lambert, the principal architect of the scheme, a man of bold ideas and sharp intellect, found inspiration in the work of Sir Robert Dudley, the Elizabethan adventurer and cartographer, the illegitimate son of the 1st Earl of Leicester and a woman who bore the first name of Douglas. Dudley's *A Proposition for his Majesty's Service to Bridle the Impertinences of Parliament*, written in 1614, had been republished in 1629 as *A Project How a Prince may make Himself an Absolute Tyrant*. Dudley's tyranny, with its strong military hue, was to be supported by 'a decimation, being so termed in Italy, where in some parts it is in use, taxing a tenth of every man's estate, to be paid yearly to the Crown as rent'. This may be the font of the infamous decimation tax, which would be imposed on Royalists to sustain the major generals' rule. It may also be the case that Lambert saw the establishment of the major generals on a permanent basis as a means to shore up his power base as successor to Cromwell, a likely scenario at that point in the Protectorate's evolution. Certainly that was the belief of the Irish MP Vincent Gookin, who, perhaps as a consequence, became a strong supporter of plans to crown Cromwell and revive the Ancient Constitution. 'Lambert is much for decimations', Gookin warned the Protector's son, Henry.[14]

If Lambert was the scheme's principal theoretician, elements of it had already been seen in practice: as knowledge of a Royalist rising increased, in February 1655 Cromwell had granted the Mayor of London and regime loyalists such as Philip Skippon and John Barkstead authority to raise militias to suppress agitation, seize arms from government opponents and disarm Catholics. Though the army's physical presence had declined from 1654, when it numbered around 41,000, it maintained a strong presence in London. The capital became a testing ground for a new kind of administration, which would spread to the provinces, where the regime faced additional problems. First, the justices of the peace, the backbone of the nation's legal administration, peacekeepers and enforcers of the law, tended to be alienated from the regime. They were not, as a rule, entirely committed to the Puritan world-view, being relatively relaxed about such matters as licensing alehouses, an important source of local income, and wider issues of moral laxity. Second, the standing army, never popular with the wider public, was tied up: keeping the peace in Ireland and Scotland and faced by the constant threat of war – whether with the French or the Dutch or – as was soon to become a reality – with Spain. Other means of keeping the peace domestically were required.

From March 1655, on the eve of the Royalist rising, twenty-two commissioners with militia-raising powers were appointed nationwide, from Durham to Dorset and from Lancashire to South Wales. The size of the militias raised was, usually, in proportion to the size of the region's population. The militia commissioners were given similar powers to those of Skippon in the City of London and ordered to cooperate with – and perhaps 'encourage' – local sheriffs, justices of the peace and magistrates in their endeavours. It was a bold new mix of the civilian and the military, supported by a tax raised on those inveterate Royalists who refused to accept the regime. The commissioners' main concern was to police their allotted region. But what if the threat of armed insurrection returned? For that, something more would be required, for which a blueprint also existed.

When news of the Penruddock Rising spread, John Desborough had taken his regiment of regular soldiers into the west, where he was joined by the forces, already there, of Colonel

James Berry. Though the insurrection was put down by Captain Croke before either Desborough or Berry could fire a shot, the pair had engaged in its aftermath with the local administrators – justices of the peace, for example, as well as the newly appointed commissioners in Dorset – to track down and imprison those Royalists involved, as well as many who were not. By May, Desborough, impressing his superiors, not least his brother-in-law, had been appointed 'major general of all the militia forces raised and to be raised within the counties of Cornwall, Devon, Somerset, Dorset, Wilts, and Gloucester'. We can date the very model of a major general – Desborough as the 'Major General of the West' – to that point.

While Desborough strengthened his position from his base at Exeter, others were encouraged to follow his model of cooperating with commissioners on a regional basis. Berry was establishing a similar project around Lincoln, while Hezekiah Haynes, a veteran of Dunbar, took up position in the East Anglian town of Bury St Edmunds. Both were to play significant senior roles in the Protector's new project.

The final, detailed arrangements for the scheme were thrashed out, away from the public eye, during the late summer of 1655. The subcommittee responsible, an elite who knew best, comprised Lambert at its head plus Desborough and Sir Gilbert Pickering, an Anabaptist* member of the Council of State. They worked alongside Cromwell to finalize instructions for the county militias. By 22 August Lambert had presented a

* Anabaptists are a religious grouping opposed to the baptism of infants. Only candidates who confess their faith in Christ and actively seek baptism are acceptable.

draft of instructions for ten new military governors. Their brief extended, it was soon made clear, far beyond military matters. As well as working closely with the county militia in the suppression of insurrection, their remit included the surveillance of 'disaffected persons', the disarming of Catholics and Royalists and the prevention of illicit gatherings, whether in private houses or at events such as race horse meetings, cock-fighting and bear-baiting, which attracted and bound the Cavalier and the conspirator. Vagrants and other 'loose' persons could be apprehended and put to work or expelled from the locality.

Finally, in addition to the role of general policing, the major generals were 'in their constant carriage and conversation to encourage and promote godliness and virtue and discourage and discountenance all profaneness and ungodliness'.[15] For Cromwell, the security of the regime was dependent ultimately on the moral reformation of the people; it would only be secure when godliness became the norm. 'I think reformation, if it be honest and through and just... will be your best security.' The major generals' role was to habituate the people to a new, reformed England. A reformation of manners would make the people and their nation virtuous. Henceforth there would be a war on illicit sex, a war on drunkenness, a war on gambling: wars unwinnable. Moral policing of the people of England was to prove a disastrous addition to the Protectorate's political programme.

But the major generals' formidable task of the moral reformation of an entire people was about to be given even greater urgency. For, in the late summer of 1655, news began to filter back to London of a military disaster on the other side of the world. It would be interpreted widely – and in Cromwell's case painfully – as God's damning judgement of a nation gone astray.

7

False News and Bad News

The Lord help us to know what our sin is.

MAJOR GENERAL CHARLES WORSLEY

BACK IN ENGLAND, the fate of the Western Design, though already sealed, remained a source of intrigue, rumour and conjecture. Its success was anticipated, but remained unconfirmed. For seven months after the fleet's departure, the Western Design's fulfilment or failure, like its origins and intent, remained a mystery. Communication across the Atlantic was slow and insecure. Six weeks was the absolute minimum crossing time from England to Barbados, during which a game of Chinese whispers could unfold, exaggerated by interested parties, from the spin of government officials eager to shape a positive narrative, to the *Schadenfreude* of Royalist exiles hoping that bad news would bring shame to a regime they despised and herald its fall. Inevitably, rumour, fantasy and wishful thinking filled the gaps left by an absence of reliable facts. The seedbeds of misinformation were watered by presses at home and abroad, by networks of diplomats and intelligence agents, and by friends and enemies of the Cromwellian regime. False news – and fake news – flowed in a steady stream. Some reports hailed a string of victories, others dwelled on disaster and defeat. The government was almost as ignorant of the truth as everyone else. Its principal conduit was the shape-shifting pamphleteer Marchamont Needham. His weekly newsbook, *Mercurius Politicus*, whose egregious lack of objectivity would do credit to a twenty-first-century tabloid, became the Protectorate's mouthpiece.

At first, even Needham said little of the Western Design, writing only 'God continue their course, with prosperous gales for the Expedition'. The target of the Design was kept quiet for obvious reasons. Lorenzo Paulucci, Venetian envoy at Westminster, seems to have been both ahead of the pack and prescient, reporting that a 'large island' in the West Indies was the ultimate focus of the Design, a fact acknowledged somewhat reluctantly by *Mercurius Politicus*, when it revealed that the Design was 'to make some attempt upon the Territories of the King of Spain'.[1] Some Royalists had discovered the Design's final destination. Thurloe's spy in Madrid reported that 'it is not unknown to the Spanish ambassador who is mad at it and has acquainted his master with it'. Spain's Council of State concluded that 'the English have some hankering after the island of Santo Domingo'.[2] Their suspicions were correct, but, since Spain was at war with France, they could not afford to withdraw Spanish ambassador Alonso de Cárdenas before a rumoured attack became established fact, as Cromwell might be tempted to ally openly with France. Cromwell was thus able to proceed with the Western Design *and* continue talks with France and Spain without fear that his plans would cause the ambassador to leave London. Despite pestering from an anxious Cárdenas, Cromwell refused to be drawn. The deafening silence on the Protector's part prompted Philip IV to dispatch a new governor, Count de Penalva, to Hispaniola in preparation to defend the island, along with an additional 200 soldiers.

If Cromwell was circumspect about his intentions and Philip

IV suspicious of them, the men of the Western Design remained largely ignorant when the fleet arrived at Barbados in February after a six-week voyage, which, according to commissioner Winslow had been remarkably smooth. His reports to Thurloe were remarkably upbeat, positively Panglossian. Though victuals had not yet arrived at Barbados and doubts had been raised about the quality of the troops raised there, they were:

> Resolved to cast ourselves into the arms of Almighty God, whose providence we trust will be ever for good and will owne us as instruments in his right hand to execute his determined vengeance upon that tyrannous and idolatrous and bloudy nation that hath inflicted so many cruelties upon the nations of the earth.[3]

Such buoyant news was no doubt welcomed at Westminster. There were solid grounds for victory. Hadn't Drake himself captured San Domingo with an infinitely smaller force? To tie in with the imminent good news, Gage's *A New Survey of the West Indies* was reprinted, this time with a newly commissioned map to help readers identify the distant lands of which he wrote, soon to be within Albion's imperial grasp. In the *Mercurius Politicus* of 31 May, Gage was identified, with some celebration, as the Protestant chaplain serving with Penn's fleet. No one in England yet knew that he had died of dysentery in distant Jamaica.

More troubling news was soon to reach Thurloe's ears. In May, agents in Madrid reported that Philip IV, well aware of the Design's intentions, had prepared accordingly, determined that 'all the English that are in Spaigne will suffer'.[4] War between the two nations seemed imminent and anti-Catholic sentiment in England increased as a consequence. Anti-Spanish – and anti-papist – rhetoric reached fever pitch in anticipation of the Design's victorious conclusion and the transplantation west of

Irish Catholics. When around 2,000 Waldensians were massacred in Piedmont after they refused the Duke of Savoy's orders to attend Mass or abandon his realm, the poet John Milton expressed his disgust in an angry sonnet that called on Protestant Europe to 'Avenge, O Lord, thy slaughtered saints, whose bones / Lie scattered on the Alpine mountains cold...'

By July 1655, rumours were circulating among European agents and diplomats, including Paulucci, that Hispaniola had been taken from the Spanish. He corresponded with his counterpart in Paris, Giovanni Sagredo, discussing the implications for Catholic Europe of an English victory in the Caribbean. An England ascendant in the New World, enriched by the seizure of the *flota de Indias*, would imperil the papacy itself. Exiled Royalists took comfort where they could. If Cromwell's England became the principal enemy of Philip IV, there was every reason to believe that a Habsburg–Stuart alliance would be in sight. The time had come to pull together in conspiracy, before Cromwell tipped the balance of power and providence in the New World towards Protestant England.

The first reports from the fleet arrived in London on 24 July 1655. They focused, intriguingly, upon Jamaica. Penn, in particular, dealt swiftly with the debacle at Hispaniola in matter-of-fact, staccato prose, while writing at length on the second-order prize. Indeed, as the military reports emphasized, the force had rallied, despite the 'setback' of San Domingo, to bring a strategic and economic jewel of the Spanish Caribbean into England's orbit.

The conquest of Jamaica was of little consolation to Cromwell. After years of victory, relentless and decisive, God, it seemed, had withdrawn His hand. Almost 10,000 troops carried in to the New World by a vast fleet had met ignominious defeat at the hands of a small band of Spanish soldiers and settlers. They had shown themselves to be unworthy of the legacy of Drake, who had routed the defenders of San Domingo with a fraction of the force. Why had England been abandoned and why now? Why had providence been lost? Was it not the mission of God's elect nation to invade the waters of the Caribbean and topple proud Spain, rock of the Roman church? For Cromwell, there was never to be such glad confidence again. The members of the expedition had been marked by 'extreme avarice, pride and confidence, disorders and debauchedness, profaneness and wickedness'. Conditions must be created where 'virtue and godliness could flourish'.[5]

A fast, held in secret and attended only by the Protector and his Council, was held in Whitehall on 25 July, the day after confirmation of the grim news arrived. Lambert's objections to the Design had been realized. The ship that had brought the news of the humiliation at Hispaniola was quarantined; no one was allowed to come ashore for fear, not so much of disease, but that word of the debacle might spread. Despite such action, word leaked and rumour and fact inevitably intermingled and worked their way into the warrens of Whitehall and beyond.

Two days later, on 27 July, the news-sheet *Certain Passages of every Dayes Intelligence* acknowledged defeat but, in what would become the classic English trope of heroic failure, reported that the defeated troops 'declared them selves valiant and true English men'. The *Faithfull Scout*, however, most fawning of the organs of the Protectorate press under its editor Daniel Border, continued to insist on an English victory, claiming that a number of forts as well as 450 prisoners had been taken on Hispaniola. Other reports conflated Hispaniola and Jamaica, declaring that the latter belonged to the former in the same way that the Isle of Wight was English. How much of this false news was born of ignorance or creative optimism it is impossible to say, perhaps a bit of both. But the idea that the conquest of Jamaica was part of the initial Design was spun with ever greater frequency.

By the beginning of August, Needham's *Mercurius Politicus* was claiming that Jamaica was targeted in preference to Hispaniola, that the commanders of the Design 'relinquished Hispaniola, were landed at Jamaica, and became Masters of the Island'. Jamaica was 'more commended every day' than Hispaniola, 'for the fertility of the place, and the goodness of the fruits and plants'. That the statement would turn out to be true – eventually, long after the protagonists were dead – was, in this case and so many others, more contingent than considered. But those who wrote of the 'advantages of Jamaica', though motivated by post hoc justification, were not wrong in their judgement that Jamaica would 'produce as good a trade as any island in America... the most convenient island the Spaniards have for my lord's design' and for settlement. But as Paulucci noted, Cromwell was:

> far from satisfied with the results achieved in America, so much below his hopes. To avoid discouraging the people he is trying to make out that the advantages are great by the continued occupation of the conquest made by the English fleet there.[6]

Jamaica was to be settled, and under the Protector, to whom, as the *Weekly Post*, the work of the *Faithfull Scout*'s Daniel Birder, urged, 'let us humbly submit'. General Blake will, in time it implored, wild in its optimism for the conflict to come, 'prove as famous as Sir Francis Drake'.

Reports that the English forces had been repelled at Santo Domingo were not confirmed in Spain until early September. War between England and Spain, long rumoured, was a reality. Whether it could be contained was another question. Would it spread to Europe? Cárdenas, in conversation with the Swedish

Ambassador to London, Christer Bonde, believed it would. Cromwell was driven by providential fervour, while Philip IV was determined to preserve and maintain his 'treasure-chamber in the Indies' at all costs. Once England's failure to take Hispaniola became widely known, English concerns about the Spanish reaction to the Western Design fuelled rumour and conjecture.

Cromwell's speeches had not been printed in full since the dissolution of the First Protectorate Parliament, for fear of them being misused. They had been summarized instead in *Mercurius Politicus*. Such paranoia can only have been made worse by the failure of the Western Design. The Royalist William Dugdale, writing to John Langley, the head of St Paul's school, on 9 October 1655, thought as much: 'It seems our "superiors" are not pleased that so much of these matters [Western Design] should be communicated by the press; for they have restrained all pamphlets by *Politicus*, which is to be viewed by the Secretary of State [Thurloe].'[7] Needham defended such restrictions on the press in the *Mercurius Politicus* of 4 October. It was necessary, he argued, to limit the number of news outlets to loyalists such as him in order to prevent the 'falsehoods, and great Confusion', which led to the 'abusing of the People, and the dishonour of the Nation'.

But English setbacks were piling up. William Goodson failed in his mission to capture the *flota* in the Caribbean as it set out from Havana. Blake, greatest of Cromwell's admirals, was ordered to intercept it as it reached the Mediterranean. Though the order was secret, such an act had long been anticipated: Paulucci reported, even before news of the Design's failure reached London, that England's 'animosity against the dominions and property of the Catholic seems steadily on the increase'. Quirini, the Venetian ambassador to Spain, reported that 'In the mean time a good proportion of the English of Malaga, Cadiz, Seville and San

Lucar, who may amount to some fifty families, have embarked by night on the fleet, taking their money with them, all things which indicate some upheaval and the very worst intentions.'

Blake's operation came to nothing. His ships were prevented from pursuing the Spanish fleet because of heavy fog. Reports carried in newsbooks such as the *Weekly Intelligencer* that Blake had captured or sunk twelve of the fourteen Spanish vessels in the *flota* were entirely false. Such an achievement was not something Cromwell would have kept quiet.

Even the *Faithfull Scout* was finding it hard to have much faith in good news from the New World: 'The truth is', it reported in September 1655, 'the loss of the English is far greater then [sic] was expected, for since the quitting of Hispaniola, and taking of Jamaica, many brave spirits have lost their lives perishing merely for want of sustenance and provisions.' Paulucci, well informed and incisive as ever, wrote that:

> Although the losses suffered at Hispaniola are concealed as much as possible, yet a letter has appeared from a husband to his wife reporting the loss as serious and that in Jamaica they are short of the most necessary things, such as bread, salt and meat, and although the island abounds in the last they can only have what they take by force.[8]

English merchants in the Caribbean became anxious when Philip IV announced a trade embargo on England; Cromwell authorized attacks on Spanish shipping in response. This would hardly make up for the loss of Spanish trade, the merchants argued, as Spanish captains would simply destroy their own vessels if they were in danger of capture. The wide-eyed idealism of the Design, unplanned and casual in its execution, was coming to be seen among the English public as 'fruitless', an adventure in which many lives had been 'lost for no purpose'. Paulucci wrote of his regret that 'if instead of going to the Indies the English had sailed to the Levant in defence of the Christian faith, they would have been loaded with glory, have found an easier task and possibly a more profitable one'.[9]

Royalists relished the irony that the same presses that once lauded the parliamentary forces, now held Cromwell to account as he had done the king. The Protector was 'putt in mind now to suppress them, there being matter to be written against his advantage'. The Cornish Royalist Joseph Jane also noted that despite the positive spin put on the conquest of Jamaica, 'it is not difficult to discern they have but sorry comfort in it'. This did not stop Royalists with too much time on their hands from indulging in paranoiac conspiracy theories: Marmaduke Langdale insisted that an Anglo-Spanish alliance, uniting the unlikely bedfellows of Cromwell and Philip IV, would carve up the Caribbean to the detriment of France.[10]

In fact, Philip IV's response to the English aggression on his Caribbean possessions was patient and considered, though pirates from the ports of Ostend and Dunkirk were given carte blanche to attack English shipping. Exhausted by the long war with France, Philip chose to be canny. He could not afford open combat with the Protector's powerful fleet; Spain had become a foe that could 'neither fight nor trade'.

As more reports arrived, it became ever more difficult to feel optimistic about Jamaica, despite the gloss offered by Needham, whose reports acknowledged serious challenges but expressed little doubt that 'the Lord will yet blesse us'. Correspondence compiled by Major General Sedgwick and Vice Admiral Goodson described soldiers on the island 'as sad and deplorable... as ever poor Englishmen were... the soldiery many dead, their carcasses lying unburied in the high-ways, and among bushes'. Those still alive 'walked like ghosts or dead men'. More than 100 soldiers were dying every week in Jamaica, most of them of disease. If this was England's jewel in the New World, it would take years to burnish.[11]

Venables, furious with Penn for leaving Jamaica without him, had attempted to overtake his fellow commander on his voyage back on the *Marston Moor*. He failed, making it to Portsmouth on 9 September, 'almost a skeleton'. Both he and Penn were sent to the Tower (via Traitor's Gate, noted the Swedish ambassador). Released at the end of October, Venables lost his commission and lived out the rest of his life in mildly comfortable disgrace.* His wife, returning from a less than happy honeymoon, blamed everyone but her husband for the failure: 'For the work of God was not like to be done by the devil's instruments. A wicked army it was, and sent out without arms or provisions.'

Major General Worsley asked: 'The Lord help us to know what our sin is, and what his pleasure is, that were so crossed and vested in Jamaica.' Enemies muttered. Arthur Vane compared Cromwell with William the Conqueror, bringer of the Norman yoke and the bogeyman of Levellers and Commonwealthsmen: the 'root and bottom on which it stood' was the 'private lust and will of the Conquerour'. Cromwell had succumbed to such vices, too. He and his nation stood admonished for all the world to see, humiliated in their hubris.

The failure of the Western Design crushed the Protector, a man who up till now had known only victory. The Civil Wars had been won by 'an army despised by our enemies and little less

---

* Writing another work on fishing, *The Experienced Angler, or Angling improved* (1662), which, held in high regard by Izaak Walton, went into five editions before Venables' death in 1687.

than despised by our friends', but on the side of the saints, which its soldiers themselves became in the light of victory. Now the army had tasted defeat for the first time. The man who had 'accomplished in three years what English monarchs had failed to in over a hundred' – the conquest of Ireland and Scotland – had been brought low.

Cromwell had written to Vice Admiral Goodson that: 'the Lord hath greatly humbled us in that sad loss… we have provoked the Lord, and it is good for us to know and to be abased for the same'.[12] In a move typical of Cromwell, he retreated from public life and, in one of his many anguished dialogues with his God, begged to be brought to an understanding of how the present, disastrous state of affairs had come about. How had he and his government failed in their duty before Him?

Cromwell interpreted the debacle in providential terms. Why had the God who had been at his side in fierce battle abandoned him, his saints, his nation? 'The hand of the Lord', he observed, 'hath not been more visible in any part of this rebuke.'[13] The saints of the New Model Army had been elected to carry out God's purpose on Earth and their military success was the outward dispensation of their inward grace. Divine providence explained entirely the spectacular military success of Cromwell, who was, we should not forget, an amateur general, who had embarked late upon a career of dazzling achievement. Naseby was credited to 'none other than the hand of God'.[14] After the 'miracle' of Dunbar, the high point of English Puritan providentialism, Sidrach Simpson, a minister, told Cromwell: 'God had stepped out of heaven to raise those who were even as dead, and to judge his adversaries.' And now He had returned there, to leave His chosen people to their fate. It was manifest that the English nation had called down God's wrath on itself. But in what way was its conduct at odds with His plans for it?[15]

The reason Cromwell lighted on was one shared by many of his Puritan comrades: they had failed in their divinely appointed task of carrying out the moral transformation of the English people. Cromwell wrote to Colonel Richard Fortescue, now commander of the army in Jamaica, that the only way to regain God's blessing is that 'all manner of vice may be thoroughly discountenanced and severely punished; and that such a form of government may be exercised that virtue and godliness may receive due encouragement'. It was a mission that could be postponed no longer. With a plan now in place to hand control of England's every region to those most zealous in godly reform, Cromwell would impose the Puritan world view on the masses and save the nation. They could not rely upon God's dispensation – every opportunity for moral betterment must be grasped, for 'to neglect... slight, or condemn any lawful means, is a tempting of God, that man that shall cast off all means, and say he will rest upon providence, neither believes there is indeed an overriding providence, nor can rest upon providence'. A day of solemn fasting and humiliation was ordered for 6 December 1655. 'We have provoked the Lord', admitted Cromwell, 'and it is good for us to know so, and to be abased for the same... we should... lay our mouths... in the dust.'[16]

Divine providence had been lost; it must be regained.

The idea of providence is difficult for the modern mind to conceive, though its traces live on in phrases such as 'God willing', 'small mercies' and the occasional, figurative attribution of a successful outcome to divine intervention. Providence could bring mercies and deliverance; it could, prompted by adultery, fornication, blasphemy and drunkenness, bring forth plague and famine and death. Every event, good and bad, was grounded in a cause. Everything had an explanation. There was no such thing as chance, the French theologian Jean Calvin had proclaimed, 'but whatsoever cometh to pass in the world, cometh by the secret providence of God'.

Perhaps all ages are ages of anxiety, though some are more so than others. The seventeenth century was marked by what Keith Thomas described as 'a new insistence upon God's sovereignty'.[17] The deity not only intervened, but he did so in a ubiquitous, all-encompassing, inescapable way, especially in the lives of the more fervid sort of Puritan. Calvin's religious teachings of predestination told of a fixed, unchanging division of mankind, decided before the beginning of time, into those saved and those damned. According to this troubling, trembling dogma, God had created humanity knowing that its majority would suffer hellfire for eternity. His attentions extended to matters of seemingly infinitesimal banality, for it was 'certain that not a drop of rain falls without the express command of God'. Among Oliver Cromwell's most treasured biblical quotations was the passage from Matthew 10:29–30 – 'Are not two sparrows sold for a penny? Yet not one of them will fall to the ground outside your Father's care. And even the very hairs of your head are all numbered.' It was God's hand intervening in the minutiae of life that gave his presence such power: inescapable, immanent, all-seeing, the cosmic observer, from whom there was no escape.

'Men who have assurance that they are to inherit heaven, have a way of presently taking possession of earth.' These words, by the American historian William Halle, illustrate the energy of puritanism. Puritans sought evidence of their having been chosen by God in their worldly enterprise, that they were of God's precious elect. They were judged by their fruits, for 'nothing is more industrious than saving faith'. As Calvin wrote to Thomas Cranmer, the architect of the Anglican alloy of Calvinist theology and Catholic rite: God would 'by no means have these persons inactive whom He Himself has placed on the watch'.

The relationship was a two-way street. While God watched, those observed sought to discern his wishes so that they might act in a way that reflected his grace and reassure themselves that they were members of the elect. Psalm 28, a touchstone of puritanism, warned that: 'Because they regard not the works of the Lord, nor the operations of his hands, he shall destroy them.' Another verse much invoked was Jeremiah 17:5: 'Thus saith the LORD; Cursed be the man that trusteth in man, and maketh flesh his arm, and whose heart departeth from the LORD.' In the absence of intercessors, such as bishops or priests, the watched were, simultaneously, the watchers. Every event, major or minor, was to be interpreted within the overall plan of God's providence. Ralph Josselin, an Essex minister sympathetic to the Protectorate, recorded his belief that the death of one of his children was due to his 'unreasonable playing at chess'. Puritans were riddled with anxiety and submitted themselves to pitiless self-examination. Yet Josselin, even when life unravelled and hurt, remained grateful for 'His wisdom and providences'. It was a surveillance society of the soul and it is no wonder that it cultivated anxieties and paranoia.[18]

The concept of a tirelessly interventionist and inescapable God might be compared to modern social media, resulting in comparable levels of anxiety and paranoia. Facebook, Twitter, Instagram are realms of round-the-clock surveillance, where one's thoughts and actions, beliefs and appearance are posted and preserved for all to see and subjected to constant comparison and judgement. On occasion, the shame, vindictiveness and piety that social media generates would not have felt out of place among seventeenth-century Puritans. But one can opt out of social media, however addictive. There was no such option in the world God had created, nor in the next.

Because God revealed his working in the minuscule as well as the massive, devoted Puritans recorded the smallest elements of their lives in order to follow the line and pattern of their relationship with God. Cromwell was typical in this. He would spend days and weeks in contemplation, especially when bad news struck, evoking Christ's question of despair at the Crucifixion: 'My God, my God, why hast thou forsaken me?'

Scripture and prayer were the means to interpretation. The Western Design's failure had been a result of God acting 'for reasons best known to himself'. Cromwell, the saints, were challenged to discern what God alone knew. But the Creator did occasionally play tricks. The Old Testament is full of examples of God raising a people or a person only to destroy them. 'What God doth providentially, He not always approves.'[19]

England, the elect nation, said Cromwell, 'hath been the Noah's ark, safe and secure, when all other nations have been drowned with a sea of blood.' But the belief in an elect nation also led to governance marked by improvisation and a wilful flexibility. Cromwell was not 'wedded and glued to forms of government'. Man's rewards were never merited, but were graceful gifts of God; unlike afflictions, which were always wholly deserved. The Civil Wars were a catastrophe resulting from moral squalor and iniquity, of licentious sexual incontinence, drunkenness and irreligion. The nation they were visited upon was in urgent need of repair, of moral reformation. In mid-seventeenth-century England, the idea of providence attained a level of intensity unsurpassed before or since – powered by the impulse, born of the Protestant Reformation, to give a 'new insistence to God's sovereignty'.

Cromwell's long run of success had been the path to hubris. Royalists had lost because of their sinful pasts, as they were all too aware, but Cromwell and his circle, especially after Dunbar, were prone to consider God's will less, perhaps, than once they had: the certainty of their election became their undoing. Their countrymen had barely probed it at all. Most English people of the early modern period were committed to an unspectacular orthodoxy founded upon the consolations, ritual and beauty of Cranmer's Book of Common Prayer. Despite the revisionism of recent decades, one can still abide by the historian Diarmaid MacCulloch's assertion that the English Reformation, especially the *via media* trod by the Elizabethan church, had been a 'howling success'. But the Puritan was different, an outlier, whose harsh creed was now at the centre of English politics. Their faith was as much about internal wranglings and eternal vigilance as it was about outward manifestation and it was prone to be inward in its obsessions. There were no intermediaries between their vulnerable soul and God. They were dependent upon God's grace and anxious of its withdrawal. Their fate – whether damned or redeemed – had been decided at the Creation. How would their salvation manifest itself on earth?

As the Puritan Thomas Taylor pointed out, Protestantism did not offer 'a gentlemanlike life or trade, whose rents come in by their stewards'. There was nothing between you and God, no transactions were available by which one's salvation might be secured. While Catholicism, with its intercessions and hierarchies, set up what the Puritan theologian Richard Sibbes described as 'the will of man to maintain stately idleness', Protestantism was an active, enabling creed, though one always in danger of being rendered sclerotic by anxiety. But, at its best, as one of Cromwell's most famous phrases put it, you trusted in God, but it was up to you to keep your powder dry. God helped those who helped themselves. Cromwell, born of a Puritan family, had imbibed such ideas not just with his mother's milk. His grandfather, in the year after the Armada, had written: 'God doth not always deliver his people by miracles; it behoveth us to reform ourselves.' It would be his grandson's task to reform a nation, a mission made more urgent by the failure of the Western Design.[20]

8

England's New Elites

Mean and profligate rascals.

ROGER COKE

IT WAS NOT until 21 September 1655 that Cromwell, re-
covering from illness (brought on, in part perhaps, by the
failure of the Western Design), was well enough to be able to
consider two drafts from Lambert's subcommittee. These were
the general commission for the major generals and the orders
for both them and the county commissions, alongside whom
they would work. The primary reason for their elevation to the
rank of major generals, the first of the documents stated, was
to guard against the 'restless and implacable in their malicious
designs against the peace of the Commonwealth'. They were
invested with powers to maintain their local militia 'in good
discipline' and to 'conduct them to fight against all enemies'. In
time of insurrection or invasion they could 'raise the inhabitants
of the said counties, and to exercise, arm, muster, and conduct
them to the places where we shall direct you in case of rebellion'.

Nineteen major generals were appointed in October 1655,
sixteen of whom served in one of the ten 'Associations' into
which the country was to be divided. The men were chosen from
among Cromwell's closest, most trusted military colleagues,

characterized by 'fidelity, wisdom and circumspection'. Lambert, inevitably, was appointed major general of the north of England, though as he was often required to attend the Council's meetings at Whitehall, two deputies were to serve under him: Charles Howard, the youngest among them, raised a Catholic, who was responsible for Cumberland, Northumberland and Westmorland; and Robert Lilburne, brother of the Leveller activist and ideologue, John, who oversaw Durham and Yorkshire. Similarly, Charles Fleetwood and Philip Skippon had seats on the Council and were granted deputies: Skippon maintained his relationship with the governor of the Tower, John Barkstead, in their firm rule over the City of London, Westminster and Middlesex; while Fleetwood had the experienced Hezekiah Haynes to assist him in East Anglia, William Packer, a religious firebrand, in Oxfordshire and Hertfordshire, and his own brother George in Buckinghamshire. Charles Worsley, who took charge of Cheshire, Lancashire and Staffordshire, was maniacal in his pursuit of reformation and would die within a year as a result of his exertions. Edward Whalley, a rare religious moderate among them, held sway over the East Midlands, the ferocious William Boteler took Bedfordshire, Huntingdonshire, Northamptonshire and Rutland, and Thomas Kelsey Surrey and Kent. The millenarian William Goffe was responsible for Berkshire, Hampshire and Sussex, while the Independent James Berry, who had dabbled with Fifth Monarchists and Baptists, retained hold of Wales and its Marches (assisted by John Nicholas and Rowland Dawkins). The original model for the major generals, John Desborough, a man with Baptist leanings, retained his command of the whole of the south-west, from Cornwall to Gloucestershire and Wiltshire.[1]

Such was England's new ruling elite, a number of whom had gained substantial estates from sequestered Royalists, which placed them at some distance from the ordinary soldiers who had fought alongside them in the Civil Wars: 'parks and new houses and gallant wives choked them up', it was claimed. Such displeasure, and envy perhaps, of the common man made good would play its part in the Restoration of Charles II. Lambert, grandest of all, had bought Wimbledon House, south-west of London, for more than £16,000 in May 1652, which gives some measure of the wealth and property he had accrued, in Yorkshire and Scotland in particular, as he rose to political prominence. He especially enjoyed the gardens at Wimbledon, which were among the most extensive and beautiful in the country. Mocked as the 'Knight of the Golden Tulip', Lambert was seriously green-fingered, becoming associated in particular with *Nerine sarniensis*, the Guernsey lily. Ironically, the horticultural land-scape Lambert tended with such care in the 1650s had been the creation of Queen Henrietta Maria.[2]

It is well known that Charles I was an aesthete, his artistic and architectural legacy a considerable one. Inigo Jones, the first Englishman to master the formal classical concepts of the great northern Italian architect Andrea Palladio, created the Queen's House in Greenwich for Henrietta Maria, as well as the Banqueting House, Whitehall, with its magnificent Rubens ceiling, *The Apotheosis of James I*, through which, with bitter irony, his son was led to execution. Yet there was, perhaps, less of a gulf between the tastes of Cavaliers and Roundheads than one might imagine, certainly so far as those at the apex of power were concerned. The wretched iconoclasm of the Civil Wars and the fire sale of the 'late king's goods', Charles's superbly curated collection of European masters, which was flogged around Europe after the king's execution are notorious.[3] There was a splendour, too, however, at the 'court' of Oliver Cromwell; in 1655 a Great Seal was cut, bearing the Protector's personal coat of arms and an imperial crown. 'Oliver P' became his signature.

The Protector's court centred on the warrens of Whitehall and the ample riverside majesty of Hampton Court. He rarely, if at all, left London and its vicinity. Cromwell and his family moved into the suite of rooms that had served as the Royal Apartments in Whitehall in April 1654, probably after rushed – and expensive – renovation, for they had been neglected since Charles I had fled London in January 1642. John Embree, Cromwell's surveyor general, spent more than £10,000 a year on refurbishments throughout the duration of the Protectorate, a sum comparable with the Stuarts' annual expenditure. The renovation of Hampton Court was a considerable and challenging project. The roofs leaked, the water supply was far from satisfactory and the gardens had been neglected (what must Lambert have thought?). Cromwell and Embree had ambitions for the site. A huge marble fountain was brought from Somerset House to become the focus of Cromwell's private garden. Originally commissioned as the centrepiece of an assembly of classical figures, it, too, was designed by Inigo Jones for Charles I, in the 1630s. This 'Diana Fountain' could hardly be less puritanical in its symbolism, decorated with nymphs, dolphins and sea monsters, the supporting cast to a statue of Diana atop. The Puritan Mary Netheway was appalled by 'those monstres' and wrote to the Protector to remind him that 'while the altars of the idols remained untaken away in Jerusalem, the wrath of God continued against Israel'.*

The interiors received as much attention as the outdoors. Clement Kinnersley, Cromwell's keeper of the wardrobe, was lavish in his spending. Between February and November 1654

* The fountain remains on display in nearby Bushy Park, to where it was moved in 1713.

he spent more than £12,000 on such items as a bed for the Whitehall apartments, 'after the Indian fashion', most of which had been part of the royal collection, along with an impressive array of paintings and tapestries. Whitehall, after all, was part of the public face of the regime, where ambassadors and emissaries from across Europe would seek audience with Cromwell. Whatever the ideology of regime, it would seek to offer similar splendour to its allies and rivals across the Continent: it was the seat of the head of state and, as the Venetian ambassador Giavarina reported, the ceremony that took place there was that of the 'obseqious and respectful form observed to the late king': ambassadors would approach the Protector in a highly formal series of choreographed steps, addressing him as 'Your Most Serene Highness'.[4] Such ceremony should not be seen so much as a reflection of Cromwell's personal taste, but more the trappings of a regime that sought legitimacy through the adoption of conventions shared throughout the courts of Europe and beyond. Greeting the Protector as his highness beneath Rubens's massive apotheosis of Stuart monarchy must have been a sobering experience for visitors. Breaking with protocol, Cromwell's insistence that letters from fellow heads of state should address him as 'brother' was disliked by France's chief minister Cardinal Mazarin, an architect of absolutism.

For an understanding of Cromwell's personal aesthetic, Hampton Court is the more revealing. This was his retreat, as well as that of his family and closest allies. It was also the location for the wedding of his daughter Mary. Its interiors were more likely to be decorated according to his personal taste rather than reasons of state. They do not reflect the aesthetics of the Puritan stereotype.

The tapestries at Hampton Court, a particularly expensive form of decoration, depicted the sinful, adulterous figure of Venus.

Those in the aptly titled Paradise Room went even further in their dabbling with sinful narratives, celebrating the Triumphs of the Seven Deadly Sins. Cromwell's collection of paintings was no less decadent in its themes. Artemesia Gentileschi's depiction of Bathsheba washing herself, was unlikely to fulfil Puritan requirements of decorum, while Andrea Schiavoni's *Madonna and Child with St Elizabeth* and Luca Cambiaso's *Assumption of the Virgin Mary* were deeply Catholic devotional works, which sat ill with Cromwell's professed protestantism.

Men of substance close to Cromwell also sought to surround themselves with splendour. Edmund Prideaux, the attorney general, had a new seat built at Forde Abbey, a former Cistercian monastery in Dorset; Oliver St John, Cromwell's cousin, instructed the architect Peter Mills to design Thorpe Hall near Peterborough;* and John Thurloe rebuilt and refurbished Wisbech Castle in Ely. Prominent courtiers such as Viscount Lisle also built up substantial art collections, perhaps feeling that Cromwell's own collection gave them the latitude to do so. It is important to remember that most of these men, though not aristocrats, were of the gentry class. Their tastes were those of educated gentleman who had achieved wealth and power. Cromwell's master of horse, John Claypole, who married the Protector's favourite daughter, Elizabeth, took delight in the country pursuits of a gentleman, such as hunting and dog fighting.

The major generals were young, energetic men, most of them under forty, usually with strong links to the regions to which they were assigned. Only three of them – Fleetwood, Howard and Lilburne – were from wealthy landowning families, while

---

* Mills was to design the triumphal arches for the coronation of Charles II and was one of the four surveyors appointed to rebuild the City of London following the Great Fire of 1666.

Worsley was the son of a prosperous Mancunian merchant. Most were minor gentry, though some were of very modest birth indeed; the accusation that they were low-born upstarts, used against them from the off, had some basis in fact. Barkstead, 'a thimble maker', and Kelsey had been London tradesmen. Berry had been a clerk in a Shropshire ironworks. Tobias Bridge, who replaced Worsley in Cheshire, Lancashire and Staffordshire at his death in 1656, was disparaged as a 'common dragooner'.

The task set for these men was nothing less than the nation's moral regeneration. They could call on not only the new county militias, raised in early summer, but, from late October 1655, the 'commissions for securing the peace of the commonwealth', a post which superseded the militia commissions established earlier in the year. Depending on the size and population of the county, somewhere between ten and thirty commissioners would be appointed, a mix of civilians and militia men judged to be 'well-affected' supporters of the regime, acting as its eyes and ears, though such intrusions were not wholly popular with the local populations. Like the major generals, the commissioners, too, tended to be of relatively modest background – 'the stress of this business must lie on the middling sort', Goffe noted. There were some of greater substance, drawn from the established county elite, while a few mirrored the likes of Barkstead and Berry in their humble roots. In Cheshire, the commissioners recruited by Worsley included a 'prominence of low born men', providing more ammunition for Royalists such as Roger Coke, who judged the recruits in his county of Suffolk to be 'mean and profligate rascals'.

Recruitment was easy enough, though some of those asked to take on the role of commissioner were wary; a few – such as Thomas Sanders, a Derbyshire colonel – refused outright. Occasionally excuses were made; Desborough reported to the

Protector that two of his commissioners cried off with convenient bouts of toothache and gout, respectively. In some cases,
genuine concerns were raised, born of thoughtful consideration
of the consequences of the scheme. Thomas Grove, described by
Desborough as 'tender', wrote that he could not 'undertake any
business till I have had some serious thoughts about it and have
debated it with mine own weak judgement, that so men's conscience may be clearly satisfied in what I do'. These were the scruples
of a good man, but a potentially poor commissioner; Grove's
political trajectory suggests he was ultimately disapproving.
On a few rare occasions, a commissioner would serve in order
to undermine the regime and to protect their political allies.
One such was Christopher Guize, a louche figure from a well-
established Royalist family, unlikely to be mistaken for a Puritan,
who tried, with little success, to help friends evade the decimation
tax. He aroused the hostility of Desborough, who would launch
a fierce, physically hostile attack on him in the parliamentary
election of August 1656. Guize's case was, however, exceptional.
Most commissioners were as ideologically committed to their
task as the major generals; as Samuel Rawson Gardiner, the
great historian of the Civil War period, put it, exaggerating
only slightly, 'the utmost harmony prevailed' between the commissioners and the men that commanded them, a judgement
borne out by the comments of the major generals themselves.

Frictions arose between these arrivistes and the traditional
administrators, the 'natural leaders' of the regions, the justices
of the peace and the magistrates. From the scheme's unveiling,
the major generals accused the civilian administrators of apathy
and obstruction. As early as June 1655, Berry had complained
to Cromwell that his magistrates in Lincoln were 'idle, and the
people all asleep'. There was much work to be done and purges
were threatened. Some major generals, such as Whalley in the

East Midlands, even added the role of justice of the peace to their own brief, probably because they had little faith in the traditional administrators.*[5]

The commissioners appear to have hit the ground running. James Berry, who presided over Herefordshire, wrote of their 'readiness' and 'joy'. Even Boteler, a more abrasive and demanding figure, spoke highly of those who aided his rule of Bedfordshire: 'God hath wrought a good promptitude in the hearts of our honest friends in other places to this great work; yet I am apt to think more than ordinary in these gentlemen.' His commissioners were zealous to 'purpose such a way for settling the hearts and quieting the minds of all good people by this course now proceeded in'. Kelsey spoke of the 'very hearty and cordial' commissioners he was assigned. Of course, there could be an element of flattery at work here, common to those new to a position and eager to please. But Boteler's men responded in kind, writing to Thurloe of their enthusiasm for an undertaking aimed at 'settling the hearts and quieting the minds of all good people by this course'. Most of them set to their tasks with zeal; especially in their dealings with Royalists.[6]

The major generals were given twenty-one official instructions by the government, the second document of which divided Royalists into three specific categories. First, and of urgent import, were those who had taken an active role in the events of March that culminated in the Penruddock Rising. Imprisonment, banishment and the sequestration of estates were to be their fate. Assigned to the second category were those who appear 'by their words and actions to adhere to the interest of

---

* Alternatively, actions such as Whalley's might be interpreted as a conciliatory move to work within and among the traditional organs of county government.

the late king or of Charles Stuart his son'. They, too, could be imprisoned or banished, but, unless they had returned from exile without permission, their estates were safe. By far the most contentious of these classifications was the final one, wholly at odds with the Act of Oblivion, passed by the Rump Parliament in 1652, with Cromwell's support, even if it was 'clogged with so many provisos'. The Act of Oblivion had offered all those Royalists who agreed to live at peace with the Commonwealth a pardon for any actions they were involved in before the Battle of Worcester in September 1651. But now Royalist culpability was backdated, quite arbitrarily, to include all those who had fought against Parliament since 1642. Even though many of them had done nothing to oppose the regime in deed or word, they were now obliged to pay a tax of 10 per cent – the 'decimation' – on any land worth £100 per annum or property valued at £1,500 or more. It would be paid to the government specifically to fund the new militias. So much for 'healing and settling'.

A declaration issued on 31 October 1655, the official inauguration of the rule of the major generals, began: 'Providence, having by the issue of the civil wars, declared against the Royalist party, the victors signalised their triumph by extremely mild measures towards the vanquished'. The 'extremely mild measure' was the Act of Oblivion. 'All such pardons and leniency', the declaration continued, 'were conditional upon good behaviour for the future. Referring to Penruddock and other alleged conspiracies and plots, it was judged that 'the royalists having failed in such behaviour the government was no longer bound to be lenient'. And the government presumed the support of the wider population in its harsher treatment of Royalists (though did not consider the people's opinion of moral reformation): 'It will not be thought strange that we have laid a burden on some of the estates beyond what is imposed upon the rest of the nation towards the defraying of the charge which they are then occasion of.' Referencing once again the unholy alliance of Royalists and Levellers, the declaration referred to a 'new and standing militia of horse', the expense of which was to be 'defrayed to the rebels'. The new tax was imposed on the 'whole of the royalist party, because the insurrection evidently involved the whole party by implications'. And yet this was despite the fact that many, perhaps most, Royalists passively accepted Cromwellian rule, if only because of the lack of any realistic hope of an alternative.

The disarming of Catholics and Royalists – frequently the same thing, for the old religion was four times more common among the nobility than the wider population – was carried out swiftly and with some vigour in the early days of the scheme. Edward Whalley, it was claimed, left Sir Roger Burgoyne with little more than a 'birding piece or a sword'. There was an element of vengefulness in the behaviour of some local commissioners, who relished the chance to settle scores with old enemies. Boteler was no doubt delighted to report that his commissioners were more than happy to 'make it their business to find out and give me notice of all their profane and idol gentry and other whose lives are a shame to Commonwealth'. Hard cases, such as Boteler, menaced local magnates. Though he found his commissioners 'a little timorous' at first in their pursuit of the decimation tax, he soon bent them to his will, recording that, 'they have all of them put their hands to the plough; and shame will not let them now look back'.[7]

Bonds for good behaviour were imposed upon 14,000 Royalists, with an additional fine of £5,000 if they erred. A register office was established in London, where any Royalist visiting the capital was obliged to report within twenty-four hours of arrival. Similar registers were established in the major ports. From December 1655, anyone arriving in England, foreign or not, had to appear before the local major general or a representative, tell him where they had come from and where they were going and, if travelling to London, register locally on pain of imprisonment.

Money matters, even to the godly, and so the first priority of the newly installed major generals and their commissioners was the assessment and collection of the decimation tax, a challenging task given that, in theory at least, it had to be collected in its entirety by 21 December 1655. On the whole, the commissioners were strict in their pursuit – up to thirty individuals might be summoned and investigated in a week – especially when spurred on by personal animosity. The decimation was no 'extraction of vitals', the commissioners of Buckinghamshire insisted, but the 'correction of distempered humours that the whole body may be brought into a right frame again'. This was to pay no more than lip service to the idea of national healing. Many commissioners, happy to trumpet their victory over their Royalist neighbours, saw the rule of the major generals as the 'instrument of our deliverance from that implacable generation of men'.[8] The decimation tax in particular was seen as a corrective means to reduce the burden on the 'good and peaceable people... who have a long time born the heat of the day'. The commissioners of Cheshire admitted to Cromwell that they had 'long been desirous that the first and continued causers of the disturbances of our peace might not equally have shared our so dearly purchased freedom'. The sentiment was echoed in Nottinghamshire, whose commissioners lauded the 'wisdom and equity of justice in charging the guilty and easing the guiltless'. The Royalist Sir Edward Nicholas reported from exile in The Hague that he and his kind were 'under the lash', and that the commissioners were 'very severe' in their pursuit of the levy. Some Royalists, he thought, 'are now meditating how to get out of England speedily'.[9]

'Vindictive zeal' was not ubiquitous, however. In Somerset, for example, assessments of the decimation tax were based on interviews with a bailiff representing the powerful Seymour family, who had been wisely reluctant to play a role in the Rising in the West. The commissioners responded 'very mildly', awed no doubt to some extent by the prestige of the name. Thomas Crompton, a commissioner in Stafford, assured his socially superior friend, Sir Richard Leveston, that he would deal with him 'with what civility my commission and instructions give me leave', offering to come to his house rather than let him be inconvenienced by 'difficult and tedious' weather conditions. Such behaviour was hardly typical; the commissioners' Puritan zeal immunized many of them from feelings of social inferiority, of any notions of 'impostor syndrome'. They were God's elect, after all, and that trumped any status an earthly power could bestow on them. The Cheshire commissioners were especially thorough, no doubt egged on by the fatally energetic Worsley, comparing the Royalists' estimates with those of recent estate surveys and commissioning new ones when disputed.[10]

Of the records that remain, for about a third of the counties of England and Wales, between 1,500 and 2,000 Royalists were decimated, which may have raised around £50,000 for the government coffers. If so, that was around £30,000 short of the income needed to pay for the new militias. From the first, it appears that more thought had been given to the punishment of the regime's largely passive 'enemies' than had been given to the administration of the tax or the sums needed to sustain the new system of military rule. However hard they were squeezed, the nation's Royalists simply didn't have sufficient funds to make much difference to the nation's debts. Most had paid up in good faith; refusals were rare and were met with severe, occasionally violent, action. Some of the major generals were more disliked than others. Boteler, arrogant and high-handed, had imprisoned the Earl of Northampton towards the end of 1655 for refusing to offer security for his future good behaviour. This despite the fact that the earl had petitioned Cromwell, who had agreed that Northampton could give security for one year rather than the usual lifetime guarantee. Boteler did eventually back down, but reluctantly and only after he had been warned repeatedly by the Council. He was delighted that his men in Bedfordshire, a Puritan stronghold, 'make it their business to find out and give me notice of all the profane and idle gentry and others whose lives are a shame to a Christian Commonwealth'. His reputation persisted long after the rule of the major generals had been abandoned: in 1659, as the Protectorate unravelled, one MP declared that Boteler's 'crimes are generally all over Northamptonshire cried out against'.[11]

Those tasked with collecting the decimation tax thought its threshold had been set 'far too little', as Worsley complained to Thurloe. Those royalists with less money, smaller estates, or none at all were perceived to be just as 'dangerous and disaffected to the present government as those of higher quality', as the plotting of the events of March 1655 suggested. But such complaints had surprisingly little purchase the nearer they got to the centre of power. One of the ways in which Royalists legitimately reduced what they paid – and sometimes even avoided the decimation altogether – was by appealing to the government in London, which, it was discovered, took a much more relaxed approach towards petitions and appeals for leniency than did the major generals in the regions. The Earl of Devonshire, William Cavendish, was among the more notable figures treated with less stringency by Cromwell and his Council, though Devonshire's temporary respite from the tax was annulled by his local commissioners. Such 'implacable officers' did not look kindly on their superiors' indulgences. Thurloe was warned by Whalley that his commissioners would be greatly annoyed to see Royalists embraced 'into your bosoms, especially eminent ones, before the Lord hath wrought real change and work of grace in their hearts'. Commissioners sometimes took action in their locality against those exempted by central government: William Russell, the Earl of Bedford, was chased for a payment of £300 by the commissioners for the City of London, despite proceedings against him having been suspended by the Council.

Ultimately, the Royalists' greatest ally in their struggle against the decimation was not the leniency of Cromwell and his Council but the sheer magnitude of the task set by them for the major generals and their commissioners. They may have performed the 'greatest and sharpest persecution now falling upon the whole Royal party that they ever yet felt' – but time and resources were against them.

If no more money could reasonably be raised though the decimation tax, the government concluded, the costly militias might have to be reduced in size. There was a regional dimension to this. Some major generals – those in Wales and Norfolk, for example – had fewer Royalists to fleece. Others, in Lancashire, with its strong recusant population, could raise very considerable sums. Though the sensible solution to such variations would have been to pay the militias in each region equally, from general taxation, in February 1656 the Council of State decided that the militias in a number of counties should be reduced, from 100 to 80 men in each troop. By April, this policy was being applied to all regions and the major generals were granted an income from the decimation tax with which to pay their men. The system was tightened up, centralized, made more accountable. The major generals were also entrusted with the regulation of weights and measures, even the regulation of time. Major General Whalley wrote from Nottingham in April 1656 of his concern that the town's market bell rang too late: 'If his highness and council would issue out a proclamation throughout England, commanding all mayors, aldermen, and bailiffs of cities and corporations to cause their market bell to ring by ten or eleven of the clock at furthest, the major generals would take care it should be observed.'

A preference for a blanket of mild tyranny over the chaotic discomforts of anarchy is a political mindset not limited to seventeenth-century England. The imposition of po-faced piety, however, is something else entirely. According to S. R. Gardiner, 'it was as discouragers of vice and encouragers of virtue that [the major generals] aroused the most virulent opposition', a conclusion shared by the most distinguished modern historian of their rule, Christopher Durston. The security of the realm was widely considered to be of immense importance, and while the financial burden of the system was shouldered by a minority – and a 'malignant' one at that – it was generally advantageous to the regime. Cromwell, in particular, was rather proud of any ruse that tempered popular resentment. 'It was a most righteous thing', the Protector was to declare, 'to put the charge upon the party that was the cause of it.'

The absence of further rebellion, as the Penruddock affair receded into the distance, led to a slow demilitarization of the regime's response. In its place came a renewed emphasis on the regulation of manners. The major generals, from their inauguration, had been instructed to crack down on horse racing, cock fighting and bear baiting, not just because of the intrinsic immorality of such activities,* but because such events, along with the den of vice that was the theatre, were places of shadows, where Cavalier conspiracies were hatched. This took on a new urgency. Godliness and virtue were to be promoted, poor churchmen and schoolmasters 'ejected', drunkenness and blasphemy targeted for their sinfulness. The crackdown was not applied consistently, however. Major General Whalley was approached in March 1656 by the Earl of Exeter, who asked him whether a horse race competing for Lady Grantham's Cup might go ahead. Possibly influenced by the earl's exalted social status, Whalley gave permission for the event to proceed. He wrote to Cromwell informing the Protector of his decision, presuming that 'it was not your highness's intention... to abridge gentlemen of their sport, but to prevent the great confluence of irreconcilable enemies'. Others railed against the proscriptions of the major generals. More in frustration than anger, the Cavalier Sir Ralph Verney, a former MP who met with exile and imprisonment, wrote: 'I love old England very well, but as things are carried here the gentry cannot joy much in it.'[12]

The less exalted were rarely treated with such indulgence. The licensing of public houses had, since Tudor times, been the responsibility of the JPs, who tended to be rather lenient in their view of public morality. Now they were to be regulated more stringently, according to both size and character. But many public houses were not even licensed. In Coventry as many as fifty unlicensed premises came under the zealous scrutiny of the town's mayor, Robert Beake, who had a habit of sending out his militias to crack down on anyone travelling on the Sabbath. The problem was that, when licensing was enforced with the

---

* The regime's objections to such sports were predicated on Puritan disapproval of gambling rather than on any concern for animal welfare.

necessary Puritan vigour, revenues went down, sometimes dras-
tically. Yet the major generals carried on with their war on joy and
iniquity. Worsley, forcing the good people of Chester into line,
boasted to Thurloe in February 1656 of the kinds of alehouse
that would soon run dry: 'those hostile to the government; those
whose owner had other means of livelihood; such as were in big
and dark corners; those of bad repute and disorderly; those suspected to be houses of ill-fame'.

There was no major general who took to the mission of
moral reformation with greater zeal than Worsley, who in his
brief embrace of arbitrary power demonstrated a pathological
adherence to the Protector's cause. Worsley had asked the Independent congregations of Cheshire, Lancashire and Staffordshire to put together a wish list of reforms they wanted carried
out in their region and to spill the beans on their less than pious
neighbours. It was a Puritan's dream come true: the perfect
package of virtue and vindictiveness. The especially enthusiastic
congregation of the Church of Christ in Altham, Lancashire,
were eager to purge the parish of the 'profane and heretical
ministers who fill most pulpits in the country', to act against
those who were less zealous than they – which was just about
everyone – and to suppress any activities in which pleasure might
be found. No doubt this was one of the settlements Worsley
was referring to when he spoke of towns that 'take a very strict
course'. According to the arguably unhinged energetic major
general, 'God hath already put into his people a praying spirit
for this great and good work.'[13]

Within three months of Worsley's arrival, Lancashire's prisons
were jam-packed with transgressors, while 200 unlicensed alehouses had been closed in the Altham area of the county. The
picture was much the same in neighbouring Cheshire. But there
particular pride of Puritan place was given to those imprisoned

for marrying in established religious ceremonies, which had been banned by the Civil Marriage Act of 1653. Worsley's judgement of his achievements might serve as his epitaph: 'Those things give matter of rejoicing to the good, and is a terror to the bad.' He would need an epitaph soon enough. Charles Worsley died in June 1656, presumably exhausted by working for the public good, and leaving his admirers to mourn his 'sincere, zealous and upright endeavours'.

In August 1654, an ordinance had been passed 'for ejecting scandalous, ignorant and insufficient ministers and school-masters'. Committees had been established on a county basis to hear the cases of individual clergy, whose behaviour or preaching had been considered dubious. The ejectors, though, had remained largely inactive. The rule of the major generals was seen as an opportunity to correct this and the ordinance was reactivated, to allow them to purge inadequate ministers and imprison those who refused to stop preaching. Some of the major generals, especially Desborough, Lilburne and Haynes, took this task more seriously than others. Haynes was especially ruthless in Essex, where he took delight in decimating the estate of his elder brother, Robert. His friend Ralph Josselin, minister at Earls Colne, who was broadly sympathetic to the Protectorate, records in his diary – one of the most complete and incisive sources of the period – his concern at the rigour of the ejectors and the hostility they displayed towards him and his fellow clergymen:

> For my part I saw no beauty in the day, neither do I joy to see ministers put under the lay power, and thus on their head. Such is the affection of some that would be counted the first friends

of God [who] hopes we should have been sent from thence to Barbados.

Yet in neighbouring Suffolk, among the most Puritan of counties, cordial relations developed between Haynes and local magnates, such as Sir Thomas Barnardiston. Haynes even wrote to Thurloe that: 'I did not expect it [the ordinance of ejection] would have had so good an acceptance with them.'

An especially egregious example of pious persecution concerns Thomas Holbech, a rector in Fleetwood's realm of administration, who had by all accounts been passive since his ejection from his Epping church during the early days of the Civil Wars. But malicious enemies with long memories informed the authorities of his Royalist past and he was ejected again. Although Holbech appealed to Fleetwood, nothing was done to correct what was clearly an injustice – 'he acts not at all in person', was Holbech's judgement on the aloof major general. Examples of such inequity are rare, though not because of the mercy of the Puritan commissioners. In truth, the procedures of investigation were often long-drawn-out and there was little support for them among local populations that, on the whole, remained quietly Anglican and wedded to the Prayer Book. Despite the hostility of some commissioners, few ministers were ejected under the rule of the major generals.[14]

The reality was that the moral policing of the major generals and their commissioners, while irritating to many, had only a limited impact. There is little evidence that, on their watch, sexual offences were reduced, nor that rural sports were successfully proscribed. And, although England – thanks to the Elizabethan Poor Laws – had, arguably, the most successful system of poor relief in Europe at the time, vagrancy, which had risen considerably as a result of the devastation of civil war, remained a problem. Some major generals made considerable efforts to tackle the issue, using the brutally effective method of rounding up vagrants for transportation, but they discovered that central government had failed to organize the ships required to transport these unfortunates overseas. As a consequence, most were released back on to the streets.

There were those, however, who believed the system *was* working. Whalley informed Thurloe that the people of the East Midlands 'look upon it as a favour to them to have us in their county'. He was not alone in thinking so. In Wales, Rowland Dawkins thought the results of their labours were 'very obser-vable' and that the good people of South Wales regarded their rule as 'very necessary and just'. It is worth remembering, how-ever, that the major generals came into contact largely with commissioners, who shared not only their world view, but also their overly optimistic account of what they were achieving. Both the major generals and their commissioners would face a public judgement on their rule soon enough.

9

Electing the Elect

'Our enemies being much terrified,
our friends encouraged.'

ROLAND DAWKINS

T HE RULE OF the major generals appeared to be settled
on firm foundations, at least from the perspective of those
closest to it. The generals and their commissioners had transformed many aspects of provincial administration. Militias
had been raised, trained and set to securing their particular
province. Measures against the enemies of the regime – real or
not – had been imposed; the decimation tax had been assessed
and collected with some efficiency; church ministers perceived
not to be up to the job had been ejected; and – a far greater
challenge – the campaign for the moral reformation of the nation
was underway. The Protector looked upon their achievements,
and he was pleased. Or so it seemed.

The regime's perpetual financial crisis had not gone away,
and had become more pressing with the war against Spain – the
inevitable fallout from the Western Design – declared officially in
October 1655. The decimation tax had never provided enough
money for the militias. Debt was increasing. Money was also
needed to sustain garrisons in Scotland, Ireland and the West

Indies. By the beginning of 1656, the military was devouring more than half of the regime's annual expenditure, a figure of almost £2 million. The Instrument of Government instructed that 'in case of future war with any foreign state, a parliament shall be forthwith summoned for their advice concerning the same'. But Cromwell did not want to call one – he feared that Protector and Parliament would pull in opposite directions.

In May of 1656, Cromwell held a number of meetings with Councillors in London, to which all the major generals were summoned. These meetings sought to address the financial crisis that threatened to undermine the regime – and in particular, the army that underpinned it. The gatherings were deemed so important that William Goffe was mandated to attend, despite his request to be excused to deal with urgent family matters.

A number of revenue-raising ideas were considered, including a substantial increase in the monthly assessment tax, and the extension of the decimation tax. Increases in taxation are rarely palatable, even when the greater burden rests on a vanquished minority, especially so when imposed by an unaccountable executive. Which is why the prospect of a new Parliament arose and, for some, especially the major generals, grew more attractive. Cromwell liked the idea of parliaments but was less enamoured of them when they became reality: elections had a habit of returning troublesome MPs. Twice bitten, by the Nominated Assembly and the First Protectorate Parliament, he shied away from gambling on a third.

But his major generals insisted that this time, things would be different. They knew the temper of their territories with some intimacy, they claimed, and they believed that the moral reformation of the country was well under way. They had their ears to the ground and believed that the make-up of Parliament would be transformed by new elections – the MPs returned on this occasion would be infinitely more sympathetic to the regime and its ambitions than their predecessors. It appears not to have struck them that they had misread the country, susceptible as they were to the flattery of those zealous commissioners they worked alongside: like many elites, they rarely looked beyond the reinforcing opinions of their own kind. Yes, the scheme *had* produced positive results – even in Wales, one of the 'dark corners' of the land. There, according to Berry's deputy, Rowland Dawkins, 'our enemies being much terrified, our friends encouraged, our peace… secured, and sin and wickedness suppressed'. Though they were generally more heavy-handed than brutal in their rule, the major generals were less than subtle in their engagements with local customs and the social fabric of the regions over which they presided. They had abandoned the ancient constitution beloved of an effective, stable gentry class, which had long maintained responsibility for local government and the raising of taxes for an ever hungrier exchequer.

Cromwell was in bad shape physically, the arduous toll of his cavalry career was catching up with him and he was wracked by self-doubt following the failure of the Western Design. The debates between the Protector, his civilian councillors and the major generals had been full and frank. According to the Venetian ambassador, Giavarina, 'sharp words were passed' between those gathered, 'upon points they have never been able to agree about'. Normal courtesies had been abandoned and the Council reduced to an inner circle, as the debate centred increasingly on Lambert, Fleetwood, Desborough and Thurloe, who held private meetings in which their concerns were expressed in increasingly bitter exchanges. But an agreement of sorts was reached. Most of the major generals – Desborough, for one, took a more pessimistic view – were convinced of their impending success and popularity. They managed to convince Cromwell to call the Parliament at which, there could be no doubt, their favoured candidates would sweep the board. Cromwell was to recall that the decision, 'advised by his Council', was, 'in his own judgement, no way seasonable'. With the legitimacy provided by electoral endorsement, they would impose the means to put the government's finances on a sounder, if not entirely secure, footing. The rule of the major generals, the 'cantonization' of England and Wales into semi-military fiefdoms, might even become permanent.

Hardline republicans such as Henry Vane, knowing of the regime's financial anxieties and the growing calls for a Parliament, had already sensed an opportunity to restore something akin to the Rump and be rid of 'swordsmen and decimators'. Vane appealed to anti-military sentiment with his elegant tract, published in May 1656, *A Healing Question Propounded and Resolved*, which reiterated his appeals to the Good Old Cause:

> *Where there is then a righteous*
> *and good constitution*
> *of Government, there is first an*
> *orderly union*
> *of many understandings together,*
> *as the publique and*
> *common Supream Judicature or*
> *visible Soveraignity,*
> *set in a way of free and orderly*
> *exercise, for the directing*
> *and applying the use of the ruling*
> *power or the*
> *sword, to promote the interest and*
> *common welfare*
> *of the whole, without any*
> *disturbance or annoyance,*
> *from within or from without. And*
> *then secondly,*
> *there is a like union and readiness*
> *of will in all the*
> *Individuals, in their private*
> *capacities, to execute and*
> *obey (by all the power requisite,*
> *and that they are able*
> *to put forth) those soveraign Laws*
> *and Orders issued*
> *out by their own Deputies and*
> *Trustees.*

Vane, for his sins, was summoned before the Council, accused of subversion. A bond of £5,000 was sought, after which he would 'do nothing to the prejudice of the present government, and the peace of the commonwealth'. Vane refused to comply, citing the similarities to Stuart absolutism and arbitrary rule. He was imprisoned for a short period on the Isle of Wight, beyond the reach of habeas corpus.*[1]

Other leading republicans and Commonwealthsmen were also targeted. John Bradshaw was relieved of his position as chief justice of Chester and his other judicial positions in Wales. Edmund Ludlow, who had circulated opposition literature while lieutenant general of the army in Ireland, confronted Cromwell in person. 'What can you desire more than you have?' asked Cromwell. 'That which we have fought for,' replied Ludlow, bluntly; 'that the nation might be governed by its own consent.' And where was that consent to be found, amid a landscape of sectarian division? 'Amongst the prelatical, Presbyterian, Independent, Anabaptist, or Levelling parties', argued Ludlow. But, in truth, Cromwell remained the sole fragile unifying force. Ludlow was ordered to provide a bond of £5,000, though an emollient Cromwell allowed him to retire to Essex, far from his West Country stronghold, the bond unpaid.[2]

Despite Cromwell's misgivings, writs for an 'extraordinary' Parliament were issued in July and elections took place in August 1656. They became, in essence, a referendum on the rule of the major generals. Despite Desborough's warning that the godly were 'like to meet with great opposition', the major generals and their commissioners campaigned with gusto and Puritan preachers gave their full backing to amenable candidates representing the new order, exhorting the faithful to vote for the

* The historian Ronald Hutton described Vane as 'one of history's most notable examples of that perennial type, the radical intellectual from a privileged family.'

godly interest. William Gurnall, firebrand rector of St Peter and St Paul's Church in the Suffolk town of Lavenham, believed that the elections would unearth the 'temper of this nation': 'I cannot look upon it otherwise than as our owning or disowning God... Oh how unhappy are thou England, if thou mayst still have thy God and will not.' In campaigning language as likely to alienate voters as attract them, Gurnall damned anyone who voted against the Puritan interest as a 'forsworn wretch', an enemy of the people.[3]

The electorate of England and Wales proved rather more independent of mind.* Though all but one of the major generals was returned to the House – George Fleetwood was the sole exception – it soon became obvious that Cromwell, or at least his 'Godly Governors', were out of touch with the mood of the country.

Haynes, his optimism dwindling, had written to Thurloe: 'I now begin to fear Suffolk, finding so malignant a grand jury, who will have a great advantage to possess the country.' The organized opposition to the regime in East Anglia – a Puritan stronghold – consisted of a 'clear combination' of Cavaliers and Presbyterians campaigning vigorously together. John Balleston, one of Haynes's Norfolk commissioners, wrote that 'Many of our seeming friends proved very feint [sic].' Similarly, in Kent, as Kelsey reported, conservative Presbyterians had allied with

---

* The Instrument of Government had altered the franchise and the distribution of votes quite notably. The number of MPs from towns and boroughs, thought to be unduly influenced by the gentry, was reduced, though cities such as Leeds and Manchester gained representation for the first time. The number of MPs from counties was increased. However, in opposition to Leveller demands, the franchise was restricted to persons with land or property valued at £200 or more. Catholics, known Royalists and those deemed guilty of 'licentiousness', a term used to describe those belonging to extreme sects, were disenfranchised.

Cavaliers. Some candidates, many of whom were elected MPs, had even declared 'down with the Maior Generalls and Decimators and the new militia'. Concerns were raised about the composition of the forthcoming Parliament, and the word 'purge' was heard. It remained the duty of Cromwell and his Council to maintain the interests of 'God's people' – by any means necessary. There was still precious little healing and settling in the nation; if anything the rule of the major generals had opened up wounds afresh.[4]

The quintessential feature of the rule of the major generals was not that it was army rule, nor that it was London rule, but rather that it was godly rule, and it was as such that it was decisively rejected by the great majority of the English and Welsh people. Criticisms, often expressed – like those of the lawyer William Prynne – in visceral, condemnatory language, were twofold: first, the old assertion that the major generals themselves were arrivistes, low-born men moulded and elevated by war, who lacked understanding of traditional social structures; in other words, they lacked 'natural' authority. Second, that what authority they did have was entirely dependent upon the military and as such they were the architects of a martial state, even a tyranny. Their power was centralized, disregarding and contemptuous of local government and its wide variety of customs and relationships that had existed time out of mind.

Prynne, again, drew historical parallels with the rule of William Longchamp, the vice regent of Richard I, who placed 'mercenary soldiers in every county to over awe and enslave the people'.[5] The truth is, Cromwell's rule was nowhere near as insecure as he imagined, or perhaps rather pretended it to be. A first-class intelligence network and strong army and navy made any threat from overseas implausible, while opposition within tended to be resentful and passive rather than optimistic and proactive. The first historian to seriously investigate the rule of the major generals, David Watson Rannie, whose seminal study was first published in 1895, reached a conclusion that remains convincing more than a hundred years on. The old hierarchy of aristocratic and gentry families retained a great deal of power at local level; the best the major generals could manage was to compromise with the traditional structures of justices of the peace, sheriffs, mayors and constables. As one modern historian of seventeenth-century England, Anthony Fletcher, points out: the 'rule' of the major generals was never that; they 'never did rule'. Even Ronald Hutton, a historian with Royalist sympathies, argues that the major generals caused 'no great trauma for the ruled'. Barry Coward, a historian of different political bent, judges their impact to have been 'very slight indeed'. But that was not how it was perceived at the time, and perception in politics is the greater portion of the game. And so the election of another Parliament hostile to the regime became a reality.

On 17 September 1656, Cromwell travelled to the opening of the Second Protectorate Parliament in the company of Lambert, with 300 soldiers in their vanguard. At ten o'clock the newly elected MPs had assembled in Westminster Abbey. There they heard a sermon delivered by John Owen, Cromwell's theological adviser and Dean of Christ Church, Oxford. Moving on to the Painted Chamber, Cromwell treated them to a long address in stifling heat. For up to three hours he spoke, sometimes rambling and incoherent. But despite the electorate's less than ringing endorsement, the major generals must have been reassured by Cromwell's opening speech. It was full of fear and warning, conjuring up once again images of 'Papists and Cavaliers' in league with the levelling sort. Much of the speech was devoted to 'security'. Cromwell looked back to the Gerard Plot of 1654 and the Penruddock Rising of spring 1655. He praised his 'poor little invention' of the major generals to the hilt, playing to his audience, reminding them that the plots on his life and threats of invasion were 'no fable'. The scheme he had set in place was as honest as any he could conceive of. He acknowledged some resistance to the project of moral reformation – a 'grudging in the nation that we cannot have our horse races, cockfightings and the like' – but he claimed that all those who opposed these men of 'known integrity and fidelity' were 'against the interest of England'. Their rule had been born of necessity, by the need to counter a very real Royalist rebellion.

Cromwell dismissed opposition to the rule of the major generals in a particularly damning way: 'if there be any man that hath a face averse to this I dare pronounce him to be a man against the interest of England'.[6] Serious concerns about the legitimacy of the decimation tax were blithely swept aside: 'if nothing should be done but what is according to the law, the threat of the nation may be cut till we send for some to make a law'. There was no alternative.

He was vigorous in his justification of the war with Spain, for which he would be granted subsidies until January 1657. Regarding the failure of the Western Design, which had not turned out to be the self-financing project he had hoped it would, he argued that 'Being denied just things, we thought it our duty to get that by the sword which we could not otherwise do. And this hath been the spirit of Englishmen.'[7] The spirit of the Elizabethan privateer lived on – 'your great enemy is the Spaniard'. By conflating foreign and domestic policy, Cromwell hardened his anti-Catholic rhetoric. When he accused the Spanish of being the enemy of 'all that is of God that is in you', he alluded to their influence at home: could it be that 'un-English-like' Catholics and Cavaliers 'shake not hands in England'? The pursuit of moral reformation must continue: 'The liberty and prosperity of the nation depend upon reformation, to make it a shame to see men to be bold in sin and profaneness, and God will bless you. You will be a blessing to the nation.'

It is, as so often with Cromwell, difficult to distinguish between the sincere and the manipulative, the hyperbolic and the realistic. One wonders if the Protector found it any easier. 'If this were to be done again, I would do it,' he declared; but his actions were to suggest otherwise.

When the newly elected MPs finally arrived at the House of Commons, they were met by soldiers, led by three militant colonels, Bisco, Lagoe and Mills, who issued tickets to approved MPs and excluded the rest. During the purge of the First Protectorate Parliament, just twelve MPs had been purged, as they could be under Articles 14 and 15 of the Instrument, should they be active Royalists or Catholics. But this time, in a major shift, Article 17 was also invoked, which excluded those who fell short of being 'persons of known integrity, fearing God, and of good conversation': this was the vaguest of designations, and one that allowed the exclusion of MPs on the whim of the executive. And so this time the actual number of excluded MPs, though never confirmed, was in excess of a hundred, with another sixty or so refusing to attend in protest.

Few of those excluded had been Royalists. Most were gentry of no particular loyalty, other than to the 'ancient constitution', and Presbyterians who had never felt fully part of the show since the execution of Charles I, but whose basic loyalty to the regime was in little doubt. All opposed, though rarely explicitly, the rule of the major generals. There was widespread anger and dismay, with some commentators drawing uncomfortable parallels with Charles I's attempt to exclude five MPs in 1642 – the trigger

1. Oliver Cromwell, by Robert Walker, 1649. Walker derives his style from Anthony van Dyck, Charles I's great court artist, but his work is a poor relation of Caroline portraiture. Cromwell, too, adopts cuirassier armour and a baton of authority.

2. Signature of Oliver Cromwell, Lord Protector, 1655. An homage, perhaps, to his historical idol Elizabeth I?

3. Cromwell at Dunbar, by Andrew Garrick Gow, 1886. An idealized Victorian painting of the much mythologized 'Miracle' of 3 September 1650, reflecting the religious zeal of Cromwell and his 'Saints'.

4. John Lambert, after Robert Walker, *c.* 1650, the second-most powerful figure of the Protectorate and long considered Cromwell's obvious successor. A brilliant soldier, Lambert was a political idealist whose religious beliefs remained elusive.

5. Edward Hyde, 1st Earl of Clarendon, after Adriaen Hanneman, c.1655. The first historian of the 'Great Rebellion', Hyde was a pragmatic Royalist who played the long game with success.

6. John Thurloe, anonymous painting after a 1650s original. Cromwell's head of intelligence and worthy successor to the Elizabethan spymasters, Thurloe, it was claimed, was a 'genius' who replaced 'mere competence'.

7. A view of Whitehall by Hendrick Daucherts, 1670s. Its rickety warrens are in stark contrast to the Banqueting House at the left of the painting, the site of Charles I's execution in January 1649.

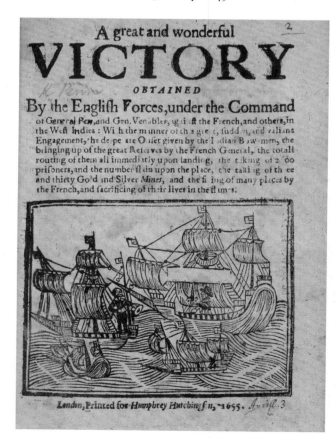

8. 'A great and wonderful victory obtained by the English forces', printed in London for Humphrey Hutchingson, 1655. An optimistic and ill-informed account of Cromwell's 'Western Design' against Spain's colonies in the West Indies.

9. James Nayler's entry into Bristol in October 1656, portrayed in a contemporary German print. Nayler's actions would have serious consequences for both him and the government.

Soldan's Palace.

Gyant Desborough.

Meek Knight. Lamberto.

Don Juan Lamberto. 1659

10. 'Gyant Desborough', a satirical print of 1661. Cromwell's brother-in-law, the model for the Major Generals, was a fierce opponent of the offer of the Crown to Cromwell. A fine soldier, his political judgment was poor.

11. Roger Boyle, Lord Broghill, after an anonymous portrait of 1650. A 'great parliamentary manager', Broghill's vision of a broad, conservative Protestantism drew the opposition of army radicals.

12. Elizabeth Claypole, by John Michael Wright, 1658. Cromwell's favourite daughter was married to John Claypole, his master of horse. Elizabeth's agonizing death in August 1658, aged twenty-nine, was followed by that of the Protector a month later.

13. George Monck, 1st Duke of Albermarle, after Samuel Cooper, *c.*1660. The pragmatic, ruddy commander of the army in Scotland was a 'monarchical Cromwellian', whose decisive actions led to the Restoration of Charles II, earning him substantial lands and a dukedom.

14. William Penn, by Peter Lely, 1665–66. Penn returned in disgrace from the Western Design, serving time in the Tower. His fortunes changed with the Restoration, when he became commissioner of the navy and made frequent appearances in the diaries of Samuel Pepys.

15. The Embleme of England's Distractions, or Cromwell Between Two Pillars, 1658. A paean to Cromwellian rule and the commitment of the Protector – who stands upon the Whore of Babylon – to the rule of law and the Protestant faith.

for civil war.* The reason for its calling, after all, was much the same: a lack of money. Why had England suffered more than a decade of bitter division if the result was the same disdain on the part of the executive for free, elected Parliaments? Disillusion was widespread and reached far beyond the political class. The exclusions were arbitrary and illegal and were symptomatic of the fact that the regime had failed to win the active loyalty of the country, which had expressed its anger in an election where the military candidates had fared especially badly.

But if the Revolution was to achieve its aims, the saints must continue to rule, alone if necessary. 'Consider what a Parliament you might have had,' said Lambert, the architect of the Instrument.

> If a Parliament should be chosen according to the general spirit and temper of the nation, and if there should not be a check upon such election, those may creep into this House, who may come to sit as our judges for all we have done in this Parliament, or at any other time or place.[8]

Lambert and his military allies in the Council of State – Desborough, Fleetwood and Skippon – had declared their hand. An elect knew what was best for the elect nation. Those revealed as outsiders had no part to play in the politics of the nation. The military wing of the ruling class had spoken, their cards were laid out. But it would be their undoing, for their opponents were marshalling their forces, those of persuasion and quiet intrigue, closer to the aspiration of the nation at large. The conflict would finally come to a head in the spring of 1657.

---

* Dorothy Osborne had drawn the parallel as early as 1653, when she asked: 'I wonder what he would think of those proceedings, and whether this would appear as great a breach of the privilege of parliament as the demanding of the five members.'

The events of September 1656 convinced a group of Cromwell's civilian supporters – the 'new courtiers' – that no stable settlement could be reached under the terms of the Instrument of Government. Typically, Cromwell had been largely absent from the proceedings and ambiguous amid the major generals' certainties. He was biddable at least and, while there is a shortage of sources on this matter, Cromwell himself may well have opposed the exclusions, a claim he was later to make at the meeting of a 'hundred officers' in February 1657. He had become disillusioned, like the rest of the country, by the rule of the major generals, who had failed in their attempts to raise enough money even to support local militias. They could at least be trusted to overplay their hand.[9]

The Second Protectorate Parliament was a docile one. Heselrige and Vane, Cromwell's most vociferous opponents, were now absent, though there was some official protest. Sir George Booth, the day after the opening of Parliament, presented a petition signed by seventy-nine of the excluded MPs, which led to five days of debate during which councillors justified their actions by reference to the Instrument. Most remaining members seemed satisfied, or at least quiescent by the response. Indeed, the Parliament, at least in its first session, was to present seventy-one Acts in all to the Protector; seventy-one more than the First Parliament, many of them concerned with the pursuit of moral reformation. Cromwell was quick to praise such activity: 'though you have sat little time... you have made many good laws'. Cromwell was keen for this Parliament to raise money for the floundering conflict with Spain. He needed, too, to justify his experiment, that 'little poor invention', of the rule of the major generals, as much to himself as to Parliament. Security, though, remained a concern, and action was taken almost immediately against the regime's enemies. In the background was an issue that had troubled the rule of many of Cromwell's royal predecessors, not least Elizabeth I: though the title of Protector had gained parliamentary legitimacy, how was the question of the succession, the age-old problem of English governance, to be solved? Who would follow Cromwell?

The day after the Parliament's opening, on 18 September 1656, Councillor Charles Wolseley introduced an Act for 'disannulling the pretended title of Charles Stuart... for the better establishment of Peace of this Commonwealth', which would 'fully, freely, absolutely and for ever' – the Act left little room for ambiguity – 'disclaim and renounce all Fealty, Homage, or Allegiance, pretended to be due Charles Stuart' and those bearing the name from becoming ruler of 'Great Britain'. Anyone who contrived to support attempts to return the dynasty to the throne would be adjudged to have committed 'High Treason'. To reinforce the point, another piece of legislation was introduced five days later 'for the security of the Lord Protector his Person, And Continuance of the Nation in Peace and Safety'. The Act addressed directly the Elizabethan peril of an uncertain succession, the stark reality that the fate of the nation – and the regime – 'very much dependeth... upon the Security and Preservation of the person of his Highness'. A body of commissioners – not judges, note – were now enabled to convict and sentence those who would 'Attempt, Compass or Imagine the death of the Lord Protector' with the same authority and powers as in 'cases of High Treason'. The intention, as the Venetian ambassador Francesco Giavarina realized, was clear and explicit: 'to consolidate the government and make it durable and longlived' – to maintain its lifespan beyond that of Lord Protector Cromwell.[10] There was a knowing embarrassment about mentioning Cromwell's mortality, which Wolseley's Act had at least confronted. Parliament would need to follow his pursuit of a solution, but it was one that would prove divisive and wounding. Despite the scale of the exclusions, Parliament was still troubled by disagreement, especially on the matter of religious liberty, the very question that had brought down the First Protectorate Parliament. Cromwell and some of his closest Councillors remained committed to the toleration of Independents, Baptists, even Quakers and other marginal sects.* Others, however, took a different view. Divisions within the regime were beginning to make themselves felt, and new faces were emerging who sought answers to some increasingly urgent questions.

The brilliant political philosopher James Harrington had offered a detailed radical political and economic solution to England's crisis in his *The Commonwealth of Oceana*, addressed explicitly to Oliver Cromwell, of whose 'new monarchy' it was immensely critical. Registered at Stationer's Hall on 19 September 1656. Harrington hoped it would be discussed and debated by the new Parliament, but it did not appear in print until around early November, its manuscript having been temporarily confiscated. Unlikely to be adopted in any case, it had rather missed the boat. As a document, however, and as a political proposal, it is fascinating. *Oceana* rejected the nostalgia

---

* Cromwell's attitude to religious liberty (and alcohol) is captured in a letter criticizing the behaviour of the zealous Scottish Covenanters which he wrote to the governor of Edinburgh Castle: 'Your pretended fear lest Error should step in, is like the man who would keep all the wine out of the country lest men should be drunk. It will be found an unwise and unjust jealousy, to deprive a man of his natural liberty upon a supposition he may abuse it.'

for the 'ancient constitution', proposing a new system resting on 'mighty foundations' taken from the best examples of political systems, ancient and modern. Israel, the 'original' of all the subsequent commonwealths, was cited approvingly, as was Sparta. Harrington's scheme was also full of checks and balances and secret ballots heavily influenced by republican Venice. It was a wonderfully imaginative and erudite concoction, though it could hardly be said to provide a way out of the mire into which the political nation was slowly sinking.

Harrington, who had been Charles I's groom of the bedchamber during the king's captivity in 1648 and was of ecumenical mind, argued that it was the distribution of property that determines what kind of government a nation has, whether it be monarchical, aristocratic or republican. Such was the dispersal of land under the Tudors that England could only work as a commonwealth. As the 'popularity of government' expanded to freemen and property owners beyond the aristocracy, it became important to balance political power with economic means. An 'agrarian law' should be introduced, Harrington proposed, which forbade the inheritance of land worth more than £2,000 per annum, reducing economic and therefore political competition within the realm. This more egalitarian settlement was combined with a Venetian system of governance, in which the legislature was to be divided between two houses: a senate of around 300 men worth over £100 a year, which debated and proposed laws; and an assembly of more than 1,000, selected by looser property requirements, which would ballot for and against the senate's proposals. This would be marked by the 'exquisite rotation' of politicians, a third of whom would be replaced each year. There would be no monarch. The system, somewhat Byzantine in its complexities, would encourage republican virtue while acknowledging the flaws of human nature and make Oceana – England – a 'rightly ordered' polity, which would prove itself 'as immortal, or long-lived, as the world'.

For all its bravura and allegorical brilliance, the flaws of *Oceana* are not hard to discern. For one, it was presumed that the assembly would simply get on with the job, regardless of ideology, a hopelessly idealistic vision, especially given the divisions on display. It depended on a rigid system of rotation, which was unlikely to appeal to the country's elites, already put out of joint by the experience of the major generals. Worst of all, it assumed that 1,000 or so assembly members would be happy to keep quiet while they considered the proposals of the senate. The poet John Milton described with typical contempt the unlikely process as 'to convey each man his bean or ballot into the box, without reason shown or common deliberation'.[11]

One increasingly active figure, growing steadily in importance, held more prosaic, though more pragmatic visions of the future: the Anglo-Irish peer Roger Boyle, Lord Broghill.[12] As a young man, he had proved himself in war with his defence of Lismore Castle in County Waterford, whose garrison he had commanded against Viscount Mountgarret in 1642, during the Irish Confederate Wars. The historian Hugh Trevor-Roper credits Broghill with the organizational skills that eluded the dithering, though sometimes commanding improvisations of Cromwell, who 'created a vacuum of leadership'. Broghill, by contrast, was a 'great parliamentary manager', whose prudent conduct in the troubled context of the Second Protectorate Parliament is comparable to that of the earls of Warwick and Bedford in the parliamentary struggles of 1640–41; the latter had been a friend of his father Richard Boyle, Earl of Cork. Broghill bridged the affairs of Ireland, Scotland and Westminster, supporting the dream of his father, the Boyle Group and the Irish Independents, that the Protestant interest in Ireland was best served by its absorption into the 'English Empire', which Cromwell's rule made possible. He was never an advocate of the level of religious liberty proposed by Cromwell, but was personally loyal to the Protector. His was a vision, epitomized by his friendship with Richard Baxter and Archbishop Ussher, the Primate of All Ireland, of a conservative and broad protestantism. The majority, conformist and moderate, were to be embraced, the minority of radical enthusiasts were to be 'discouraged'.

Broghill's Irish concern is evident enough, but he was no less committed to union with Scotland, too. His mother, the Countess of Suffolk, was Scottish; his sister was married to the future Earl of Newburgh; his brother, Viscount Kinalmeaky, had married Elizabeth, sister of the Marchioness of Hamilton. When he arrived in Edinburgh in 1655 to serve as Cromwell's Lord President of the Council in Scotland and member for Edinburgh, he found a land ravaged by civil war, conquered by the English, its Protestant population divided between Resolutioners – who favoured leniency towards their Royalist compatriots – and Remonstrants, or Protesters – a hard-line grouping, which sought to purge their former enemies from church and state. His smooth-talking pragmatism was never more evident than when he brokered an arrangement behind closed doors, in which he gathered Resolutioners, committed to public prayer for Charles Stuart, and Council members together to come up with a compromise in which neither lost face. Thurloe, for one, had been impressed: he told the Protector's son Henry Cromwell that the 'Council of Scotland have wrought a great wonder there, in persuading the ministers to leave praying for C. Stuart'.

In his ambitions to create a broad coalition in support of the Protectorate, or at least the Protector, Broghill made enemies in Ireland among the radicals of the army and their Westminster allies; in Scotland he was opposed by Cromwell's military commander-in-chief General Monck and the Protesters. Yet Broghill had shown, with his work in Scotland, that moderate government could be established, that the army could be tamed, that religious fanatics could be neutered and that Royalists could be brought back into the fold. The same had been attempted in Ireland. But it was in England that the radicals had gained real power. The rule of the major generals was a 'radical innovation' unprecedented in English history, manned by 'socially obscure' men of uncertain background acting wholly against precedent and traditional social structures. The governance of Scotland and Ireland was deeply threatened by this English innovation and Broghill knew it. While Fleetwood remained Lord Deputy of Ireland and Monck the commander-in-chief in Scotland, Broghill's moderate aims and those of his allies, most notably Henry Cromwell, were unlikely to be realized. The conflict between moderates and radicals, although conducted via political channels, was a deep-rooted one, and clearly had the potential to take a violent turn. Patrick Little, a historian of Cromwell's Parliaments, has pointed out that Broghill had in mind that war might break out in future. On his journey back to Westminster from Edinburgh in September 1656, he called on his relatives and allies, the earls of Warwick and Suffolk, both of whom were also Presbyterians, to consider the future of the three kingdoms. Broghill had become a genuinely British politician, one of the first. His political aims were threefold: to create a national church; to reduce the power of the army; and to return government to an ancient and settled constitution, including, ultimately, the return of monarchy, probably in the person of King Oliver. This holy trinity would be the first foundation for the settling and healing desired not just by Cromwell but by the nation. What is more, it would secure a permanent post-Stuart settlement.

Significant figures were attracted to Broghill's light. Though most of his political network was in Ireland and Scotland – he could count on the support of almost fifty MPs in the new Parliament – he was treading the innermost corridors of White-hall, working closely with Thurloe, the 'door' to Cromwell, and counted the Protector's close political associates Bulstrode Whitelocke and Edward Montagu among his friends. Signifi-cantly, Sir Charles Wolseley, who had retained his Staffordshire seat, was sympathetic to his world view and was to become the first MP to make moves towards a settlement compatible with Broghill's vision.* The battle lines were being drawn between those 'civilians' for whom a national conformist church and traditional forms of government were the ideal, and those including the major generals, the 'military', who had literally fought for and would bitterly defend their interests.

* Wolseley, an ecumenical figure, whose father was created a baronet by Charles I, had married Ann Fiennes, Lord Saye and Sele's youngest daughter.

IO

The Quaker Jesus

There was not so dangerous an enemy to the Presbyterians
as this brood of their own making.
THOMAS HOBBES, *BEHEMOTH*, 1668

T HE GROWING DIVISIONS within the Cromwellian regime,
so far kept private, were exposed to the nation in the final
months of 1656, when, in an act extraordinary even for an age
of millenarianism, a charismatic Quaker performed a reckless
piece of religious theatre.[1]

Rain is no stranger to the West Country and on 24 October
1656 the port of Bristol, among the largest and most prosperous
cities of seventeenth-century England, was enduring a deluge.
Unperturbed, a group of men and women, eight in all, had
gathered at dawn in the Somerset village of Bedminster, a mile
to the south of the city, and walked through Redcliffe Gate into
the 'mire and the dirt' of Bristol's streets, singing hosannas,
waving palms. James Nayler, recently released from Exeter
gaol, where he had been held as a vagabond, was mounted on a
horse, led on each side by one of two female disciples: Martha
Simmonds, a vicar's daughter and sister of Giles Calvert, one of
the most active pamphleteers of the day; and Hannah Stranger,
the wife of a London comb-maker. They were recreating Christ's

entry into Jerusalem on the first Palm Sunday as described in St Matthew's Gospel. 'Holy, holy, holy, Lord God of Israel,' sang the heretical ensemble as they headed towards Bristol's High Cross and on to the house of their fellow Quaker, Dennis Hollister. Here they were apprehended by the city authorities.

This dishevelled crew created a sensation that would gain the attention of the nation. Even the great political philosopher Thomas Hobbes recorded the event: 'James Nayler appeared at Bristol,' he wrote. 'He wore his beard forked, and his hair composed to the likeness of that in the *Volto Santo* [Christ's holy face]; and being questioned, would sometimes answer "Thou sayest it".'[2] Theirs was a wicked act in the eyes of most who witnessed it, though not perhaps as unique as their opponents portrayed it. Nayler's performance had an antecedent in the actions of Sarah Goldsmith, who in May 1655 wandered around Bristol in a long, hairy coat, attended by two young women. All three women were committed to London's Bridewell prison for the correction of wayward women. Nayler, however, owing to a contingent concordance of time and place, was treated with rather greater severity, as a subversive presence. He had committed an outrageous and deliberate provocation worthy of the most grievous punishment. A few people, some of them perhaps members of the regime, and certainly those who had strewn palms before the Bristol procession, understood the intended meaning of Nayler's 'Sign': that there was something of Christ in us all, a belief fundamental to Quakers. But it was a revelation for which he would pay a terrible price.

The image and sometimes the reality of the Quakers in the mid-seventeenth century was very different from that of the pacific souls who gather in Friends Meeting Houses today; not until 1661, in the wake of the Restoration of Charles II, did Quakers offer their first 'official declaration of absolute pacifism in all circumstances'. It had not been a characteristic of the movement in its earliest days, but 'was forced upon them by the hostility of the outside world', a hostility that would soon descend on Nayler.[3]

Quakerism, a movement known to its members as the Children of Light long before it adopted the more prosaic Society of Friends, was the creation of George Fox, a cobbler by training from rural Leicestershire in the East Midlands. It had its roots in the bands of Seekers, who, shunning the churches they deemed corrupt, roamed the north-west of England seeking a 'desert wildernesse condition' as they awaited the return of Christ. In 1652 a former Seeker, Margaret Fell of Swarthmoor Hall in Lancashire, converted to Quakerism under Fox's influence, and gained a level of protection from her husband, Judge Thomas Fell. Together, the Fells became well-connected guardians of the movement, their substantial home a haven from a hostile world.

During one of his periodic bouts of depression, Fox, in 1647, claimed to have heard a voice proclaiming 'there is one, even Jesus Christ, that can speak to thy condition'. Such experiences of conversion – or 'convincement' – would become a feature of Quakerism; details of Nayler's strikingly similar epiphany were revealed during his interrogation for alleged blasphemy in the Westmorland town of Appleby in 1653: 'I was at the plough, meditating on the things of God, and suddenly I heard a voice saying unto me, "Get thee out from thy kindred, and from thy father's house".'

Fox and his Friends rejected the Trinity, which made them heretics. They had been described and defined by their enemies in Thomas Edwards's influential, encyclopedic heresiography *Gangraena*, published in 1646, as the growth in millenarianism movements, inspired by a remarkable period of the free exchange of religious and political ideas, via preacher and printer, spread alarm. The young John Locke thought them 'madd as jugglers', worthy of mirth and derision rather than persecution. Oliver Cromwell and his Council suggested that Quaker perversity arose from a defect in understanding rather than 'malice in their wills'. In 1650 a Derby justice, when sentencing Fox to one of his occasional periods of incarceration, noted that his followers were said to 'quake and tremble' during their meetings. And so 'Quakers' they became.

Quakerism became especially strong in the north of England. Its opponents drew attention to a passage from the Book of Jeremiah: 'That out of the north an evill shall break forth upon all the inhabitants of the land.' 'Northern locusts' and 'Morice-dancers from the North' were among the epithets granted them. Unlike most forms of radical Protestantism, Quakerism was a largely rural phenomenon, strongest in pastoral rather than arable regions and among those who travelled a great deal, such as clothiers. There were many women among them (Quakers were unique in allowing women to preach regularly) and they tended to be young. As the Presbyterian reformer Richard Baxter wrote: 'Very few experienced, humble, sober Christians that ever I heard of turn to them; but it's the young raw professors, and women, and ignorant ungrounded people that were but novices and learners in the principles... being wise in their own eyes.' Such converts to Quakerism, in Baxter's view, had the arrogance of youth.[4]

Their numbers grew rapidly following a gathering in June 1652 near Firbank Fell in the Lake District, where Fox addressed a crowd of more than a thousand: there were soon as many Quakers in England as there were Catholics. By the late 1650s there were no fewer than 35,000 Quakers and perhaps as many as 60,000, a figure exceeded only by the Baptists among the religious sects of post-Civil War England.

From the start, Quakerism was equated with political and social protest. Salvation, Fox and his friends claimed, was open to all, not just an elect: 'God woulde have all men to bee saved. Marke all men.'[5] They believed that every individual should follow their 'inner light' – the willingness to accept the suffering Christ into one's body – which Fox and his followers regarded as the voice of God and superior in authority to the Bible, for which, unusually in an age of scripture, they had little time. Quakers embraced antinomianism, the belief that external moral laws should be replaced by internal, spiritual truths, as Nayler had outlined in his pamphlet *A True Discoverie of Faith*, published in 1655: 'My covenant is the new one, and the law in the heart, and here Christ is the rule of me for ever, and my law is spiritual and not moral.'

As a definition of antinomianism it could hardly be bettered. Quakerism was, for some, a more attractive religious option than the Calvinism of the Presbyterians and Independents, a harsh creed, intrinsic to which was the notion of an elect, chosen at the dawn of creation, who were to be saved while everyone else was damned, denied of all hope for eternity. Calvinism, wrote Fox, would have God 'the most Cruel of all Beings'. Quakers sought to restore the church to a pure, primitive model, one in which Spirit trumped Scripture, the knowledge of which only served to reinforce the hegemony of a learned elite. While there was an anti-intellectual strand to the movement – 'This learned generation have been the stirrers up of all strife and bloodshed' – Quakers, particularly its core of relatively affluent founders, known as the Valiant Sixty, were articulate, albeit in a blunt, obstreperous way. They refused to doff their hats to social superiors: 'When the Lord sent me forth into the world', said Fox, 'he forbad me to put off my hat to any, high or low.'[6] They addressed social superiors with a 'thou' rather than the more formal 'you'. They opposed the taking of oaths, so hindering, even endangering the legal process; advocated the abolition of parish tithes – which 'kept priests in their idleness' by the 'labours of poor people'; and encouraged female preachers, thereby inverting the patriarchal order. As the Royalist cleric Thomas Fuller pointed out: 'Such as now introduce Thou and Thee will (if they can) expel Mine and Thine, dissolve all property into confusion.'[7] But this dynamic creed of social egalitarianism proved especially attractive to artisans and small landowners, to whom Nayler, the movement's most prolific pamphleteer and its most eloquent orator, invoked in Paul's Letter to the Corinthians:

> He that is called of the Lord being a servant, is the Lord's freeman; likewise he that is called being free, is Christ's servant.

This was levelling talk and it aroused fear and opposition. In the eyes of its opponents, it was a recipe for social, political and religious chaos. According to Baxter, who would later mellow in his attitude towards them: 'Quakers were but the Ranters turned from horrid profaneness and blasphemy to a life of extreme austerity on the other side. Their doctrines were mostly the same as the Ranters.'* Another commentator thought them to be 'of the same puddle'.[8] In some areas of Britain evidence of a man's Quakerism was enough to have him turned out of the army, out of his home, to lose him his tenancy, even to have his vote disputed, were he of sufficient social standing. During the early years of the movement missionary activity was invariably accompanied by unrest and hostility. In the villages and towns of

---

* The Ranters were another antinomian (which derives from the Greek, 'against law') Christian sect who emerged in England in the mid-seventeenth century. They denied the authority of both scripture and clergy.

Cumberland and Yorkshire in the 1650s, Quakers were frequently set upon by groups of assailants armed with staffs and clubs. In Lancashire, said George Fox, referring to his own unfortunate experiences, it was the custom 'to runn 20 or 40 people upon one man'. Further south, in Evesham in 1655, when they attempted to hold meetings, Quakers were stoned, spat at and urinated on.

Yet most Quakers were largely uninterested in practical politics; their more astute critics, such as the Puritan minister Thomas Weld, who had returned from Massachusetts to advise Cromwell, recognized their 'forsaking of the world'. The Quaker movement, despite the fears it aroused in contemporaries, was where people headed when radicalism was in retreat. Take the example of the former Leveller John Lilburne, who became a Quaker in 1655 after reading Nayler, whom he described as 'that strong, or tall man in Christ'. The Quakers were fundamentally apolitical, for perfection was not of this world, which they rejected. As Nayler himself wrote: 'The best expedient for the preserving of this nation is for all people in the nation to turn to God, that by his light you may be led to repentance and newness of life.'[9]

As Quakerism grew, so did its geographical reach, as preachers spread the message of the Inner Light to parts of southern England. Charles Marshall, from Bristol, attended more than 400 meetings in thirty-six different counties in just two years. Indeed, Bristol gained a reputation as a Quaker hotspot, with the city's garrison acting as both patron and protector of religious and political dissent. By the end of 1654, it was not just the city's garrison commanders who were among its converts, but a former MP, the wife of an assize judge, and a high-ranking civil servant.

John Audland and Thomas Airey had been the first Quakers to visit Bristol, in June 1654. Returning in September of that year, Audland was accompanied by his co-religionist, John Camm, who had previously gained an audience with Cromwell, albeit a disappointing one: 'He holds that all the worships of this nation is the worship of God,' Camm wrote to Margaret Fell. 'But the blind cannot judge of truth.' Quakers could be intolerant, too.

Audland and Camm found strong support among the radical soldiers stationed in Bristol and their preaching attracted crowds of up to 1,500 locals: 'many hundreds were by the word and testimony of truth by them published convinced'. Tensions rose in the city, where a military–civilian split, echoing the growing division in the Protectoral government, was becoming apparent.[10] The governor of Bristol, Colonel Adrian Scroope (one of the commissioners who signed Charles I's death warrant), recognized this schism as a microcosm of the fragmented nation: 'Here, as in many other places, a clear distinction between the godly party, and the enemies of God' was all too apparent. The growth of sectarianism was visible, too, to the Venetian ambassador to London, Alvise Sagredo, who noted at the time that the English were 'divided into as many faiths as there are heads, and the number of religions equals the number of men'. Cromwell's wish for religious liberty was being fulfilled, but at the cost of his competing desire for a settled, stable nation, healed of the wounds of civil war.[11]

The city's divisions became explicit in the elections for the First Protectorate Parliament in August 1654, when military and civilian factions lined up in fierce opposition. The army was represented by George Bishop, a Quaker convert, former soldier, advocate at the Putney debates of placing Charles I on trial (it was he who christened Charles 'that man of blood') and intelligence expert 'of some credit' in London. He allied with Colonel John

Huggett, the head of the city's militia. For the civilian interest stood Robert Aldworth, the city's recorder, and Alderman Miles Jackson, an unrepentant Royalist who had managed to cling on to power. The election was held against a backdrop of allegations of intimidation and sharp practice. Aldworth and Jackson won the vote, though not before Bishop and Huggett had appealed against the result. When that was lost, they made no secret of the fact that they sought 'occasions to blast the cittie by all possible meanes'. The will of God – necessity – trumped that of the people. One is reminded, not for the first or last time during this period, of Bertolt Brecht's observation: 'Would it not be simpler if the government simply dissolved the people and elected another?'*

The arrival of the Quakers had nourished further the unorthodoxies that flourished among the port's population, peripatetic by early modern standards. The city's vibrant popular culture proved resistant to the city authorities' ban on theatre and cock fighting – sensual, visceral pleasures, symptomatic, thought some, of liberty's all too easy transformation into licence. Bristol's notoriety for excess contrasted with the godly exemplars of towns and cities such as Gloucester, Coventry and sublime Kidderminster, the reformed 'Ramoth-Gileath of the Good', where, according to Baxter, its energetic and eloquent minister, there was 'not a separatist, Anabaptist, antinomian etc. in the town'.

The religious diet of the godly was a rich one, consisting of daily dishes of psalms, Eucharist and spiritual exercises, though not, officially, the Lord's Prayer. Many ministers, including Richard Baxter continued to use the Lord's Prayer and the Creed, for their 'perfect method and satisfactory comprehensiveness'.

---

* These words come from Brecht's poem 'Die Lösung' ('The Solution'), inspired by the 1953 uprising against the Communist government of East Germany.

Their weekly recitation served as a lodestone for the ordinary churchgoer. Baxter was a hugely successful religious reformer, who was modestly proud of the changes he had wrought at the Worcestershire town of Kidderminster: 'I bless God for the change that I see in the country; and among the people, even in my own charge.' Ralph Josselin was more sanguine: his flock at Earl Colne in Essex were, but for a godly core, indifferent to his efforts at reform.[12]

The state took a heavy-handed view of immorality; it may be that the Republic was harsher on sexual practices than any British government before or since. The 1650 Act laid down the death penalty for adultery by a married woman and her partner, though few were indicted.* A married man and a single woman were spared such harshness. The plain injustice requires no further comment. Death was also the price paid by those judged to have committed incest and prostitutes in the habit of reoffending. This brought English law into line with that of the Old Testament and was endorsed by the wilder churchmen: 'God would have put the adulterer to death', preached Thomas Warson, a Presbyterian of the most ardent sort, at St Paul's in 1656, citing the Old Testament book of Deuteronomy.

The 1650 Act also enshrined the new criminal offence of fornication, previously handled by the spiritual courts. It was notoriously difficult to prove, though when it was, sentencing became more rigorous during the Protectorate. In Manchester in January 1657, constables were ordered to arrest all those who had recently become single mothers and detain them for a year in the house of correction.

---

* According to the historian Bernard Capp, there were at least thirty-six prosecutions at the Old Bailey, though judges were reluctant to enforce the ultimate penalty.

Sodomy, a felony since the reign of Henry VIII, was popularly viewed as an exotic, 'arabic' practice, a perception 'confirmed' by the case of Michael Ben-Alexander, who, in 1651, had been hanged at Tyburn for 'buggering a boy'. Thomas Vayham, a schoolmaster in Lincolnshire, was also hanged for buggery with one of his pupils. The fact that this 'beast of a man', in the judges' words, proclaimed himself a Catholic convert at the gallows only served to confirm Puritan prejudices.

Such harsh legal strictures appeared to have little effect on licentious, fissiparous Bristol and tensions continued to rise. Apprentices rioted against the Quaker presence on 18 December 1654 and there were further disturbances on Christmas Day, the celebration of which – or not – was yet another source of dispute.

As Bristol's reputation sank, Cromwell himself was forced to intervene. Major William Boteler, soon to forge a fearsome reputation as one of the Protector's major generals, was sent to investigate the crisis. Boteler, a 'cruel persecutor' of Catholics and Quakers, put most of the blame on the activities of the soldiers: 'With some griefe and shame on the behalf of my fellow officers especially I am forced to let you know, they have carried things very imprudently, and to the dishonour of religion, your highness, and army.' Following the vanquishing in the West Country of the hapless Royalist Penruddock Rising in 1655, Bristol's garrison was broken up and moved on. Into this toxic mix, entered James Nayler.

'Of ruddy complexion, hair brown and slank', Nayler was leanly Messianic in appearance, wearing a 'hat that hung over his brows' to the apparent delight of his female followers. This charismatic preacher, in his late thirties, referred to himself as the 'Sun of Righteousness, the Prince of Peace, the only Begotten, the fairest of ten thousand'. Humility was not prominent in his make-up and he was considered vulnerable to pride; he had been warned by his colleague Richard Nelson, not to 'steal men's hearts away from God to thyself', for his followers might 'take thee as a demi-god'. It was a prophetic warning, and one ignored.[13]

Born in 1618 near Wakefield a radical and prosperous part of Yorkshire's West Riding, Nayler was a farmer and landowner of reasonable means who had joined the parliamentary army in 1643. He was a good soldier, who served in John Lambert's elite regiment of horse, where he attained the rank of quarter-master. It was a role of considerable responsibility and of vital importance in a land ravaged by crop failures and food shortages, demanding an organized mind and considerable personal charm. There was much delicate negotiation with local populations, especially during the ultimately successful though precarious Scottish campaign of 1650. Both Lambert and Nayler, exact con-temporaries, were products of the West Riding's cussed religious milieu and his commander thought highly of this veteran of the three sieges of Pontefract Castle, of Marston Moor and the miracle of Dunbar. When Nayler was tried before Parliament following his arrest in Bristol, the second most powerful man in England was to declare him:

> A very useful person. We parted with him with great regret. He was a man of very unblameable life and conversation, a member of a very sweet society of an Independent church.

It was the Westmorland Friends who had first drawn the atten-tion of the regime to Nayler following his interrogation in that county in 1653, when they petitioned Parliament, Cromwell and Lambert on his behalf:

> Our dear brother James Nayler lies in prison in Appleby, who

served the Parliament under the command of Major General Lambert between eight and nine years, as we believe some of the Army can witness.

Lambert's northern regiments had been packed with Quakers, their beliefs formed, as with so many religious and political radicals, in a hothouse atmosphere of 'ideologically committed militancy' mixed with military discipline.* Captain Amor Stoddard became one of the most productive figures in the dissemination of Quaker texts, while the governors of the garrison on Holy Island off the Northumbrian coast converted wholesale, like their brethren in Bristol, to the lively new creed.

Little is known of Nayler's whereabouts once ill health, probably consumption, forced him out of the army in 1651. He became a member of an Independent congregation at Horbury, a village close to Wakefield, where he was charged with blasphemy and expelled by its pastor, Christopher Marshal, who accused Nayler of 'uncivil and wanton carriage' with a married woman, Mrs Roper. 'It was his Opinion', said Marshal, 'He might with any Woman that was of his Judgement.'

After a period of vagrancy in Cornwall, where unorthodoxy, even Catholicism, was indulged, Nayler dwelt in the Somerset town of Chew Stoke. There he was accused of spending a night in 'a Chamber with three Women of his Company' (his wife Anne, whom he married in 1643 and with whom he had three daughters, is notable for her absence from his much of life). The Puritan minister Thomas Weld, who had returned from Massachusetts, noted Quakers' habit of 'forsaking

---

* Such a combination is always of concern to authority. It is not by chance that the unparalleled reforms of the 1945 UK Labour government took place as troops returned from victory overseas.

the world (though to a sinful neglect of their callings and families)'.*

Nayler arrived in London in June 1655. It was in the capital that he made the most of his national forum, delivering a tireless flow of exuberant speeches. Such was his loquacious oratory and output of writing, he began to surpass Fox as the voice of the Quaker movement. It was a dangerous moment for Quakers. A month later, James Parnell, just eighteen years of age, was arrested after he caused a disturbance in a church in the Essex town of Coggeshall. He was fined £40, which he didn't pay, and so was marched off to Colchester Castle, where he was beaten and starved to death, possibly following a hunger strike. His fate was widely mocked in song and pamphlet, reflecting the growing hostility to the creed. The Quaker card had been marked.

Even by the standards of early Quaker verbosity, Nayler had been a prolific propagandist for the cause, publishing almost fifty pamphlets, a relentless barrage of invective, between 1652 and 1657. James Gough, a former parliamentary officer, recalled that he was 'struck with more terror before the preaching of James Nayler than I was before the Battle of Dunbar'.

The radical London Baptist Rebecca Travers was equally impressed by Nayler's verbal assaults on her co-religionists. On meeting Nayler, she was 'confounded and ashamed that a Quaker should exceed the learned Baptists' and was sufficiently awed to convert on the spot, leaving with Nayler's advice ringing in her ears: 'Feed not on knowledge... it is good to look upon, but not to feed on, for who feeds on knowledge dies to the innocent life.'[14]

* One can see why Christopher Hill, the great social historian of the mid-seventeenth century, drew favourable comparisons between the likes of Nayler and the libertines of the 1960s and 1970s counter-culture; a comparison that, in the light of more recent revelations, no longer appears quite as bewitching as it once did.

It was a succinct credo of Quakerism, with its emphasis on feeling over thought, the irrational over the rational.

Nayler's residency in London, that 'great and wicked place', made him a celebrity, the 'fairest of ten thousand'. People of the highest social standing went to hear him preach, including Henry Vane, the republican critic of Cromwell's abandonment of the 'Good old cause'. Nayler, like Vane, felt the revolution had been betrayed. In his pamphlet *To the Parliament of the Commonwealth of England* he wrote of walking along London's South Bank, the traditional home of its theatres, and of his horror at seeing 'men upon scaffolds', players 'acting such abominable folly in words and actions'. He wrote of the wound to his heart caused by such spectacles, 'that ever such things should be tolerated under your government'.

Yet his moralizing did not stop the likes of Lady Darcy, in an early example of radical chic, inviting aristocrats, politicians and others well born to hear Nayler from 'behind a ceiling [*sic*]'. Even his opponents testified to his powers. The Anglican priest John Deacon, a veteran of many sharp encounters with Nayler as well as his first biographer, described him, shortly before the entry into Bristol, as 'a man of exceeding quick wit and sharp apprehensions, enriched with that commendable gift of good oratory with a very delightful melody in his utterance'.[15]

His popularity in London may have turned Nayler's head; he was a rock star *avant la lettre*. He gathered a loyal group of disciples around him, many of them women. One of Nayler's most ardent supporters was the belligerent and brilliant Martha Simmonds. She became the most prominent and vocal member of a small group that began to disrupt Quaker meetings, shouting 'Innocency' at the congregation. They held Nayler to be superior to Edward Burrough and Francis Howgill – both members of the Valiant Sixty – who had been seen as the leaders of London's Quakers.

Simmonds, the 'turbulent woman', demanded that Nayler confront Burrough and Howgill. As a consequence, wrung out by fame, fasting and fierce opprobrium, he had some kind of breakdown, physical and mental, during he which lay on a table for a number of nights, shaking and babbling. Simmonds was accused of using witchcraft to cast a spell on him. Friends of Nayler took him to Bristol to escape Simmonds's grip, but she followed in pursuit. He tried to reach Launceston in Cornwall, where Fox was imprisoned – unable to stand trial because, as required by his faith, he refused to take the oath. But Nayler never got there. On his journey west he was arrested as a vagabond and imprisoned in Exeter.

In a letter of 23 June 1656, fellow Quaker Thomas Rawlinson had warned Fox of his colleague's excited state. 'James Naylor is here with me... He hath been in a fast. He eat no bread but one little bit, for a whole month; when I came to him he took no manner of food, but some days a pint of white wine, and some days a gill mingled with water, but now he eats meat.'[16]

While Nayler fasted for weeks in gaol, losing flesh and maybe even his mind, Simmonds made it to Launceston, where she confronted and abused the imprisoned Fox to his face: 'She came singing in my face, inventing words', Fox recalled. Released from gaol in September, Fox visited Exeter to confront Nayler, who 'had ran out into imaginations, and a company with him, which raised up a great darkness in the nation'. Fox sought his subservience, offering his hand to be kissed in redemption. The half-starved Nayler insisted Fox kiss his feet instead. The movement was ruptured. Nayler, gorged on millenarianism, had become the 'wicked spirit' recalled in Fox's memoirs, 'risen amongst Friends to war against'.[17]

Could the Quakers survive? The summer of 1656 had witnessed a national crackdown on the movement by the authorities, which mirrored earlier assaults on the Levellers and the Ranters, with whom they were deliberately conflated: 'They hold that all things ought to be common, and teach the doctrine of levelling privately to their disciples', wrote one magistrate. More extreme Quakers even claimed that 'wheresoever Christ came, he came to destroy all property'.[18]

Simmonds, extraordinarily, had become nurse to the wife of Major General Desborough, Cromwell's brother-in-law. Jane Desborough called on 'His Highness' to release Nayler from Exeter gaol, a request granted on 20 October. Four days later, Nayler would enter Bristol, with Simmonds and six others by his side.

Having shocked the burghers of Bristol with his provocative entry, Nayler and his companions were interrogated by the city's magistrates. He denied his divinity, though his followers were less cautious in their proclamations, declaring him the 'anointed king of Israel'. Dorcas Erbury even claimed that Nayler had raised her from the dead while he served time in Exeter gaol.

Nayler was found to be carrying a copy of the *Epistle from Lentulus to the Roman Senate*,* with its description of Christ with hair coming down to his shoulders and a short beard, a look, it was claimed, that Nayler had knowingly cultivated in imitation of the Saviour. The magistrates in Bristol, familiar with and fearful of the Quaker menace, considered their authority inadequate to deal with such an outrage and appealed to Parliament, 'that your honours would now take up the reins of government into your hands, which have too long lain loose in this particular, and curb

* A letter of unknown origin, published in Italy in the fifteenth century and containing a physical description of Jesus Christ.

the insolencies of all ungodly persons'. Nayler would not face justice, as precedent would suggest, at a local court. He was to be made an example of at a show trial in the capital, where he would face the prospect of execution.

Judge and Jury

There is a power in me from above.

JAMES NAYLER

O N 31 OCTOBER, one week after their profane procession through Bristol, Nayler, along with his followers, was brought to London to appear before a parliamentary committee. They arrived at Westminster singing the same hosannas. Two resolute opponents of the Quakers, Robert Aldworth, the victor over the army and Quaker interest in Bristol, and Thomas Bampfield, recorder of Exeter and future Speaker of the Commons, chaired the committee. It consisted of fifty-five, eventually rising to fifty-eight, of the most powerful and distinguished figures in England.

One can barely imagine how intimidating such a setting was for the relatively low-born Nayler, but he was lucid and apparently fearless throughout his interrogation, conducting himself with grace and dignity. When asked if he had raised Dorcas Erbury from the dead while in Exeter Gaol, he replied, echoing Job: 'I can do nothing of my self... There is a power in me from above.' He was God's vehicle, perhaps, that he would admit; but he was not the Christ. Bampfield asked who provided for him, how was he maintained on his travels?

'Him that clothes the Lilies,' Nayler replied, revealing that he had fasted for 'two or three' weeks.

His final statement to the committee was a concise and consistent summary of his position:

> I do abhor that any honour due to God should be given to me, as I am a creature. But it pleased the Lord to set me up as a sign of the coming of the Righteous One, and what has been done as I passed through these towns, I was commended by the Lord to suffer such things to be done by me, as to the outward, as a sign, not as I am a creature.

The Quaker Anthony Pearson wrote to Margaret Fell, who by now was married to George Fox, that 'Nayler answered all the questions with so much wisdom, meekness and clearness... that the whole assembly (except some violent ones of the committee) were strangely astonished and satisfied with his answers.' But there was to be no shortage of malice in response. The men of the committee saw the hand of God at work in the 'timing of discovering this business'.[1]

The Committee's thirteen-page report was read out before Parliament on 5 December 1656 and concluded: 'First, James Nayler did assume the gesture, words, honour, worship, and miracles of our blessed Saviour. Secondly, the names and incommunicable attributes and titles of our blessed Saviour.'

He was a 'grand imposter and seducer of the people' who had taken on 'the gestures, words, names, and attributes of our Saviour Christ'.[2]

Parliament's commitment to liberty of conscience was never as sincere or expansive as Cromwell's; certain creeds, such as those which denied the Trinity were proscribed, though even Anglicans were persecuted. England's Catholics, the nation's original nonconformists, whose right to practise their religion was already denied by the Instrument of Government, often came off worst and, as the 1650s progressed, the atmosphere had become even less tolerant of them. The idea that peace with France might improve the position of English Catholics, a hope shared by Cardinal Mazarin, was cancelled out by the war with 'Black' Spain. 'The Papists in England', said Cromwell, 'have been accounted Spaniolised ever since I was born. They never regarded France... Spain was their patron.'[3]

Up until the mid-1650s, it might be argued, Catholics had been treated with a certain neglect – albeit hardly of a benign nature – by the Protectorate: the old Recusancy Acts, passed under the reigns of Elizabeth, James and Charles I, had been abolished by Parliament in 1650. But conflict with Spain had hardened Protestant hearts, and a bill for the 'discovering, con- victing and repressing of popish recusants' was introduced in November 1656. If it were passed – and its spiteful hostility led forty-three members to oppose it – judges could summon suspected Catholics not only to take an oath renouncing the pope's authority, but to deny beliefs central to Catholicism, such as transubstantiation and the existence of purgatory – actions in firm opposition to any concept of religious liberty. If they did not, two-thirds of their estates were to be forfeited. Those Catholics who attended mass at foreign embassies, to which a blind eye had been turned, were now liable to a fine of £100. Catholicism was, once again, deemed 'unEnglish'. The brutish Boteler looked upon recusants as 'other than Englishmen. I look upon them as enemies'.[4] Such encouragement of aggression and intolerance did not escape the attention of Mazarin, who ordered his envoy, Antoine de Bordeaux Neufville, to intercede on behalf of England's Catholic community. The Protector wrote to the Cardinal in regretful tones: 'I may not... as the face of my affairs now stands, answer to your call for toleration.' But he reminded his correspondent that he had 'plucked many out of the fire' and that it was his intent 'as soon as I can … to make a further progress, and discharge my promise to your Eminency'. France's chief minister seemed to be mollified by the Protector's words. In the history of the Protectorate, only two Catholics were executed for their faith.[5] But the regime was not averse to persecuting those beyond the tolerated Presbyterians and Independents.

After the report on Nayler had been read out, Major-General Philip Skippon, a member of the Council, whose motto, *Ora et pugna* ('Pray and fight') embodied his simple, muscular Presbyterianism, rose to his feet. Skippon was a lauded veteran of the Civil Wars. At the battle of Turnham Green in 1642 his cry of 'Come my boys, my brave boys', had inspired the London Trained Bands in their fragile defence of the capital's western boundary; and at Naseby in 1645, where he was badly wounded, his drilling of the New Model infantry had proved a decisive factor. Skippon's governance of London, with an ever tighter grip, had brought him into repeated conflict with the Quakers. For this 'Christian Centurion', politics and religion were one. Nayler's crime embraced both the sacred and the profane and raised fundamental questions about the very idea of 'toleration'. The Quakers had flourished in the soil of Cromwell's liberties and Lambert's Instrument.

Skippon, normally an 'infrequent and unskillful speaker', looked around and marked the chamber's stillness. 'I do not marvel at this silence', he began,

> Every man is astonished to hear this report… It has been always my opinion that the growth of these things is more dangerous

than the most intestine of foreign enemies. I have often been troubled in my thoughts to think of this toleration... Their great growth and increase is too notorious, both in England and Ireland; their principles strike both at ministry and magistracy. Many opinions are in this nation (all contrary to the government) which would join in one to destroy you, if it should please God to deliver the sword into their hands.[6]

The regime was gambling with God's providence, Skippon believed. If the government acted against His will in allowing such blasphemy as Nayler's, then it and the nation it ruled would deserve its fate. 'Should we not be as jealous of God's honour as we are of our own?' Skippon pleaded. The concerns of this world and that of God could not be separated. Skippon and his hardline allies were determined to secure His peace and providence, which were inextricably linked, and harass their enemies to their death.

'I am of the opinion', said Skippon, judging Nayler's actions, 'that it is horrid blasphemy and ought to be punished as horrid blasphemy.' Nayler should be shown no mercy and the law must not stand in the way of his punishment: 'I have been always against laws for matters *ex post facto*; but, in this, I am free to look back, for it is a special emergency.' Skippon was arguing for retrospective judgement, a bad law for a hard case.

The zealous William Boteler, 'most odious of all Cromwell's Major-Generals' and Independent champion of the 'gathered churches', whose dislike of Quakerism can be traced back to his time in Bristol, was equally dismayed by what he had heard of Nayler: 'My ears did tingle, and my heart tremble, to hear the report.' The Quakers were 'despisers of your government', he told the House. They condemned magistracy and ministry – church and state – 'and trample it under their feet'. George

Downing, the MP for Carlisle, a town familiar with the perils of Quakerism, added with ominous finality: 'We have gotten enough out of him.' They had evidence enough to nail Nayler.[7]

Parliament's conservative majority were clearly eager to demonstrate the limits of Cromwell's relatively capacious religious settlement and hold the errant Nayler to account. As Colonel Cox was to assert: 'The world abroad says it is liberty of conscience has brought this fellow before you. I am of the same opinion.' Boteler, whom Fox had once declared a 'cruel prosecutor', called for Nayler to be stoned to death, in accordance with Mosaic Law: 'The law made against blasphemy in Leviticus is as binding to us this day as surely as that against murder, which follows in the next verse.'

The House had now to consider three important questions. The first of these concerned whether it should accept the report of the committee and, by doing so, accept Nayler's guilt, or should it hear from the accused first?

Cox, despite his claim that he was 'as much for liberty of conscience as any man', thought that Nayler's action 'exceeds that liberty' and that, therefore, the Quaker did not deserve to be heard. Colonel Sydenham, a noted opponent of anti-Quaker legislation who was close to Cromwell, responded, asking whether it could be right for a man to be accused 'by the bare Report of a Committee, to have the sentence of death passed upon him without further hearing?' This could be 'any man's case, hereafter', he protested. Sydenham's judicious approach met with the approval of the Oxford MP Richard Croke. If Nayler claimed his actions were not blasphemous, argued Croke, 'I would have him called to the bar.'

The House voted to bring Nayler in, to the frustration of Bampfield, who appeared to be personally offended by their decision: 'You believe your Committees' Report in all other matters, that concern the lives, liberties and estates of three nations', he insisted. 'So why not this?'

Nayler took up his position before Parliament in its majesty. No great issue was made of his refusal to kneel or take off his hat, which was removed politely by the serjeant. The Speaker, Thomas Widdrington, addressed him and, in reply, Nayler confirmed that the committee's report was accurate bar the details of his affair with Mrs Roper. 'It might be she kissed me,' he said, struggling to recall the details. 'It was our manner.' But he was adamant that he did not have sexual relations with that woman. 'I abhor filthiness.'

The charges were read out to him and Nayler allowed them to stand, declaring his faith in his judges. He was then asked to provide an explanation for his actions in Bristol. 'There was never anything since I was born so much against my will and mind as this thing,' Nayler confessed. He was well aware that to be 'set up as a sign', to parade through Bristol, were dangerous activities, likely to be judged harshly by the authorities: 'I knew that I should lay down my life for it,' he admitted. But he did not seek to foment civil disorder, nor to blaspheme: 'I am one that daily prays that magistracy may be established in this nation. I do not nor dare affront authority. I did it not to set up idolatory [*sic*] but to obey the will of my Father.'[8]

Having brought Nayler into their company and given him hearing, MPs now confronted a second, knottier issue. Was there a law that dealt specifically with Nayler's offence? Indeed what *was* his offence? The Blasphemy Act of 1650 appeared to be the obvious one under which Nayler should be charged. But there was a problem, for the hardliners at least, as Skippon and Boeteler made clear. Under the Blasphemy Act, first offenders were liable to no more than six months in prison, while even repeat offenders faced no greater punishment than banishment.

The Instrument of Government was even less stringent. Its Article 37 stated:

> That such as profess faith in God by Jesus Christ (though differing in judgment from the doctrine, worship or discipline publicly held forth) shall not be restrained from, but shall be protected in, the profession of the faith and exercise of their religion; so as they abuse not this liberty to the civil injury of others and to the actual disturbance of the public peace on their parts: provided this liberty be not extended to the Popery or Prelacy, nor to such as, under the profession of Christ, hold forth and practice licentiousness.

Skippon was disgusted by this intolerably tolerant interpretation of the instrument. 'God deliver me from such liberty,' he thundered. He warned his fellow MPs, with Lambert especially in his sights:

> I am afraid there will nothing come of this business, and then sin and judgment lie at your doors... These Quakers, Ranters, Levellers, Socinians,* and all sorts, bolster themselves under thirty-seven and thirty-eight of Government.

Even those formerly committed to the aims of the Instrument, such as Major General Goffe, admitted that, if Skippon was right and the Instrument did 'hold out anything to protect such persons I would have it burnt in the fire'. Goffe held a long-standing hatred for Quakers – they would 'tear the flesh off the bones of all that profess Christ' – and had been zealous in his persecution of them in southern England. He suggested that

---

* Socinianism was a movement that emerged during the sixteenth-century Reformation, and which rejected the orthodox Christian doctrines of the Trinity and the divinity of Jesus.

Nayler had fulfilled at least one prophecy, but not one that would gain him the affections of the court: 'He has fulfilled a scripture, that false Christs should arise.'[9]

But splits emerged among the army grandees. Lambert, author of the Instrument and Nayler's former commander and compatriot, was insistent on the rule of law; Parliament could not have unlimited judicial power. Yes, he too was appalled by his former quartermaster's actions: 'It is very much sorrow of my heart, and I hope nothing shall quench my zeal against it.' But due process must be followed. As Lambert put it, with soldierly gruffness: 'I would have it regular.'

Captain Baynes, MP for Leeds, took up the challenge laid down earlier by Skippon. 'The Instrument of Government says all shall be protected that profess faith in Jesus Christ, which I suppose this man does.' Would Parliament, *could* Parliament, act against the provisions of the written constitution?

The third and final problem the House had to consider was under what terms they should judge Nayler. They could take the legislative option and pass a bill of attainder, an ex post facto law, though this risked angering the Protector, who was committed to the Instrument. Or they could take a judicial approach, arguing that the power to judge held previously by the abolished House of Lords, the highest court in the land, had devolved to the Commons. George Downing argued that it could. If Cromwell had seen the case, he argued – with all the evidence to the contrary – 'I am confident he would have been zealous in it and extended the law.'

Walter Strickland, who had helped negotiate the end of the conflict with the Dutch, sought a belt and braces approach. If Nayler was guilty of blasphemy, horrid or not, then the judgement must be explained clearly: 'I would have your proceedings justified as much as may be, and him left inexcusable.' And

Strickland offered a warning to the hardliners: 'that which sticks with me the most is the nearness of his opinion to that which is a most glorious truth, that the spirit is personally in us'. Strickland was close to Cromwell and his observation may well have reflected the views of the Protector, as did those of Sydenham, who offered a historical perspective, that those sitting previously 'in our place... would condemn us for heretics'. This position was backed by Colonel Holland: 'Consider the state of this nation, what the price of our blood is. Liberty of conscience, the Instrument gives it us. We remember how many Christians were formerly martyred under this notion of blasphemy.'[10]

Oppposing such arguments, Robert Beake, who appeared to believe that Parliament had the freedom to create whatever laws it wished, went even further than Skippon and Boteler in the fate he proposed for the unfortunate Nayler. Parliament, he said, was 'so sovereign, that it may declare that to be an offence, which never was an offence before'. He then made a bizarre appeal to Classical precedent for Nayler's punishment, citing the obscure example of the Roman Consul Publicius Malleolus. When he was found guilty of parricide in 102 BC, the Senate had ordered Malleolus to be 'sewn up in a leathern sack, with a dog, a cock, a viper, and an ape, and so thrown into the Tiber'.[11]

Despite the various objections raised and words of caution uttered, the House of Commons – showing scant regard for precedent and using reasoning that was dubious at best – resolved to adopt the powers of the Lords, whose judicial powers, it was argued, it had inherited. The House was to be Nayler's judge and jury after all.

John Desborough, Cromwell's brother-in-law, looked mercifully upon Nayler. If anything, he argued, it was Nayler's followers that were guilty of greater blasphemy, of idolatory, 'if we judge by Christian rule'. He would not vote 'to call him a horrid blasphemer'.

Strickland took a similarly nuanced view: 'I look upon him as a man exceeding scandalous, proud and sinful; but to say he is a blasphemer, I cannot agree.' Deluded, proud, yes. Blasphemous, no. Perhaps he could be charged as a 'seducer', argued Strickland, or sent 'to Biddle in the Isles of Scilly'.[12] Strickland was citing the example of John Biddle, a distinguished, though controversial, biblical scholar, who had come under suspicion for his adherence to antinomianism and for his highly technical theological arguments denying the Trinity. Cromwell had intervened personally to save the life of Biddle, whom he thought 'full of modesty, sobriety and forbearance, no ways contentious'. Cromwell did not seek out martyrs, despite a plenitude of candidates amid the religious ferment of the age. Banishing Biddle to the Scilly Isles in October 1655, the Protector allowed him 'a hundred crowns per annum for his existence'. Though Cromwell was more concerned with order than toleration when the crux came, his personal interventions in private religious matters were striking. As well as his merciful role in the Biddle case, Quakers were released on his instruction and Anglicans were more than tolerated (Cromwell paid for the funeral of Archbishop Ussher at Westminster Abbey in April 1656). He also refused to restrict admission to Catholic services at the Venetian ambassador's residence and protested against the execution of the Jesuit John Southworth. Unfortunately for James Nayler, his case had become too public for the Protector to drag it back into the shadows. And furthermore, the times had changed.

The serpentine debate over Nayler's fate meandered on, to the obvious frustration of many MPs, but few opinions budged. Dr Thomas Clarges proposed that they cut the Gordian knot:

'Let us all stop our ears and stone him.' Predictably, Nayler was judged guilty of 'horrid blasphemy'. He was convicted, too, as a 'grand imposter and a great seducer of the people'.[13]

Some suggested sentences that were appropriately harsh in nature but fell short of the death penalty. Judge George Smith cited the precedent of the Ranter Jacob Bottomley. One of the few convicted under the Blasphemy Act of 1650, Bottomley had his tongue bored through as a punishment for publishing a pamphlet called *The Light and Dark Sides of God*. When Beake proposed that Nayler's tongue and right hand should be cut off, Desborough argued that this would endanger his life. But his was a lonely compassionate voice. Many continued to call for Nayler's death: Colonel Robert Wilton warned his colleagues against the pitfalls of lenience by resorting to another biblical precedent, this time from the Book of Samuel, in which Eli spared his sons the punishment requested by God, only to lose them, the Ark of the Covenant and his own life. Colonel Thomas Cooper countered with the perceptive observation that vengeance and martyrdom would cement the Quaker legend: 'if you take this man's blood', he argued, 'you do certainly lay a foundation for them. Instead of taking away Quakerism, you establish it.' When Dennis Bond, the member for Weymouth and Melcombe Regis, spoke approvingly of the grim, prolonged execution of a Quaker by the authorities in Bordeaux, he was challenged by Major Parker, who asked why he was bringing up the case of a 'company of papists in Bordeaux... It may as well be said the Spanish Inquisition may rise up in judgement against us.'

Major General Edward Whalley struck a conciliatory tone: 'I would have this agreed upon in peace and charity', he suggested. 'That these that are for a low punishment might not be censored for coldness, nor these for a higher punishment censured for preposterous zeal.' He thought Nayler should receive a death sentence, but be allowed six weeks in which to repent, before any sentence was carried out. His fellow major general, the ultra-millenarian Goffe, responded: 'It is the law of this nation, of all nations, and written upon every man's heart that a blasphemer should die.'[14]

On 15 December 1656, as MPs gathered to make their final judgement, Robert Rich, a prominent Quaker, handed out letters to them as they entered the chamber. 'There is no blasphemy in the light which is truth', they read, 'and to witness the light is no blasphemy.' Yet subtlety and ambiguity remained the focus of a few. Most wanted to make an example of Nayler, in the most brutal terms.

The Speaker put the question to Parliament. 'That the punishment of James Nayler, for his crimes, shall be death; and that bill be prepared and brought in for that purpose.'

The next day, 16 December 1656, despite the brimstone cast by the likes of Skippon and Boteler, MPs voted against his execution by ninety-six to eighty-two. Perhaps they were wary that they had already pushed process far enough; they did not wish to risk the tongue of the Protector.

With death no longer an option, a variety of lesser punishments were mooted, including the bizarre suggestion of colonels Barclay and Coker that Nayler have his hair cut off. Whalley objected: 'That will make the people believe that the Parliament of England are of opinion that our Saviour Christ wore his hair so [like Nayler's long, lank locks], and this will make all people in love with the fashion.' One would not wish to make a fashion of such a distinctly Cavalier style. Downing proposed that the House 'ought to do something with that tongue that has bored through God', while Alderman Foot urged that 'his head may be in the pillory, and that he be whipped from Westminster to the

Old Exchange'. Should Nayler be confined 'from all people', whether in Bristol, Orkney, the Scilly Isles, Jamaica, or even the Isle of Dogs, no relief should be given him beyond what he was able to earn. Bampfield recalled the rather generous treatment of John Lilburne, who had been granted 40 shillings a week in jail, 'more than he ever had before'.

Finally the House issued a statement. It had:

> Resolved that James Naylor be set with his head in the pillory, in the New Palace, Westminster, during the space of two hours on Thursday next; and shall be whipped by the hangman through the streets, from Westminster to the Old Exchange, London; and there likewise be set on the pillory, with his head in the pillory for two hours, between the hours of eleven and one on Saturday next; in each of the said places wearing a paper with an inscription of his crimes; and that at the Old Exchange his tongue shall be bored through with a hot iron; and that he be there also stigmatized in the forehead with the letter B. And that he be afterwards sent to Bristol, and be conveyed into and through the said city, on a horse bare-ridged, with his face backwards; and there also be publicly whipped on the next market day after he comes thither. And that from thence he be committed to prison in Bridewell, London, and there restrained from the society of all people and kept to hard labour, till he shall be released by Parliament; and during that time shall be debarred from the use of pen, ink, and paper, and shall have no relief but what he earns by his daily labour.

Speaker Widdrington, all too aware of the lack of legal precedent in the treatment of Nayler, asked the House what he should say to the guilty man in passing sentence. 'Shall I ask him any questions? If he speaks, what shall I answer? Shall I barely pronounce the sentence and make no preamble to it? I can do nothing but by your directions. I pray you inform me.'

Major General Kelsey thought Nayler should be allowed a response to his sentence: 'This is a new business. He has never been yet heard what he can say to it, why judgment should not be pronounced against him. You have no law for what you do.'

The vindictive Boteler tossed such objections aside: 'If it had been the case of death, I confess I should have given him all the liberty that might be to speak for himself. But in the lesser punishment, you need not put an excuse in his mouth.' A bore through the tongue and a 'B' on the forehead would do.

The sentence was finally recorded as a 'judgement' and it was resolved by 107 votes to 85 that Nayler should not be heard. The prisoner was summoned before the bar of the House for his sentencing. Widdrington addressed him: 'Now ten or eleven days have been spent in debating your crimes which are heinous. You have troubled the countries up and down and now you have troubled Parliament. Yet in your sentence mercy is mixed with judgment. It is a sentence not of death.'[15]

Having been told of his fate, Nayler attempted to speak, seeking clarification as to what his crimes were. 'God has given me a body,' he cried as he was led from the House. 'He shall, I hope, give me a spirit to endure it. The Lord lay not these things to your charge.'

The following day, Nayler's punishment commenced. He was transported the two and a half miles from Westminster to the New Exchange in the City, where the pillory awaited him. The plan was that, at each 'kennel' or crossing – and there were 311 of them – he would be whipped by the hangman. In the end, he 'only' received 310 lashes as, at one of the kennels, the hangman slipped and badly cut his hand. Rebecca Travers, the London Baptist, who had been converted to Quakerism by Nayler, attended his Calvary and described his condition: 'To my best discernment, there was not a space bigger than the breadth of a man's nail free from stripes and blood from his shoulder to his waist.' To make things worse, he was trodden on by one of the bailiff's horses that led his procession.[16]

In the aftermath of the Nayler trial, anti-Quaker feeling ran high among the public. Numerous petitions were raised urging action against them, from Northumberland, Durham, New-castle, Cheshire, Bristol, Cornwall, Dorset and even Dublin. Yet 'merciful men' made their voices heard, too. A petition was presented to Parliament, which claimed that Nayler was 'not fit to undergo' the next part of his sentence and, backed by sympathetic MPs, punishment was postponed for a week. Parliament also agreed to send five ministers to his cell, 'to save his soul if possible'. When the ministers arrived, Nayler asked that a written record of their meeting be kept. They asked him if he was sorry for his blasphemies? 'What were they,' he replied. The exasperated ministers burnt the transcript.

Nayler's sympathizers even petitioned Cromwell, appealing to his reputation for religious liberty:

> That you will be pleased and according to your former declarations and the experience we have had of your Highness' care of this tender interest of liberty of conscience to weight the consequence of these late proceedings and according to the 37th article [sic] of the said Instrument and one of the grounds you declare upon in your war with Spain, your highness will stand up for the poor people of God in this day, in doing whereof your Highness will not do more right to your petitioners than to yourself and these nations.

Further petitions arrived at Parliament. One of them, from Joshua Sprigg, an army chaplain, begged Parliament to leave

Nayler 'to the Lord and such Gospel remedies as he hath sanc-
tified... we are persuaded you will find such a course of love
and forbearance most effectual to reclaim him, and you will
assuredly leave a seal of your compassion and tenderness on the
spirits of your petitioners'. It was a forlorn hope. 'We are God's
executioners,' Downing reminded the petitioners.

John Deacon, Nayler's most lucid critic, though never able
entirely to disguise a certain admiration, described the scene of
his second bout of punishments:

> On Saturday December 27th about 11 of the clock he was in
> a coach conveyed from the common gaol of Newgate to the
> Black Boy near to the Royal Exchange, London; in which house
> he continued till the clock had struck twelve at noon, when by
> divers on with holberts he was guarded to the pillory, where when
> he came they presently put his head into the same, and having
> pinned it down, came up Martha Symonds, and with her two
> other, who was said to be Hannah Stranger and Dorcas Erbury;
> the first seated herself just behind him on the right side, the two
> latter before him, the one on the right hand, the other on the
> left, just at his feet, in imitation of Mary Magdalen and Mary the
> Mother of Jesus, and Mary the Mother of Cleophas, John 19.25,
> thereby to witness their still blasphemous and presumptuous
> and heretical adoration of him, as Jesus the Christ, as is more
> evidently expressed by that act of Robert Rich, whom I saw stick
> up a paper over his head, in which it is said was writ, 'This is
> the King of the Jews,' word by word with that in Luke 23.28...
> When he had stood just one hour and three quarters, they took
> him forth of the pillory, and having bound him fast with his
> back to the same, the executioner pulled off his cap, and having
> hoodwinked his face and taken hold fast of his tongue, with a red
> hot iron he bored a hole quite through; which having done, and
> pulling the cloth off that covered his face, he put a handkerchief

over his eyes, and so putting his left hand in his pole, he taking the red hot iron letter in his other hand, put it to his forehead, which gave a little flash of smoke; which being done, Rich licked the same, as did the dogs the wounds of Lazarus; and then sang, which he did often before, both stroking and kissing him, which he suffered with an admired impudence; so Nayler was first conveyed back to the Black Boy, and thence again to Newgate, where he rests till he sets forward to suffer deserved shame in like manner at Bristol...

A Quaker eyewitness recalled that Nayler 'never so much as winced, but bore the experience with astonishing and heart-melting patience'. It is Simmonds, Erbury and Rich who come off worst in contemporary accounts, acting like fevered fundamentalists, in stark contrast to Nayler, who, resigned to his fate and at peace with himself, maintains his dignity throughout. An anonymous Quaker text confirms that Nayler, having endured the ordeal, embraced the executioner.[17]

Returned to Bristol, Nayler was forced to ride his original route backwards through the city, a humiliation described in *Mercurius Politicus*, Needham's government broadsheet. He was stripped, strapped to a cart horse and 'there in the Market first whipped, from thence to the foot of the Bridge there whipped, thence to the middle of the High Street there whipped'. And so it went on. Again he was accompanied by the 'mad merchant' Rich and his singing. It appears, however, that his punishment in Bristol was delivered half-heartedly. The city's Bellman, when announcing Nayler's crimes, did so with modesty and the administering of the lashes themselves was obstructed by one of Nayler's followers to little objection from the man wielding the whip. He was returned to London, to an isolation cell in the City's less than salubrious Bridewell Prison.

When the Protector finally made his voice heard on the

Nayler affair, it was clear, despite his cautious tone, that he had been disappointed once again by his Parliament. Cromwell had backed its judgement, in public at least. Yet on 26 December a letter from 'His Highness' to the Speaker was read to MPs, revealing his unease at the process and seeking clarification. One can imagine the eyes of members darting suspiciously, sheepishly, accusingly at one another.

The letter, blunt in its criticism, called on the Commons to account for itself:

> Having taken notice of a judgment lately given by yourselves against one James Nayler... Although we detest and abhor the going or occasioning the least countenance to persons of such opinions or practices, or who are under the guilt of such crimes as are commonly imputed to the said person; yet we, being interested in the present government on behalf of the people of these nations, and not knowing how far such proceeding (wholly without us) may extend in the consequence of it, we desire that the House will let us know the grounds and reasons whereupon they have proceeded without our consent.

It was heard as a reprimand. The implication was clear: it must not happen again.

Downing defended the House. The Commons had 'inherited' the authority of the Lords and, after all, Nayler's punishment was merely corporal:

> The instrument of Government is but new and our jurisdiction is but new too. It is dangerous either for [Cromwell], or for us to question his; in matters that are for the public safety we must both wink. If we should enter upon such a moot point, I dread the consequences. What bred all the former differences, but points of jurisdiction?

But opinions remained divided. Francis Rous, MP and former provost of Eton was more critical of the House than Cromwell: 'Either you have done what you ought to have done, or you have not. If not, you must be whipped for whipping James Nayler.'[18]

Cromwell, remarkably and leaving no doubt of his sympathies, sought to lighten Nayler's suffering. On 20 February 1657, Nayler's neglected wife, Anne, petitioned Cromwell in person. The Protector, in response, enforced an order on the gaolers at Bridewell to stop any ill treatment of Nayler and to provide him with adequate food and drink. Cromwell's attitude is revealing: having allowed Nayler's punishment to take place, in the light of its brutal nature he now regretted having done so. Though the canary was back in the cage, Cromwell and his increasingly influential band of civilian advisers in Council and Parliament had taken notice of its song.

The Militia Bill

The quarrel is now between light and darkness.

JOHN LAMBERT

SINCE THE OPENING of the Second Protectorate Parliament in September 1656, when Cromwell had given the major generals what appeared to be his full and public backing, they had remained at Westminster, attending Parliament. It did them no good. Instead of securing their power and influence within their respective regions, furthering the cause of moral reformation, they wandered about Whitehall, where meandering thought won out over constructive action. Why they had abandoned their fiefdoms for Westminster is unclear. Was it Cromwell's decision? Was it theirs? While ugly, deep divisions had opened up among them in a very public way during the Nayler trial – with Skippon, Boteler, Goffe, Haynes and Whalley on one side and Bridge, Desborough, Kelsey and Packer on the other – they now gathered together one final time to overplay their hand.

On Christmas Day 1656 (incidentally, perhaps significantly, the same day that Cromwell wrote to the Speaker concerning the constitutional implications of the Nayler trial), a sparsely attended House was discussing the arcane matter of forest law. Despite the efforts of the regime to pour scorn on Yuletide revelry and pleasure, it seemed that MPs were as eager as ever to observe the 'superstitions' of Christmas, in line with most of the population. Those MPs who had trudged their way to Parliament noted how few shops and stalls were open and that the streets were eerily free of people. Most of the members in attendance were therefore, by definition, Puritans of the most fervid sort. 'I could get no rest all night for the preparation of this foolish day's solemnity,' complained one MP, fearing that such seasonal festivities were symptomatic of the lingering appeal of prelatism and popery.[1]

Major General Desborough sought to cement the hold of military rule when he stood up among the few MPs to introduce a bill that would establish decimation as a permanent levy in law, seeking the 'continuance of a tax upon some people for the maintenance of the militia'.[2] The sanction of Parliament was the best means of making decimation legitimate, though ironically, in the three months that the Second Protectorate Parliament had sat, not a single MP appears to have raised the issue. Desborough may have been encouraged to introduce the bill to the House by the positive response among some MPs to a petition presented on 23 December by Lord George Eure, the commissioner for Yorkshire and commander of its militias, signed by representatives of the county's godly community; the major generals, despite the setback of the parliamentary elections, had still not, it seems, learnt to be suspicious of such praise of their rule. But it is just as likely that the major generals and their supporters were alarmed by the groundswell of support among the civilian faction around Cromwell for a hereditary Protectorate, even a hereditary king. It was the 'distinguishing character', according to the Dorset MP Colonel Fitzjames, of those who would oppose the military faction in its pursuit of greater powers that they 'were for hereditary rank'. In order to secure decimation and the rule of the major generals, it was hoped that Desborough's 'short bill' might be passed before most MPs, including those of the civilian faction, returned to Parliament on Twelfth Night. Such cynical manipulation was noted by the Buckinghamshire Royalist William Denton, who wrote four days after the bill's introduction: 'Decimation had but a poor Christmas dinner, no sweet plum broth nor plum pie, for they chose that day to bring it in when *armiger* was in *patnis*.'*[3]

Even in the sparsely attended House, there was considerable opposition to the proposals of Desborough and his argument that Parliament must 'lay the saddle upon the right horse'. He pleaded that this was not simply a punitive act, but a means of reforming the Royalists, too, and that any 'that shall come in to a cheerful compliance with us' would be exempt. In a conciliatory tone, reminiscent of his role in the Nayler debates (though less sincere), Desborough argued that it was the Royalists' 'reformation, not their ruin that is desired'.[4]

The bill was seconded by the Yorkshire religious radical Luke Robinson. In a more honestly combative tone, he called for the House to unite against their enemies, who 'Grow fat and live at home; – we decrease, they increase'. It was them and us, he argued: 'If the power were in their hands, they would spare their friends and lay it upon us.'[5]

The major generals – Lambert, Sydenham, Strickland, Pickering, even secretary of state, Thurloe – offered a united front against opponents of their bill. The original bill – the Militia Bill, as it came to be known – was read and a second reading was approved for the following day by the small coterie of zealots assembled. Any optimism the major generals may have felt for their bill's prospects, however, was about to be disappointed.

* Meaning 'while the gentry are feasting'.

Opposition to the Militia Bill proved fierce: a Royalist rising was feared rather less, it appeared – and with good reason – than the permanence of the major generals. A decimation tax in perpetuity would mark a further violation of the Act of Oblivion, which was essential, it was widely agreed, to the healing and settling of the nation. William Lenthall, Master of the Rolls, argued that 'Never was an Act of Oblivion violated by a Parliament in any age of the world.' Thomas Bampfield saw the hand of Machiavelli on Desborough's shoulders, but saw even greater warning in a biblical precedent, found in the Old Testament books of Joshua and Samuel.[6]

Bampfield was referring to the Gibeonites, idolatrous rivals of the Israelites. Their story would have been a familiar one to MPs, who, like most of their educated contemporaries, shared a familiarity with scripture unimaginable today. Joshua, having become leader of the Israelites following the death of Moses, had been deceived into making a treaty with the rival Gibeonites. When the deception was discovered, Joshua was criticized fiercely by his people. However, the Israelites did not renege on the treaty:

> We have sworn unto them by the Lord God of Israel: now therefore we may not touch them. (Joshua 9:19)

Saul, Joshua's vengeful successor, ignored the promise and attacked Gibeon. As a consequence, Israel suffered famine for three years. Only when David executed seven of Saul's sons was fertility restored. Bampfield suggested to the House that this biblical passage had a clear 'parallel with the case of the Cavaliers'.

In response, Lambert painted a picture of Royalists 'merry over their Christmas pies', toasting the king, Charles Stuart, across the water. The Act of Oblivion, he said, was not just a law but a contract and Penruddock's Rising, among other examples real and rumoured, had shown that the royal party never had any intention of keeping its side of the bargain. Too many Royalists were ultimately irreconcilable – and not just the present generation. 'They are as careful to breed up their children in the memory of the quarrel', Lambert warned. Thomas Kelsey, in support, wondered why the House seemed more concerned for the welfare of its enemies than its godly friends.[7]

A vote on the second reading of the Militia Bill was taken in the half-empty House and was won by eighty-six to sixty-three, a narrow victory given the circumstances and one that prompted William Denton to comment optimistically that, when the House was full, 'much good may be hoped for'.

It was agreed that Desborough could introduce his bill, which he did on 7 January 1657, before a 'pretty full House'. This time it also contained a clause guaranteeing indemnity for the major generals and their local commissioners, though whose addition it was is unclear.

Opposition focused on two points. First, of course, the Act of Oblivion, which Bulstrode Whitelocke warned was fundamental and could not be rowed back on: 'If you shake that Act, you shake all foundations.' It was fundamental to the rule of law, which, in the light of the Nayler trial, had been shown to be vulnerable enough. Just as importantly, the threat to the Act had aroused Cromwell's ire.

Second, another opponent of the major generals, John Trevor, lamented the way in which the bill would further 'divide this commonwealth' and stressed the need to heal the nation's divisions: 'I am not ashamed to plead for my enemies', admitted Trevor, 'where justice and the faith of the nation plead for them. What do we by this but incorporate them against us, and put such a character of distinction upon them, that they will never be reconciled.' As had been seen in the Nayler case, the major generals, and the military interest in general, were keen to apply Old Testament, Mosaic justice, when it suited them. Trevor preferred to make a simple appeal to the more emollient values of the New Testament: 'To forgive our enemies is God's rule, and the only way to make them our friends.' Trevor also articulated a widespread sentiment, which had eluded the supporters of military rule: the hatred of locally raised militias and the very notion of the project of the major generals. This had, Trevor believed, 'A tendency to divide the commonwealth into provinces; a power too great to be bound within any law; in plain terms to cantonize our nation, and prostitute our laws and civil peace to a power that was never set up in any nation without dangerous consequences.'[8]

Events such as Penruddock's Rising had undoubtedly spread alarm. But it had also been clear that this and other conspiracies never stood the slightest chance of success. As the rising and its impact drifted out of popular memory, most people's concerns centred much more on the creeping militarization of the localities, a fact demonstrated all too eloquently in the elections of 1656.

A flustered Desborough insisted the major generals had no more power than the traditional lord lieutenants – an unconvincing assertion. He then stated, this time with rather more conviction, that theirs was a moral force as much, if not more, than it was a military one.

MPs listened with particular interest to the first contribution to the debate. It came from John Claypole, an MP of few interventions, but who spoke with considerable gravitas because he was the husband of Cromwell's daughter Elizabeth and, as his master of horse, was an intimate of the Protector. Many MPs assumed, therefore, that he spoke with his master's voice. Cromwell's oft-stated concern, he implied, was for the 'healing and settling' of the nation. And, already troubled by the Nayler affair, he thought the proposal unjust. According to Ludlow, who witnessed it, Claypole's speech was a 'clear direction to the sycophants of the court' to oppose the rule of the major generals.[9]

Even more significant was the intervention of Lord Broghill, the leader of the Irish interest in the House and most able and energetic of the group of civilians coalescing around Cromwell in opposition to the military. He, too, sought the 'healing and settling' of a nation tired of conflict and military rule: 'How is it possible that we should gain that party by punishment when we could not by grace? Surely this will harden them... do not make them a corporation, and make men of estates and no estates desperate.'

The debate was unlikely to reach a consensus. The government itself was split, as Desborough demonstrated when he came back at the civilian party with gusto. If anything, he said, he was too easy on the malignant party – 'I would have it higher' – and he appealed to the 'true old interest of the nation'. Lambert saw the nation's division in Manichean terms: 'The quarrel is now between light and darkness; not who shall rule, but whether we shall live or be preserved, or no.'[10]

Lambert appears to have realized that he was fighting for his political life and that of his comrades. His was the military response to a growing groundswell of support, cultivated by Broghill above all, for a hereditary Protectorate, for a reversion to the ancient constitution. Most revealing in this respect was the conversation recorded by Thomas Burton at the conclusion of the day's debates on 7 January 1657. Burton found 'Colonel FitzJames, and divers others... talking about the decimations' and FitzJames remarked that 'it was the distinguishing character of those that were against the [Militia] Bill, that they were for hereditary rank'. Amid an atmosphere of increasing rancour and division, the debate was adjourned when the Speaker of the House, Sir Thomas Widdrington, was taken ill the next day. The debate on the Militia Bill would not resume until 20 January. By then, the House had been informed of a new and alarming development, which was to transform the trajectory of the Protectorate.

13

Gunpowder, Treason and Plot

Two parties are in it, the old malignant,
and the levelling party.

JOHN THURLOE

JOHN THURLOE, Cromwell's secretary of state, rose to address Parliament on the evening of 19 January 1657, the day before the House was scheduled to resume its reading of the divisive and contentious Militia Bill, which would decide the continuity or not of the rule of the major generals. Before the debate could proceed, Thurloe brought news that would do much to focus the minds of those at the heart of the regime, whose survival depended largely, if not entirely, on the fate of a single man:

> I rise up to acquaint you with the discovery of a late heinous plot, which is in part discovered, and we are in pursuit of the rest. The place where that design was hatched is Flanders, a place fit for such designs of assassination, at the Spanish court there. Two parties are in it, the old malignant, and the levelling party. It is carried on by one Sexby there.[1]

The 'old malignant' was a reference to actively dissenting Royalists – as opposed to the more contrite 'delinquents' – in exile and at home. The 'levelling party' consisted of a few disenchanted republicans, who saw the Protectorate as a betrayal of ideals once thought to be shared. The most formidable and dangerous of them was the saturnine former Ironside, Edward Sexby. A loquacious opponent of Cromwell at the Putney Debates, now almost a decade past, he was in league with a 'considerable person of the late king's party' and another conspirator 'suspected to hold close correspondence with Charles Stuart'. Sexby had fled to Flanders in 1655, when the Penruddock Rising failed. There, he had met up with the gullible Count of Fuenseldaña, the commander of the Spanish army in Flanders, who invited him to an audience in Madrid. The Spanish court was unimpressed by Sexby's plans for insurrection, though it did offer him some financial backing. Both sides, at opposite ends of the political and religious spectrum, had united in the shadows to hatch plots to kill the Protector, believing that, with the head gone, the body politic, bound by Cromwell, would sicken and die.

Whitehall in the mid-seventeenth century was nothing like the wide, imposing 'High Street of Empire' constructed during Britain's imperial zenith of the nineteenth century, echoes of which resonate still on London's grandest avenue, with its recordings in stone of military achievement and sacrifice. In the 1650s it was a tight warren of noise and smoke. Those who could escape its clammy grasp, such as Lord Protector Cromwell, did so at every opportunity. Hampton Court was Cromwell's retreat of choice, the vast palace built by Thomas Wolsey on the airy banks of the Thames, far to the west of the cities of London and Westminster. Since its requisition by Henry VIII on the fall of his lord chancellor, it had remained a royal palace. It was one now, in all but name and, every Friday that he could,

Cromwell made his way there. Though the air was clean and its spaces open, Hampton Court could still be a place of danger. In the autumn of 1656 opponents planned Cromwell's death in the approach to the palace, the 'narrow, dirty passage', where 'coaches use to go but softly'. The assassins, armed with 'strange engines' each containing twelve bullets, intended to open fire on the Protector's coach and free England from tyranny. It was to be the first of a number of attempts on the Protector's life by this strange new alliance of Royalists, republicans and former Levellers. To unravel their conspiracies, we must return to the man who, in the opinion of C. H. Firth, the most incisive historian of the Protectorate, led the most 'remarkable career in the annals of the New Model Army'.

Edward Sexby, the son of a faded London gentleman with roots in the Puritan heartland of East Anglia, had joined Cromwell's regiment of Ironsides in 1643, where his radicalism soon became apparent: it has been suggested that the fiery Leveller tract *England's Miserie and Remedie* was his work. Certainly, as a trooper in Thomas Fairfax's regiment of horse, he gained a reputation as an uncompromising agitator, so much so that he was brought before the House of Commons in April 1647 to face accusations of writing and circulating *An Apologie of the Common Soldiers*, the first manifesto to be drawn up by representatives of the New Model Army's rank and file. Sexby gained some respect for his views among his more radical superiors and set up a printing press, which was rarely silent, with money given to him by sympathetic officers. Sexby played a part in Cornet George Joyce's seizure of Charles I at Holdenby House, Northamptonshire in 1647 and played a prominent role in the Putney Debates later that year.

In Putney's hothouse of political and theological inquiry, Sexby revealed himself to be a proponent of native rather than natural rights, preferring liberties rooted in history to those discovered in abstraction. In particular, he vigorously defended the rights of unpropertied soldiers, a view at odds with the army's more conservative leadership, and argued for a radical, egalitarian vision:

> We have engaged in this kingdom and ventured our lives, and it was all for this: to recover our birthrights and privileges as Englishmen... there are many thousands of us soldiers that have ventured our lives; we have had little propriety in the kingdom as to our estates, yet we have had a birthright. But it seems now, except a man hath a fixed estate in this kingdom, he hath no right in this kingdom. I wonder we were so much deceived.[2]

A fierce republican, Sexby had been vigorously opposed to negotiations with the king:

> The cause of our misery is upon two things. We sought to satisfy all men, and it was well; but in going about to do it we have dissatisfied all men. We have been by Providence put upon strange things... We have laboured to please a king, and I think, except we go about to cut all our throats, we shall not please him.

Sexby was comfortable with division; he prospered in it.[3]

Sexby became a leading light among the 'new agents', the cavalrymen who sought the kind of wide franchise that would not be realized in England until the first half of the twentieth century. That was 'the ground that we took up arms', he asserted, a claim that earned him a rebuke from Cromwell: 'I confess I was most dissatisfied with that I heard Mr Sexby speak, of any man here, because it did savour so much of will.'[4]

Sexby left the army following the mutiny at Ware in Hertford-shire in November 1647. Though a mere private, he maintained his contacts with both the army grandees and its radicals. Despite a growing reputation as a 'frantic anabaptist', Sexby avoided the imprisonment imposed on other radicals, such as the Leveller leader John Lilburne, who, broken in part by persistent persecution, would eventually embrace the increasingly gentler aspects of Quakerism.

Despite his well-earned reputation for radicalism, Sexby rejoined the army and was appointed governor of Portland Castle, a coastal fort on the south coast and therefore a significant strategic role, where he was ordered to monitor post from abroad. Promoted to colonel, he commanded a regiment originally bound for Ireland, which served with mixed results in Scotland. Ironically, given his appetite for egalitarianism, Sexby was cashiered for withholding pay from some of the soldiers stationed at Portland, though he was acquitted by the same court martial of illegally executing a soldier. Indeed, the army's secretary, William Clarke, thought the affair was a stitch-up, the work of 'a malicious crew of Levelling officers… which I know not how he raised up to pick as his own'.

Despite his public disgrace, a secret committee of the Council of State of which Cromwell was a member granted Sexby £1,000 to clear his debts and sent him to Bordeaux as an unofficial envoy to the Fronde des nobles, where he met the Prince de Conti, younger brother of the Prince de Condé. When their revolt was crushed by the Bourbons in August 1653, having alienated most of his French acquaintances, Sexby returned to England. No diplomat, Sexby went back to work for Thurloe, checking the spymaster's incoming post.

Cromwell's *coup d'état* of April 1653, as well as the Protectorate's quest for an alliance with Louis XIV, the nemesis of French Protestant aspiration, appears to have ended any hope Sexby had in the regime and from then on he sought the demise of Cromwell. In correspondence with his friend the perpetually scheming Leveller John Wildman, he compared Cromwell to

Nero and Caligula, an 'apostate surrounded by Janissaries'. He set himself the task of forging an alliance of Levellers and Royalists, backed by Spanish money. Sexby, more than anyone, would draw these disparate political traditions into one menacing conspiracy. 'I shall ruin him [Cromwell] from abroad in three or four years.'[5]

Sexby was not alone in feeling a sense of betrayal. In *A Politick Commentary*, fellow radical John Streater accused Cromwell of becoming a Julius Caesar: 'to be like Caesar is in effect to say they deserve to be killed by a Brutus, as he was'. A Royalist pamphlet, *An Admonition to My Lord Protector and His Council*, drew similar, threatening parallels.

Sexby fell into a shadowy world of international intrigue, of networks inhabited by spies and conspirators, with their bases in Paris and the cities of the Spanish Netherlands. He gained his interview with Count Fuensaldaña, the region's governor, from whom he sought military and financial assistance. Sexby's ultimate, and deeply naive, aim was to lead an invasion of England, oust the Cromwellian regime and restore Charles Stuart to the throne, having secured from him the liberties of all Englishmen. It was an unlikely scenario not only because Charles Stuart was hardly likely to agree to such restrictions on his restored rule. The plan could only work if a political vacuum was created: 'either I or Cromwell must perish'. The Treaty of Brussels, completed in April 1656, had agreed an offensive and defensive alliance between Charles Stuart and Philip IV of Spain. There was a vague blueprint to Charles's ambitions: for a Spanish army to invade, accompanied by internal insurrection; but it was all a pipe dream, as Edward Hyde, one of the clearer thinkers among the court in exile, knew only too well: 'If the king should land tomorrow... he will be overpowered as he was at Worcester, whilst all men sit still, and look for the effect of the first battle.' Insurrection, of a traditional form, remained out of the question.[6]

There was some Royalist support for such a plot at the margins, though few of the king's party trusted Sexby – perhaps unsurprisingly, given his past as a republican agitator. Sir Edward Nicholas was an exception in giving Sexby the benefit of the doubt: 'No man that should effect so glorious work can possibly fail of an ample reward on earth as well as in heaven.'[7]

Relations between Sexby and the Royalists were always awkward. Sexby's pathological hatred of the Cromwellian regime and of the Protector in particular, born of a deep sense of betrayal, was easily manipulated. Hyde encouraged Sexby's plans for assassination, but kept him away from any invasion blueprints. A born gambler, Sexby intended simply to take out the head and see what happened afterwards. Reckless and spiteful though this plan might have been, it stood a far greater chance of success than military invasion.

Wildman was of greater interest to the Royalists. He had been a signatory, in the summer of 1656, to the Leveller *Address to the King*, which offered terms to the Royalists, in the event of a successful insurrection, including religious toleration, the abolition of tithes, the restoration of the Long Parliament and confirmation of the Isle of Wight Treaty of 1648. The discussions seem to have come about through an intermediary, William Howard, younger son of Lord Howard of Escrick, who despite military service for Cromwell, was dismissed in 1656 and headed to Bruges, where he entered talks with Charles. Sexby had a plan, known also to Sir Robert Shirley, to bribe the governor of the Portsmouth garrison with Spanish money. At the sight of any breach between Parliament and the Protector, it was to declare for liberty and spark the tinder of insurrection. What the Royalist exiles did not know was that Wildman was yet another conspirator turned by Thurloe and he had revealed the Portsmouth plot to him. The invasion plan, always a long shot, was now an impossibility. Small scale acts of terror, with large-scale consequences, were the only options left. And Sexby had a plan.[8]

Sexby's reconnaissance had begun in the early summer of 1656. On his return to England he found a country in turmoil, riddled by uncertainties about its future. Republicans, appalled by Cromwell's increasingly regal manner, had all but ceased engagement with the regime. The army was at loggerheads with those moderates who sought a civilian settlement. The major generals had brought security to the regime, but at the cost of alienating a wide range of people who were otherwise happy to tolerate the regime and the security it offered. Cromwell appeared to be the only man holding things together. If he disappeared, so would the whole rotten edifice. But who was willing to take him out? Sexby found just such a man on his return to Flanders.

Assassination was more common than rebellion in early modern Europe, as some emissaries of the Cromwellian regime had already found to their cost.* Political murder was relatively cheap; it needed little manpower; and, if the target was big enough – and none was bigger than Cromwell – its consequences could be incalculable, especially as the problem of succession remained unresolved. If one took out the head, 'All things could come to a confusion; it being certain that the great ones would never agree who should succeed, but would fall together by the ears about it

---

* Isaac Dorislaus, a Dutch-born historian and lawyer who had made his home in England and played a minor role in the trial of Charles I, had been assassinated in The Hague while on diplomatic business for the newly established republic in 1649.

and then in that disorder the people would rise and things might be brought to a Commonwealth again.'

So said Miles Sindercombe, a barely less colourful figure than Sexby, a Kentish man who, before the Civil Wars, was apprenticed to a surgeon in the City of London. Beyond that, his early life is obscure, but it is known that he, too, became a quartermaster, in a regiment led by John Reynolds, who, like Sexby was one of the New Model Army's more prominent agitators. In May 1649, to quote Carlyle, 'daylight forsook him': he was involved in a mutiny, in which he may have played a leading role, and came to the attention of the official newspaper of the republic, *Mercurius Politicus*, which described him as 'one of the old levelling party'.[9]

Having escaped from the clutches of the military authorities, he took lodging with a hat-seller in the City of London before rejoining the army, this time in Matthew Tomlinson's regiment of horse, which served in Scotland. A born conspirator, Sindercombe took part in the Overton Plot of late 1654, which Sexby promoted. It sought to seize control of the army in Scotland from the moderate General George Monck, who was later to become a principal figure in the Restoration of Charles II. Monck dismissed Sindercombe, judging him 'a busy and suspicious person, and one who was forward to promote such ill designes'. Sindercombe fled to Flanders before the full extent of his role in the Overton Plot came to light and it was there that he came into contact with Sexby.

Both men were prepared to chance the return of monarchy, because of their optimistic reasoning that its restoration would be opposed and a new republic would emerge from its ashes. Sexby had access to money and weapons; Sindercombe a fervent desire to kill the Protector. They seemed a perfect match. Sindercombe's religious views, which may have informed his seeming fatalism, were those attributed to 'soul-sleepers', one of numerous tiny sects that blossomed in the mid-century turmoil, who believed that 'when a man dieth the soule sleepeth with the Body and it may be it shall rise again'. According to the heresiographer Ephraim Pagitt, writing in 1647, the belief of soul-sleepers that 'they should dyeth with the body is an old and despicable Heresy, raised in Arabia, about the time of Origen'. This heretic was more dangerous than most.

Sindercombe returned to England to gather around him a handful of oddballs, ne'er-do-wells and malcontents: they included John Cecil, a former soldier; William Boyes, supposedly a Royalist sympathizer, though a man who gathered serial identities; and John Toope, one of Cromwell's Life Guards. Toope was promised riches and power in a world without Cromwell, but he would soon develop grave misgivings about Sindercombe's project.

The plotters rented a house in King Street, Westminster, from where they planned to attack Cromwell's coach as it passed by en route to the opening of Parliament. The dwelling was soon found to be unsuitable, as it offered no obvious means of escape. Under the alias John Fish, Sindercombe rented another house closer to Westminster Abbey belonging to one Colonel Mydhope, which backed onto a yard overlooking the street and was judged handy for 'escaping the fact'. Cromwell was to be targeted as he made his way from the Abbey to the opening of the Second Protectorate Parliament on 17 September 1656. That day, Sindercombe, along with Boyes and Cecil, went into the yard carrying a viol case – shades of Al Capone – containing pistols 'charged with leaden bullets and slugs', and an arquebus, an early matchlock gun that rested on a tripod when being fired.

The scheme was swiftly abandoned, however, when Sindercombe lost his nerve, overwhelmed by the sheer presence of so many people.

The hapless plotters lost their nerve again when they shadowed Cromwell in Hyde Park, where, as an inveterate, albeit ailing, horseman, he frequently took the air. Cecil, also on horseback, latched on to the Protector's retinue, while Sindercombe kept watch on the fringes of the park. Cromwell, always a connoisseur in matters equestrian, rode up to Cecil to admire his mount. Fazed by the Protector's attentions, Cecil panicked, made his excuses and left. Not only had the would-be assassins failed in their attempt, they were now firmly in the sights of spymaster Thurloe's intelligence network.

Still the plotters were desperate to prove themselves to Sexby. If they couldn't murder the Protector in a face-to-face encounter, they would set fire to his seat of government, White-hall Palace, burning Cromwell and everyone within it. This, England's 'other' Gunpowder Plot, is far less well-known than Guy Fawkes's attempt to murder the Parliament of James I in 1605.*

Thurloe had received intelligence of the plot and revealed its unravelling to Parliament on 19 January 1657: 'Some great villainy was to be acted upon on the night of 8th January.' The plotters had cut a hole in a back door entry to the Commons chapel, below Cromwell's private apartments. There they had 'set a basket of wild-fire', of tar, pitch, tow and gunpowder, 'such wild stuff... fit almost to burn through stones'.

Toope, the Life Guard who remained loyal to Cromwell, had betrayed them to Thurloe. Even as they planted their device, the

---

* In 1654 the poet John Turner had warned that 'England alas almost hath quite forgot the great deliverance from The Powder-plot.'

plotters were being watched and, when they left, the 'fire-work' was made safe and Cecil was arrested some time between 11 p.m. and midnight. Sindercombe lost part of his nose trying to escape the guard sent to seize him, before being personally interrogated by Cromwell, just as Guy Fawkes had been by James I, though this time in the absence of torture. Sindercombe gave nothing away and Boyes escaped. Cecil confessed everything straight away, confirming all that Toope had revealed to the authorities about the support of the 'King of Spain' and funding from Flanders. It was not such a leap from Cromwell's warning before Parliament of the unholy trinity of conspirators: papists, Cavaliers and Levellers.

The formal legal process against Sindercombe began on Monday 9 February, presided over by the 'courtier judge' and lord chief justice, John Glynn and Justice Warburton. The indictment was served. Sindercombe, along with William Boyes and 'divers other Rebels and Trayters' had been 'moved and seduced by the Instigation of the Devill' and did 'conspire, compass and imagine' the death of Cromwell. Sindercombe was to be made an example of, a warning to all those seeking to take out the head of the regime. His was to be a grisly fate, 'condemned to be drawn at the horse's tail, hanged, drawn and quartered, the parts set up at the principal gates of London and the head on a tower in the middle of the bridge'.

Following his sentence, Sindercombe was taken back to the Tower, 'much enraged, and in a great passion', determined to escape the executioner. He asked his guard for poison, which was refused, and he made the same request to his sister, Elizabeth Herring. The lieutenant of the Tower, aware of his intentions, ordered extra security.

In the end, his body was dragged through the streets, but it was already lifeless. Sindercombe the 'chief delinquent', had gained a vial of poison on the eve of his execution, scheduled for 14 February. His guards noticed that he was 'snorting unusually' and called the 'chirurgeon', but two hours later the prisoner was dead. A coroner's inquest was held the following day. Sindercombe's skull was opened up and the two doctors reported that 'We found the brain much inflamed, red and distended with blood', the result of a 'very violent and preternatural cause'. On the eve of his intended execution, he had received three female visitors, his two sisters in the company of 'his sweetheart'. The verdict: that Sindercombe 'feloniously did snuff and draw' poison.

On 15 February, a suicide note was found, or so it was claimed, and published next day in the *Publick Intelligencer*: 'God knoweth my heart, I do take this course', Sindercombe is supposed to have written, 'because I would not have all the open shame of the world executed upon my Body: I desire all good people not so to judge amiss of me; for I do not fear my life, but do trust God with my soul.'

Cromwell, outwardly trusting to providence, had affected a public nonchalance towards the conspiracy, referring to 'fiddling little things... which I would not remember as at all considerable to myself or to you'. Others, such as William Strickland, possibly with an eye on favour and good fortune, appealed for a day of thanksgiving for the sparing of the Protector's life: 'We are obliged to give thanks to God for this and all other deliverances, without whose providence a hair cannot fall from our heads.' Thurloe was voted the thanks of the House of Commons for 'tracing out a plot', a rare moment of public recognition.[10]

For all his providential reasoning, Cromwell did not reassure minds as he once did. The thread of providence had been mislaid, if not lost entirely. The catastrophe of the Western Design, the opposition to the major generals, the iniquities and divisions of the Nayler trial: all spoke of a withdrawal of God's grace. The regime was one death away from disaster, to which the ailing body of the Protector and the threats to his person drew attention every day. The Sindercombe Plot had focused minds yet again: the regime was horribly exposed, dependent on one person. Who would succeed Cromwell when the day came, and by what process? Hereditary or elective? Protector or king?

As news of the Sindercombe affair spread, on 23 January the Commons held a thanksgiving service for the deliverance of the Protector. The Speaker, Thomas Widdrington, reminded the members that 'the Devil… will not let his emissaries be idle, but be always contriving'. The Protector, the regime and its continuity remained in grave danger. The succession had to be settled. Following a vote in Parliament on 19 January, a committee was appointed to prepare a 'Narrative of the Grounds and Reasons for setting apart for Friday Three Weeks a Day for public Thanksgiving'. Its report, anxious in tone, was published on 2 February:

> A sort of discontent spirits, called Levellers, plotting to disturb our peace… have so far degenerated, as to associate themselves with the inveterate enemies of the English nation and Protestant religion, those of Spain; and for malice and hire, to submit themselves to be executioners of their barbarous designs, and against their native country… one Boyes (a principal actor in those designs) did assure them, that when the protector was dispatched, forces were to come from Flanders, in ships to be hired with the king of Spain's money.

Here was the regime's narrative to unite a nation: political and religious extremists, backed by sinister foreign powers, were in league with the vanquished Royalists. The Sindercombe revelations played out against a background of rumour and conspiracy, encouraged by Thurloe and Needham in the pages of *Mercurius Politicus* and the *Publick Intelligencer*.

In the aftermath of the events of 8 January, a shaken regime gave thought to how best to respond, and how to ensure its future security. The day before the trial of Sindercombe, on 3 February, the Irish MP Vincent Gookin, a close ally of the increasingly prominent Broghill, had written to Thurloe about the attraction of 'reducing of the government to kingship, to which His Highness is not averse'. Circumstances might 'ripen towards a perfect settlement'.

The following day, as Sindercombe was hauled before the authorities, *Mercurius Politicus* entered what was fast becoming a pressing constitutional debate: 'Charles Stuart will hardly be able to effect anything upon England, so long as his highness is alive.' There was a desperate need to ensure 'the preservation of his highness' person, and to come to such a settlement as may secure him and us'.[11]

14

Cromwell and the Crown

*Your father hath of late made more wise
men fooles than ever.*

SIR FRANCIS RUSSELL

O N 19 JANUARY, as soon as the Sindercombe Plot had
been revealed, Parliament embarked on a discussion of two
matters of great urgency: security and succession. First of the
members to speak was the moderate Presbyterian John Ashe,
who proposed 'that his Highness would be pleased to take upon
him the government according to the ancient constitution... an
old and sure foundation'.[1] Such a settlement would, he claimed,
'tend very much to the preservation of himself [Cromwell]
and us and to the quieting of all the designs of our enemies'.
George Downing, an ally of Broghill and very much a Court
man, reminded his fellow members of the Elizabethan peril, for
'men go away' – even Cromwell – 'but constitutions never fall'.
The issue of kingship had been broached, albeit allusively, even
cryptically. Ashe and Downing had set something astir, which
demanded a full and serious debate, according to Thomas
Wroth, MP for Bridgwater. But could Cromwell, as the religious radical Samuel Highland asked, 'beget a fit governor?' His
son Henry Cromwell, perhaps, who had showed his mettle and

political maturity in Ireland. Richard, his older brother, perhaps less so.

The major generals, wedded as they were to Lambert's Instrument of Government, responded immediately to Ashe's motion, claiming that such constitutional reform would be no more than a 'slender prop', though one newsletter, which supported the military line, reported that 'a kingly and hereditary government' was the logical outcome of Ashe's proposition. Desborough asked the House to adjourn until the following day, and then 'take up the debate upon the [Militia] Bill before you'.

In a rare moment of harmony, those around Broghill assented, believing they could take the military men on in argument. Gookin, his fellow Irish MP, argued on 27 January that, if the Militia Bill was passed, 'his highness' government will be more founded in force, and more removed from the natural foundation, which the people in parliament are desirous to give him'. Gookin was convinced that the debates around the Militia Bill were crucial to the future of the regime; the continuation of the major generals' rule would ensure that the military Cromwellians would retain election to choose his successor, which owed much to Venetian practice, outlined in the Instrument: 'if any others have pretensions to succeed him by their interest in the army', then 'the more of force upholds his highness living, the greater when he is dead will be the hopes and advantages for such a one to effect his aim, who desires to succeed him'. They must not get the chance.[2]

The Militia Bill was rejected for good on 29 January by a vote of 124 to 88. According to Thurloe, who had been ambiguous about the bill initially, the major generals did 'think themselves much trampled upon by this vote, and are extremely sensible thereof'. The debate over the bill had 'wrought such a heat in the house' that Thurloe feared 'little will be done for the future', while two MPs, including the Protector's second cousin, Henry Cromwell, were censured by the Speaker for derogatory remarks about the major generals. The military scheme for settlement and succession had been defeated. The gruff insolence of the major generals and their absence from their localities had not helped their cause. Public relations was not one of their strong points. Their low-born status had been held against them, together with their lack of regard for local custom and the fabric of the communities they ruled. The diarist Thomas Burton recorded conversations around Westminster between the debates for the Militia Bill held in January 1657, in which MPs scorned the likes of John Barkstead, who had risen through deed and talent from thimble-maker to figure of authority. Similar aspersions were cast upon Kelsey and Bridge. Thomas Wolsey and Thomas Cromwell, their Tudor forebears, similarly men of 'mean extraction', who ascended the greasy pole through talent alone, had faced similar hostility – and worse fates – a century before.

Especial venom was aimed at William Boteler, major general for Bedfordshire, Huntingdonshire, Northamptonshire and Rutland, whose 'crimes are generally all over Northamptonshire cried out against'. His imprisonment of the Earl of Northampton in 1655 had earned him lasting notoriety, not least because it was done in the face of protests by both the Protector and his Council. Fiery and incorrigible, Boteler had argued in the House that *all* Royalists should pay the price for the actions of a few, which raised the ire of Henry Cromwell, who declared that 'by the same argument... because some of the major-generals have done ill, which I offer to prove, therefore all of them deserve to be punished'. Keeping company with Boteler as a target of public antipathy was Major-General Pride, whose remit included Southwark, on the south bank of the Thames, opposite the City of London, notorious for its brothels and places of entertainment. It was later claimed, by the historian Thomas Babington Macaulay, that Pride, one of the regime's natural enforcers, prohibited bear-baiting, long a Southwark fixture, 'not because it gave pain to the bears, but because it gave pleasure to the spectators'.

Boteler, however, along with the other major generals, had been convinced that he had the support of the Protector. On 9 January he had written a letter to Edward Montagu which detailed a reassuring meeting that Boteler and his colleagues had with the Protector, their former comrade in arms. The moderate Broghill had also been approached by Cromwell towards the end of January, but only to be asked why he had voted against the Militia Bill. Broghill, now a pivotal figure, was blunt in his reply: the Militia Bill, he argued, 'would have made three kingdoms rise against you; and they were your enemies not your friends who brought it in'.

There can be little doubt that the defeat of the bill came as a surprise to Cromwell. Had he been fed misinformation by the major generals who introduced it? Was this an example of their poor judgement, their inability to read the country? Or had Cromwell, having already decided that the experiment was over, been canny enough to offer his major generals enough rope with which to hang themselves? That possibility is hinted at in a letter written by Sir Francis Russell to the Protector's son Henry Cromwell (Russell's son-in-law), dated 29 January: 'Your father hath of late made more wise men fooles than ever; he laughs and is merry, but they hange down their heads and are pitifully out of countenance.' Wittingly or unwittingly, Cromwell had failed to back his major generals. Their opportunistic introduction of the Militia Bill on that fateful Christmas Day had proved the beginning of their end. The rule of the major generals had become the domestic equivalent of the Western Design: it was casually hubristic in its intentions and was ill-thought through. Desborough, a gifted soldier but politically flawed, was central to both schemes. The assumption behind both the Western Design and the Rule of the Major Generals appeared to have been that God would ensure their success. And when he did not? There was nothing to do but repent and turn inward.[3]

The introduction of the Militia Bill had exposed a chasm between the regime's more fanatically Puritan adherents who sought wholesale godly reformation, grounded in necessity rather than law, and the civilian interest, echoing the will of the wider nation, who preferred some kind of moderate long-term settlement within the traditional parameters of hierarchy and the ancient constitution. It was not a struggle the unpopular major generals had ever been likely to win. And yet, had Desborough not raised the issue of the decimation tax in Parliament, it might well have remained in place as a continuing means of both raising money and punishing Royalists, implemented in perpetuity by the major generals and their successors. As Cromwell was later to point out to them: 'You might have gone on. Who bid you go to the House with a bill, and there receive a foil?'[4]

The day after the Militia Bill was thrown out, 30 January, an elated, grateful Parliament, which Cromwell had allowed to stick around longer than many expected, voted to supply the government with £400,000, raised from general taxation, a remarkably constructive and bountiful action. The Second Protectorate Parliament had been called into being in autumn 1656 as an extraordinary parliament tasked with meeting the pressing financial demands of the war with Spain. Like Barebones, the Protector was entitled to dissolve it after three months – in December 1656 – which many feared he would. The day of the expected dissolution arrived while the Nayler trial was at its height; a dissatisfied Cromwell could pull the plug. Burton wrote on 9 November that the Commons 'sat till almost nine' debating the Nayler case, 'it being the last night of the natural life of this Parliament'. But the Protector allowed it to continue.

The Venetian ambassador Giavarina believed that, having been summoned to raise money for war with Spain, the Parliament's end would 'undoubtedly follow as soon as supplies have been secured'.[5] Yet, even when supplies were voted, the guillotine did not come down. Even though the government's agenda – as set out in the opening speech and reinforced in the wake of Sindercombe's plot in January 1657 – had been fulfilled, the Parliament was allowed to continue. The military plans for settlement and succession had been defeated, but the civilian Cromwellians had not yet presented their alternative. What constitutional package they came up with would depend on the reaction of its intended beneficiary: ideas would be paraded gently before the Protector, as signs of his assent were sought.

The security of the regime and – just as importantly – its continuity, could no longer be left to the whims of a providential God alone. Increasingly, a number of leading figures in the government wished for Cromwell to settle on the title of king, preferably in its hereditary form, a word of permanence and legal standing in contrast to 'Protector', with its whiff of the provisional, of a caretaker. Cromwell, however, had displayed little concern for titles: 'Signification goes to the thing… not the name,' he had confidently told his First Protectorate Parliament as far back as 1654.

By the time of the Second Protectorate Parliament, things had changed. Cromwell was older, weaker, his body ravaged by his years of military service and the pressures of governance, both within and above the fray. The security of the regime was in the balance, and the future fortunes of those closest to it in peril. On one side of government stood a group of 'civilians', most of them lawyers, who sought a constitutional solution to issues of security and succession; on the other were the military men, the old comrades of Cromwell, headed by Lambert. The Militia Bill had represented the military's response to the growing groundswell of support for a hereditary Protectorate. Its defeat had placed the civilians firmly in the ascendant.

Article 32 of Lambert's Instrument of Government had defined the office of Lord Protector as 'elective and not hereditary'; the concept of hereditary kingship was as alien to Lambert as it was to Cromwell. Under the Instrument, the election of Cromwell's successor was the responsibility of the Council, though, in a systemic weakness, the choice of successor was to be made *after* the Protector's death, not before; a recipe for instability, uncertainty and conflict, which the regime could ill afford. After all, as Cromwell had warned at the opening of his Second Parliament, fragility and insecurity was the 'state wherein we have stood' for too long. While the First Parliament had agreed on the election of Cromwell's successor, the Second, amid growing concerns, began to think that hereditary succession was a safer option, establishing a clearer, more secure line of succession. With the claim of Charles Stuart now removed in law and in perpetuity, was it now time to secure the claims of the Cromwells?

The settlement as maintained by the Instrument – 'the safety of it' – had first been questioned publicly on 28 October 1656, when a motion was proffered by 'an Irish gentleman' – almost certainly William Jephson, MP for Cork and Youghal, who was close to Broghill – 'to take into consideration the 31st [actually the 32nd] article of the government'. On 7 November, Giavarina recorded that Parliament again discussed the position of a hereditary protector – and that Cromwell resisted the proposals. A week later, Parliament sent a 'special deputation' to Cromwell, once again to persuade him of the hereditary principle. They, too, were rebuffed when, in an 'eloquent speech', the Protector set out the reasons which 'impel him to refuse'.

Bordeaux, the French ambassador, reported on 14 November that MPs 'made another proposal in parliament in favour of succession of the Protector [not a king, note], but the officers [the major generals] seemed as hostile as before'. The campaign by Broghill and his allies to 'settle upon the olde bottom' – the ancient constitution of king, Lords and Commons – was proving a rather exhausting experience. 'The nights are very long at Corke House', Colonel Bridges observed. In the same letter, addressed to Henry Cromwell and dated 25 November 1656, a month before the Militia Bill was introduced, Bridges revealed that he had been in a quarrel in the Speaker's chamber with Major General Berry, during which Desborough intervened. He asked Bridges to put his 'scattered notions into writing, and he would answer them'. Bridges took up the challenge and met Desborough 'in the tobacco room', where he 'offered him the grounds of my dissent'. His arguments for hereditary succession, which even Desborough admitted were 'not easily answered', put great stress on the issue of security – especially in the period following the Protector's death. If the elective form of succession embodied in the Instrument continued, Bridges believed, 'every man in the nation hath a like right to the government by the death of the Lord Protector' and therefore 'upon every change there will be a competition'. Such an election would breed insecurity, instability and resentment, with competitors coming 'to blows'. Those who were perplexed by such a situation would be tempted to look towards the Stuarts for stability. 'What can be the result', asked Bridges, other than to 'settle upon the olde bottom'? Why create an unsatisfactory Elizabethan succession crisis when one had the option of hereditary successors to the protectorship in the shape of Cromwell's sons?[6]

The divisions within the regime, apparent in such debates, had been noted by Royalist agents. From his base in Antwerp, Silius Titus wrote to Edward Hyde in December 1656: 'There are great disputes about the Government, whether it shall be successive or elective, the soldiery part of the house are for the latter, the Court partie (as they distinguish them) for the former.'[7]

The Commons met Cromwell in the Painted Chamber of Westminster on 27 November 1656, where they received the Protector's assent for the Treason Acts. Inevitably, having done so, according to Giavarina, 'some of the most devoted members tried to raise the question of the succession'.[8] Cromwell raised his hand and 'compelled them to go no further'. It was then that a new distraction had come upon the scene in the form of the Nayler trial, which, although it interrupted the advance of the succession debate, was to profoundly shape the Protector's attitude towards the creation of a second chamber, a successor to the House of Lords, to hold the Commons in check.

Giavarina, writing on Boxing Day 1656, the day after the Militia Bill had been introduced, suggested that 'parliamentarians may have cooled and changed their minds about making the Protector's office hereditary in his family, seeing how silent they have been about it all this time'. But, once the trial and punishment of Nayler had taken place and the Sindercombe Plot had been negotiated, the debate that was crucial to the future fortunes of the regime arose again.

15

A Feather in a Cap

They speak as if it were decided.

VENETIAN AMBASSADOR GIAVARINA

A DAY OF Thanksgiving for Cromwell's deliverance from the Sindercombe Plot, 'appointed for our fasting and praying together', was planned for 20 February. It was widely rumoured that, at the feast hosted by the Protector in the evening – 'the rarest entertainment ever seen in England' – he would 'be presented with the crown'; what better moment to focus minds, not least that of the Protector, on the insecurities thrown up by an uncertain succession? The urgency to settle the succession had been publicly acknowledged since Ashe's proposal before Parliament more than a month before. The civilians were convinced of the need for hereditary government, whether by a Protector or a king, as Cromwell himself suspected. Henry Cromwell, in a letter to Broghill written at the end of January, argued that his father's safety and that of the regime was imperilled 'unless he follow some such advice as your lordship gave him' – presumably to accept an hereditary title. The 'designs of the major generals' were, thought Henry, 'visibly dangerous' and he was, as a letter from son to father that found its way into the hands of Thurloe demonstrates, confiding his thoughts to the Protector.[1]

It was not just Cromwell's son who was urging constitutional change. Men such as Broghill, St John, Whitelocke and the ubiquitous Thurloe attended meetings in Whitehall in which the Protector would listen to their arguments as they sought to tie him down to the ancient office of monarch and restrict his personal rule to explicit English law, refined over centuries: kingship was known to the law. Were the old title placed upon Cromwell's head, they urged, the people would 'know your duty to them, and they their duty to you'. The argument made by eminent legal minds such as Whitelocke, the lord commissioner of the Treasury, Glynne, the lord chief justice, and Lenthall, the master of the rolls, was simple, effective and understood by all.

It was supported, too, by the 'lukewarm' majority of MPs, who had been alienated by the millenarian beliefs tolerated by Cromwell during the time of the Barebones Parliament in particular, who mistrusted his close relationship with the army and loathed the rule of the major generals. They were more comfortable with the Cromwell who passed off military rule as 'a story of my own weakness and folly... done in my simplicity', and who espoused his sincere belief in the natural hierarchy, 'the ranks and orders of men, whereby England hath been known for hundreds of years: a nobleman, a gentleman, a yeoman'. And, traditionally, at the top of that hierarchy, easily imagined by the gentleman of the shires, was a king. 'The law knowing this, the people can know it also, and the people do love what they know.'[2]

Even the government mouthpiece, *Mercurius Politicus*, on 4 February, agreed that the political nation needed to arrive at 'such a settlement as may secure him and us, and after him'. The insecurity of the regime was only highlighted by constant reports of Charles Stuart's invasion plans, believed to be reaching fruition in the spring of 1657. On 26 February, Cromwell sent 'cautionary letters' to his militias warning them of such prospects. Thurloe only partially succeeded in quelling anxiety at this worrying news, which was likely to strengthen the defeated military faction's anger at the prospect of constitutional change in such troubled times.

According to Giavarina, writing on 9 March, the matter of the monarchy had been 'brought up again' in Parliament 'some days ago and they speak as if it was decided'. The new Parliamentary constitution, replacing the Instrument of Government, was to be a hereditary one, so it was said, symbolic confirmation of the victory of the civilian faction over the interests of the major generals.[3]

It was not usually during banquets such as the Protector's deliverance feast on 20 February, however, that critical decisions were made. They were more likely to be decided 'after Dinner', when, as he had done so many times before, Cromwell loosened up and invited councillors and those MPs to whom he was closest to join him at 'the Cockpit', to set out his political agenda amid 'rare Musick, both of Instruments and Voyces'.

No offer of the crown, however, was forthcoming on the evening of 20 February. It became apparent that the much anticipated draft of a new civilian constitution, rooted in tradition, was to be presented on Monday 23 February, along with a proposal for an upper chamber – the 'Other House' – though not hereditary principle. Just four days later, at an assembly of 100 or so officers petitioning against the title of king, Cromwell was to address in explicit terms the inadequacies of the current settlement and the lack of an Other House – a 'balancing power'. He placated the officers' concerns about the apparent revival of what they might interpret as a new House of Lords, at the same time as shocking them with an assault on those army grandees, such as Lambert, who were also present: 'By the proceedings of the Parliament, you see they stand in need of a check or balancing power, for the case of James Nayler might happen to be your case.' He asked a rhetorical question of them: 'By their judicial power they fall upon life and member, and doth the Instrument enable me to control it?' The title of 'King', in comparison, was a mere 'feather in a cap', he told them, while reminding them, to the shock of some of those present, that the original draft of the Instrument had offered him just that title! He never was much for kingship, Cromwell reassured them, as the 'kinglings', those who sought to offer him the crown, were about to discover. It was, however, 'time to come to a settlement and lay aside arbitrary proceedings, so unacceptable to the nation'.[4]

The Cromwellian loyalist MP Sir Christopher Packe presented a paper – the Remonstrance – before Parliament on 23 February 1657. The paper had, he declared, 'somewhat come to hand'. He claimed that it might offer a path to the 'settlement of the nation, and of liberty, and of prosperity'. Its casual introduction masked its deliberate creation, for it was the work of the group of predominantly Irish and Scottish MPs of Broghill's circle and their English allies, such as Sir Charles Wolseley, who had introduced the Treason Act renouncing the 'pretended title of Charles Stuart'.

Since 1649 Cromwell had been utterly consistent in his opposition to the hereditary principle, and not even the eloquence of the civilian faction could convince him of its worth; a point he had probably made plain at the gathering at the 'Cockpit' three days before. Realizing this, and in some haste, the Remonstrance had to be rewritten to take this into account for its presentation on 23 February. The version presented by Packe on that day, therefore, had no hereditary clause.

Rather, 'for the preventing such confusions and inconveniences that otherwise may ensure upon your death', Cromwell was required to: 'appoint & Declare who shall immediately after your death succeed you in the Government of these Nations'.[5] The wording was dangerously vague. Because there was no formal mechanism to ensure that such a nomination took place, the chances of Cromwell dying suddenly without a designated successor remained high. The bill met immediate, and predictable, opposition from the usual suspects of the military persuasion: Lambert, Fleetwood, Desborough. A vote of 144 to 54 enabled the Remonstrance to pass to a second reading. That the amended Remonstrance was hardly different from the Instrument may have placated the defeated military faction a little.

The first clause of what was now described as the Humble Petition and Advice, which sought to establish that Cromwell and the heads of state who succeeded him would bear the title of king, was passed by 123 votes to 62 on 25 March, and Cromwell received the entire draft on the last day of the month. At this point the Protector requested time 'to ask counsel of God and of my own heart'. On 3 April 1657, Cromwell told MPs that the Humble Petition and Advice was an answer to the 'two greatest concernments that God has in the world':

> The one is that of religion and the preservation of the professors thereof, to give them all due and just liberty, and to assert the truths of God, which you have done in part in this paper, and referred to be done more fully by yourselves and me hereafter... The other thing cared for is the civil liberties and interests of the nations, which although it be, and indeed ought to be subordinate to a more peculiar interest of God, yet it is the next best God hath given men in the world, and better than any words, if well cared for, to fence the people of God in their interest.[6]

On the matter of his bearing the title of king, however, Cromwell had this to say: 'you have named me by another title I now bear', and he was unable 'to find it my duty to God and to you to undertake this charge under the title'.

He had acknowledged Parliament's importance to him:

> If the wisdom of this parliament should have found a way to settle the interests of this nation, upon the foundations of justice and truth and liberty to the people of God, and concernments of men as Englishmen, I would have lain at their feet, or at anybody else's feet, that this might have run at such a current.

But he did not believe, he told them, that he could accept the title of king.

The logic of the civilians who had made the offer was grounded in the Ancient Constitution. An hereditary king was best, an hereditary Protector next best, but a non-hereditary, elected king was better than a non-hereditary Protector. For the title of king had a legal necessity. But when the crown was offered to Cromwell, he made it clear he would not become Oliver I. God had willed the end of kingship on a freezing January morning in 1649. Cromwell had his prize, the Other House, a constitutional corrective to the deep concerns the Nayler trial had aroused in him. This man, so routinely ambiguous and evasive, really had meant it when he told those officers in late January that the crown was a mere 'feather in a man's cap'.

On 13 April Cromwell made clear his reasons for rejecting the crown in explicitly providential terms:

> Truly the providence of God has laid this title aside providentially... God has seemed providentially not only to strike at the family but at the name ... God... hath blasted the title... I would not seek to set up that that providence hath destroyed and laid in the dust, and I would not build Jericho again.[7]

Parliament backed down. The reaction of Thomas Cooper MP is revealing and, perhaps, typical:

> Having according to what light and understanding I have received from the Lord, discharged my conscience, I can and do freely acquiesce in the will of God; and though this matter, so long as it was in debate, was against my mind, yet being now concluded by the major part, I can and shall through the assistance of God, I hope, approve myself with as much faith-fullness to it, as if I had been never so much for the thing in the first promoting of it: and this I do not upon a politic but Christian account, well knowing that if a hair of a man's head fall not to the ground without the Lord's providence, much less do so great things as the governments of the world suffer alteration without special providence.[8]

More than two weeks after Cromwell's refusal of the crown, an amended Humble Petition and Advice was ratified by Parliament – with Cromwell's approval – which retained the station of Lord Protector, but would contain no hereditary clause; Cromwell would nominate his successor, though no formal process or timeline for doing so was outlined. The succession remained as fragile as ever.

There was dissent, from the highest quarters. Cromwell had won: the final outcome was his victory and his alone. His power revealed the weakness of the regime, its lack of settlement and security, its unsatisfactory succession. Lambert, the architect of the Instrument, who was the loser in all this, refused to swear allegiance to the new constitution when, on 24 June 1657, Parliament imposed an oath on all councillors. Lambert refused to attend meetings of the Council and Cromwell summoned him on 23 July and asked him to resign his commands, which Lambert did. To pour salve on their wounded relationship,

Cromwell allowed Lambert an annual pension of £2,000. Once the heir to Cromwell, Lambert was now an outcast, a status confirmed by the adoption of the Humble Petition and Advice by men who would, he believed, fail to act in the army's interest.

Thomas Hobbes, long after the event, offered an incisive reading of the deteriorating relationship between the Protector and his once uncontested heir: 'Lambert, a great favourite of the army, endeavoured to save him [Nayler], partly because he had been his soldier, and partly to curry favours with the sectaries of the army, for he was now no more in the Protector's favour, but meditating how he might succeed him in his power.' Such ambition remained.[9]

The inner circle at the heart of the regime was fractured and would be beyond healing if Cromwell were to become king. The godly and the army would have felt a profound sense of betrayal. Yet Cromwell had been a ruthless commander when called upon, a suppressor of mutinies who was more than willing to confront dissent, even from senior officers, including the ostracised Lambert.

And what did the Humble Petition and Advice consist of? The government remained that of a Protector and Parliament, which was obliged to meet at least once every three years. The control of the army was still shared between the Protector and his Council. There were more restrictions of religious liberty than the Instrument provided for: the civilian circle around Broghill would be closer to achieving their more restricted form of religious liberty. Quakers and other anti-Trinitarians could be proscribed, though there was a clause that allowed for a Confession of Faith according to the 'rule and warrant of the Scripture', which, to Cromwell's delight, offered 'all due and just liberty' to God's chosen people – though no more. It was not to be imposed, though it was an offence to criticize it in 'opprobrious words and writing'.[10] What was most attractive to Cromwell, especially in the light of the Nayler trial, was the proposal for a second chamber, called, rather prosaically, the 'Other House', which would protect against the erosions of liberty threatened during the Nayler trial and serve the 'honest interest'.

The Humble Petition and Advice provided, said Cromwell on 8 May 1657, 'for the safety and security of honest men, in that great, natural, and religious liberty, which is liberty of conscience. These are the great fundamentals.' But the greatest fundamental of any government is the defence of the realm and the security of its continuity. In that, the regime was found to be lacking.

16

Dancing and Dissent

A pattern of virtue, and a precedent of glory!

ROBERT RICH

THERE WAS an air of exhaustion around Britain's head of state, and the Protectorate continued to be plagued by debt. Although the Humble Petition and Advice guaranteed an annual income of £1.3 million, that was still around half a million pounds short of what was needed to continue the war with Spain and maintain the army and navy at its present size. Far more a man of God than of money, Cromwell remained at arm's length from Mammon: he confessed that he had 'as little skill in Arithmetic as I have in the law'. The sums were unlikely to get any better, even though the political temperature had lowered.

In November 1657, the French ambassador noted a 'different spirit' in Whitehall and at Hampton Court, at the weddings of Cromwell's youngest daughters, 'dances having been held there again during these past days, and the preachers of the older times are withdrawing from it'.

At the wedding of Mary Cromwell to Viscount Fauconberg on 19 November 1657, a musical dialogue was performed, with words by Andrew Marvell sung by a choir of men and boys.

It marked 'the revival, albeit in shadowy form, of those magnificent masques which had helped to make the courts of the first two Stuarts among the most extravagant in Europe'. Marvell's pastoral dialogue, performed just eight days after the wedding of Mary's younger sister Frances to Robert Rich, deployed classical parallels to suitably flattering effect vis-à-vis the Protector and his two newly married daughters.*

The story of music during the Protectorate is a complex one. The Westminster Assembly's shorter catechism of 1647 condemned 'lascivious songs, books, pictures, dancings and stageplays'. Lascivious anything was out (beyond the confines of Cromwell's private chambers); dancing, at least of the courtly, decorous kind, was a matter 'indifferent'; and stage plays were regarded as abominations by some, although attitudes towards the theatre softened during the Protectorate. The impresario Sir William Davenant played a role in this more emollient approach; getting around the ban on spoken theatre,[†] he commissioned five composers, including Matthew Locke and Henry Lawes, to provide music for his libretto to *The Siege of Rhodes*. Premiered in 1656, it is generally considered to be the first English opera.[‡] Edward Leigh, in *A Treatise of Religion*, published the same year, insisted that England was 'celebrated abroad as the ringing island'. During the Commonwealth, the emphasis on explicit worship had meant that polyphony, with its melange of complicated vocal lines, was looked down upon as popish

---

* Cromwell, the sole male among seven sisters, was described as 'naturally compassionate' to an 'effeminate measure' by his household steward John Maidstone.
† Theatres were closed as a wartime emergency measure in 1642, a ban that continued into the 1650s.
‡ Samuel Pepys attended its first performance. There is no evidence of Cromwell's attendance.

obfuscation of Christian comprehension. Simplicity and clarity of understanding was all. Things became more relaxed as the Protectorate proceeded, reflecting in part a more monarchical style. The third of September 1656, the day of thanksgiving, marking Cromwell's great victories at Dunbar and Worcester, was celebrated with an anthem by his master of music, John Hingston, a setting of works by the court poet Payne Fisher, with six singers and six instrumentalists.

Cromwell himself was clearly a lover of music. The Royalist Antony Wood reported that Cromwell especially enjoyed works by Hingston, who had trained two boys to accompany him in 'Mr Deering's printed Latin songs for three voices'. Chamber music was popular, usually in the form of a consort of viols, always a sociable form of conversational music making, with its inwardly circular arrangement of players, though a new instrument from the Continent, the violin, also made appearances. Wind bands were accompanied by organs, including one removed from Magdalen College, Oxford, to Hampton Court, where Cromwell employed a Mr Farmulo as his own 'virginal musician'. A Scottish politician visiting Hampton Court reported that he arrived 'just while my lord and lady was at their music'.

Some of those who had once been most committed to the regime struggled to make sense of its new face. John Owen, the leading Congregationalist minister, who had preached a sermon to MPs on the day following the execution of Charles I, was perplexed by the turn of events: 'Would anyone have thought it possible that such and such professors, in our days, should have fallen into ways of self, of flesh, of the world', he wondered, 'to play at cards, dice, revel, dance?'[1] Yet these were common pastimes in the Lord Protector's court. The moral vision of the Puritan revolution remained unfulfilled, unachievable in this world, though the polity remained stable and its institutions largely efficient. Owen was a key barometer of the republican response to the religious and political backsliding of the Protectorate. He had accompanied the army on its invasions of Ireland and Scotland, had been appointed dean of Christ Church and vice chancellor of the University of Oxford and had acted as one of the chief architects of Cromwellian religious policy. He did not take his seat as an MP in the First Protectorate Parliament, where observers noted his links with its republican critics. His disenchantment with the direction of the government had become known among the faction of army radicals associated with General Charles Fleetwood. In 1657, Owen had drafted the petition of the army officers, which protested, successfully, against Cromwell accepting the crown, after which his friendship with Owen was never the same. Owen's criticism of the regime became more pronounced and many officers, especially of the junior ranks, agreed with his barbs.

Royalism, too, remained a running sore, for all its ineffectiveness. Ormond had swept in from Ireland to foment trouble, while the Protectorate's old adversary Henry Slingsby plotted from his prison cell in Hull, where he had lain since the abortive Royalist uprising of 1655. Slingsby tried to turn some of the junior officers in this North Sea port of strategic importance. Having reported Slingsby's efforts to the authorities, the officers went along with his conspiracy. Convinced of their sincerity, Slingsby offered one of them a commission purported to bear the signature of Charles Stuart. The entrapped conspirator was charged with treason at Westminster Hall, where he claimed that officers had 'trepanned' [sic] him and that the conspiracy was nothing more than a harmless joke. If it was, the humour was lost on his opponents. Lord Fauconberg, his parliamentarian nephew, husband of Cromwell's daughter Mary and the son of Slingsby's former Royalist collaborator Henry Belasyse, appealed for mercy, but in vain. Slingsby faced the inevitable on Tower Hill in June 1658.

The army remained both the foundation of the regime and its greatest threat. John Lambert, brooding in Wimbledon, did not, as Lucy Hutchinson had insisted, simply while away his hours in his horticultural haven, 'at the needle with his wife and maids'. Though he had little direct support from the army, his ambition remained undiluted (though he had resisted unlikely Royalist approaches that his daughter marry Charles Stuart or the exiled king's younger brother, James, Duke of York). Cromwell had to move against dissent in the army, when Major William Packer and five captains, all of whom were Anabaptists, expressed their anger very publicly at the betrayal of the 'Good Old Cause'. The fact that their dismissals attracted little more than grumbles among the ranks, suggests that Cromwell – through ties of shared experience and dependency – still had the loyalty of the army, which had formally declared for him on in March 1657. No one was likely to be more meaningfully supportive of the army than Cromwell and they knew it. Around the time of Packer's dismissal, he made sure he ingratiated himself with the officers he mingled with. The ploy worked. They were still brothers in arms.

The leading Commonwealthsmen, who remained rooted in republicanism, such as Vane, Ludlow and Heselrige, remained eloquent thorns in the side of the regime, and their cries of 'betrayal' were persistent. Vane's *A Healing Question*, first published in 1656, was the Ur-text of an energised radical republican opposition. It would ultimately provide the blueprint for the Protectorate's *Gotterdämmerung*.

The government's situation was not helped by the fact that the Humble Petition had allowed for the return of dissenting

MPs, especially evident during the session of Parliament that began in January 1658. The introduction of the Other House, so eagerly sought by Cromwell, had resulted in fewer regime loyalists in the Commons, which made managing the House that little bit harder. Problems were exacerbated when former allies of Cromwell, such as Oliver St John, Lord Saye and Sele and Lord Wharton, refused to take their seats in the new chamber, which looked a little too much like the old, and despised, House of Lords, and offered further fuel for the narrative of 'Betrayal'.

Cromwell's isolation was further compounded by the fact that Thurloe, his eyes and ears, was ill throughout much of 1658. Giavarina wrote: 'His Highness is not a little distressed, for he loves the minister dearly and trusts him more than anyone else, the more so because if it was necessary to find a substitute it would not be easy to come across one possessing his qualifications, who is equally devoted to his Highness.'[2] On 25 January 1658, Cromwell, himself visibly ailing, pleaded to Parliament to bring an end to the 'divisions among us', a response to a republican petition circulated in London, one symptomatic of the increasingly dangerous alliance between the Commonwealthsmen and the army radicals, who sought the return of a single-chamber Parliament – or the Purged Parliament – and the ever-greater extension of religious liberty. When it was rumoured that the petition was to be presented to Parliament by sympathetic MPs at the beginning of February, Cromwell took it upon himself to do what Cromwell did: he dissolved the Second Protectorate Parliament, and treated them to a speech of brimstone and fire, that of a man frustrated by his own indecision and dilations, who realized that time was short: 'What is like to come upon this but even present good and confusion? And if it be so, I do assign it to this cause. Your not assenting to what you did invite me by the Petition and

Advice, as that which might be the settlement of the nation.'
The regime had never been so dependent on one man.

Cromwell's health had been in decline for years. Many of his
chronic ailments harked back to military campaigns: he had
suffered dysentery in Ireland and he had been close to death
during the Dunbar campaign, when Lambert came to prominence. He had never fully recovered from the disaster of the
Western Design, the withdrawal of providence that sowed doubt
in the minds of men who until then had known none. In February 1658, his son-in-law, Robert Rich, died of consumption.
The young man's grandfather, the once mighty 2nd Earl of
Warwick, former military commander and sometime grandee
of the Providence Island Company, replied in generous grief to
Cromwell, wishing that the Protector might 'long continue an
instrument of use, a pattern of virtue, and a precedent of glory!'
    But such desires looked hopeless. Cromwell's signature began
to falter, declining from a firm and certain symbol of authority to
a shaky and uncertain scrawl. His favourite daughter, Elizabeth,
herself gravely ill with cancer, had recently lost her younger
son, Oliver. On 6 August 1658, she, too, died, and was borne
along the Thames from Hampton Court four days later to be
buried 'without funeral pomp' in the chapel of that other great
usurper with Welsh roots, Henry VII.
    There had been a few bright moments. In June 1658, the
military forces whose financing had proved such a burden on the
Protectorate captured Dunkirk, fatally weakening the Spanish
presence in Flanders. Whatever its internal wrangling, Britain
remained a considerable military power, in little danger from
invasion. The underwriters of the fledgling fiscal-military state,
the City of London, remained steadfastly loyal, attracted to the

Protector's strong and stable rule, allergic to uncertainty and all too aware of the succession crisis that might arise any day.

Jamaica, the sole compensation of the Western Design, the reckless adventure that had called a halt on the regime's providential advance, was finally showing signs of promise. Situated in the western Caribbean, in the heart of the hostile Spanish Indies – distant from Britain's other West Indian possessions – Jamaica had benefitted from Cromwell's insistence on the rapid construction of forts on the island, 'to secure the common quarters'. The unsavoury but profitable crops of sugar and tobacco were beginning to flourish; so much so that there were fears that the Spanish would make an effort to recapture their former possession, aided by those compatriots who remained in the north of the island. The governors of Jamaica, already dealing with deadly attacks from African former slaves, had taken on reinforcements throughout 1657. When two Spanish squadrons landed at Ocho Rios on the island's northern coast in October 1657, numbering around 1,000 men in total, the defenders were willing to 'sell their lives as dear as they can'. The British soldiers had learnt how to fight in tropical conditions the hard way. A 'stiff dispute' took place around a Spanish stockade on the north-west coast, with supply lines to Cuba. More than 100 Spanish defenders were killed and their ammunition and supplies fell into the hands of the British, who lost just four men in the encounter. News of the successful defence of the island reached Cromwell in April 1658.

The following month, a more substantial force of Spanish infantry landed at Rio Novo with the intention of building a garrison, the first step to taking back the island. A confident British marine unit under the command of Governor Edward D'Oyley, with 'exceeding joy', found the Spanish fort half built and rushed in: no military action, it was reported, had been 'carried on with as much cheerfulness and sweet carriage as this was'.[3] Around 300 Spaniards were killed and those who fled were left to perish in the wilderness.

Following the rout of the Spanish at Rio Novo in June, a Captain Barry had left Jamaica for London, bearing ten captured ensigns and the standard of the King of Spain. The failed assault on Hispaniola, the source of so much anxiety and doubt, was in the process of healing. But Cromwell would not hear of the latest success. Captain Barry arrived too late for the Protector to hear good news from the Caribbean.

Cromwell's military glory was encapsulated above all in one date: 3 September. On that day in 1650, he and Lambert had experienced the miracle of Dunbar. On the same day a year later, Charles Stuart's hopes for his kingdom would be put to the sword at Worcester, after which royal exile followed. On 3 September 1658, to the accompaniment of a ferocious storm and lashing rain, Oliver Cromwell died, 'riven by gout and other distempers' including a decades-long battle with Fenland malaria, crushed by the agonizing death of his daughter Elizabeth. One of his final visitors at Hampton Court, on 20 August 1658 according to Carlyle, had been the Quaker George Fox, urging tolerance towards his co-religionists. Seeing Cromwell in the saddle, he sensed a 'waft of death got forth against him; and when I came to him he looked like a dead man'. Those around him were fearful of what was to come, in a country neither healed nor settled. 'If no settlement be made in his life time', they asked, 'can we be secure from the lust of ambitious men?'

17

Succession

I would be willing to live to be further serviceable to God and His people, but my work is done.

OLIVER CROMWELL

WHEN CROMWELL DIED, his eldest son became head of state, while his younger son ruled Ireland and his son-in-law and brother-in-law held joint command of the army. The succession arrangements left much to be desired, the accession of Richard Cromwell to the role of Lord Protector being announced only in the wake of his father's death. As with Elizabeth I, his hero and exemplar, it may have been the fear of confronting his own mortality that prevented Cromwell from making preparations for an adequate succession. Was it, like his rejection of the title of king, a fear of the sinful pursuit of family ambition? Did his constant dialogues with God offer no solutions? Did Cromwell even nominate Richard?

On 30 August 1658, just days before Cromwell's death, Thurloe 'had some discourse' about the succession. At this point, presumably, the name of Richard Cromwell was mentioned – 'but his [Cromwell's] illness disenabled him to conclude it fully'. When his condition improved the following day, there were again hopes for a formal nomination, but Cromwell continued, as he had done all his life, to seek guidance from God, believing he would provide: 'God's cause did breathe in him to the very last', it was reported. On the eve of his death, Cromwell had accepted his mortality, and the proximity of his end: 'I would be willing to live to be further serviceable to God and His people, but my work is done.'[1] Unfortunately for his country, it was left undone. The succession question remained, and the Protector's answer was a tentative one. A final attempt was made to obtain a formal nomination of his successor. Thurloe, with whom he had the brief discussion on 30 August, asked him to affirm his decision, to which he assented. Thurloe believed that to mean that Richard was the nominated successor and the eleven members of the Council present agreed. Whether they were acting on the deathbed wishes of Cromwell or their own briefly considered judgement is unknown.

It has been suggested that Fleetwood – a man Cromwell had described as a 'milksop' in the months before his death – was his preference to succeed him, though in the absence of evidence, that can only be conjecture. Others have wondered why the succession did not go to Henry, Cromwell's younger but more experienced and politically astute son. The answer lies in opposition from the two sides who were competing for Cromwell's ear and for his political legacy: the army simply did not trust Henry, whose great achievement in Ireland was a marriage of the interests of the Protectorate and the Presbyterian gentry, which they feared might form a template for the wider realm. On the other hand, those civilians around Broghill, who had campaigned for a more monarchical settlement, strongly favoured the principle of hereditary succession, which meant they must deny Henry in favour of Richard, whatever the advantage in qualities the former had over his elder brother.

Richard Cromwell was the worst prepared adult head of state in British history. He had never been mentored in politics by his father, nor, more importantly, had he been encouraged to develop links with the army, the foundation of the regime. One of the most significant, dominant and extraordinary figures in British political and military history had been replaced by an ingénu who, since the end of the Civil Wars and for almost the entirety of his father's rule, had lived on a country estate in Hampshire, happily married by all accounts to his wife, Dorothy, sharing the settled and conservative world view of the Presbyterian squires whose company he kept. Other than an appointment to the Council of State at the end of 1657, he had no experience of politics at all.

Richard had made a couple of public outings to the West Country in June 1658, which may or may not have been attempts to meet 'his people' in anticipation of his assumption of power. He was comfortable with the regime's civilian faction, though he never impressed or ingratiated himself with the army radicals; Desborough in particular, despite his familial links, despised him. Entirely unprepared for the role of Protector, he now faced a situation that even his formidable father had found challenging. It did not bode well. But the name of Cromwell gave him some purchase and legitimacy, in his early days as Protector at least, and he benefitted from a panegyric by Andrew Marvell, who wrote, perhaps more in hope than anticipation:

He, as his father, long was kept from sight
In private, to be visited by better light:
But open'd once, what splendour doth he throw![2]

Despite Richard's obvious lack of preparedness – perhaps in

part because of it, with factions competing for influence – welcome addresses of loyalty arrived from the army and the City of London, both foundations of the state. Royalists, many in exile, observing the nominally successful transition through a glass darkly, despaired at the new Protector's accession. Clarendon talked of the 'hopeless', 'desperate' state of the king and his supporters when they heard of Richard's accession, their 'utmost despair' confirmed. Supporters of a broader religious settlement, such as Richard Baxter, were delighted, as his tract *Holy Commonwealth*, which he later repudiated in order to make peace with the restored king, made clear. But trouble did not take long to arrive.

Two weeks after Oliver Cromwell's death, on 18 September 1658, Fleetwood published an address, signed by around 200 officers, mapping out a more radical path for the regime. As Fauconberg, a Cromwellian loyalist of the civilian party pointed out, such machinations would 'prove a serpent', a harbinger of things to come. Fleetwood's action had opened the doors to vigorous debate among the junior officers at their barracks in St James, many of whom were Independents of radical bent, reminiscent of those who had gathered at Putney more than a decade before. There were many new faces among the junior officers, but the old ideas ran deep and the times were ripe for radicals. Never well paid at the best of times, the junior officers' wages were in arrears and even when they had money in their pockets it did not go far, as bread prices rose to a decade-long high thanks to poor harvests.

By October, they were demanding that Fleetwood should replace Richard as the commander of the army, a demand the novice Protector could not possibly concede to, though he did, in an act of conciliation, promote Fleetwood to lieutenant general. Richard, under pressure, played his hand surprisingly well: he retained overall command of the army and kept a monopoly on commissioning new officers, whose pay he increased, making allies of senior army figures such as Whalley and Goffe. He cultivated General George Monck, commander in Scotland – an able man, adept at sensing where power lay – as well as the all-important Thurloe. His younger brother's hold over Ireland was further cemented when he made him lord lieutenant.

The festering resentment among the junior ranks was aggravated by the monarchical ostentation in evidence at Cromwell's funeral held in late November, which took place 'with extraordinary pomp and magnificence', following the 'forms observed at the burial of King James' though 'much greater'. Poor Charles, of course, had been buried in a private ceremony at the cost of £500. Cromwell's lying-in-state took place in Somerset House, England's first major classical building, the creation of another Protector, Edward Seymour, Duke of Somerset, during the minority of Edward VI. Cromwell's coffin, according to an English royal tradition that began with Edward II (and ended with the quasi-king Oliver), was laid beneath a bed upon which an effigy of the dead ruler was placed: it was literally the body politic, which stressed continuity from one ruler to another, except that now the transition was ambiguous. Had Cromwell taken the office of king, with its underlying connotation that the monarch never dies but is transformed into another body, such ambiguities would have receded. The office of Lord Protector, novel in its seventeenth-century form, was, however, untested as a title for transfer. The test would come soon enough.

At the feet of Cromwell's effigy as it lay in state, surrounded by eight pillars, decorated with 'trophies of military honour, carved and gilt', was an inscription of his life and achievements.

OLIVER CROMWELL

Lord Protector of England, Scotland, and Ireland.
Born at Huntingdon,
Of the name Williams, of Glamorgan, and by
King Henry VIII changed into Cromwell;
Was educated in Cambridge, afterwards of Lincoln's Inn.
At the beginning of the Wars, Captain of a Troop of Horse
raised at his won charge;
And by the Parliament made Commander-in-Chief.
He reduced Ireland and South Wales;
Overthrew Duke Hamilton's Army, the Kirk's Army,
at Dunbar;
Reduced all Scotland;
Defeated Charles Stuart's Army at Worcester.
He had two Sons,
Lord Richard, Protector in his Father's room;
Lord Henry, now Lord Deputy in Ireland;
And four Daughters,
Lady Bridget, first married Lord Ireton, afterwards
Lieutenant-General Fleetwood;
Lady Elizabeth, married Lord Claypole;
Lady Mary, married Lord Viscount Fauconberg;
Lady Frances, married to the Hon. Robert Rich,
Grand-child to the Rt. Hon. The Earl of Warwick.
He was declared Lord Protector of England, Scotland, and
Ireland, Dec. 16, 1653.
Died Sept. 3, 1658, after fourteen days sickness, of an ague,
with great assurance and serenity of mind,
Peaceably in his bed.
Natus, Apr. 25, 1599.
Dunkirk, in Flanders, surrendered to him, June 20, 1658.

It was a succinct précis of his rule; there was no mention of the Western Design in the obsequies.

Cromwell, rather in keeping with his elusive nature, was absent from his own state funeral. On 11 November, Lady Hobart wrote: 'My Lord Protector's body was buried last night at one o'clock very privately and 'tis thought there will be no show at all.' Cromwell had been buried quietly in a vault in Henry VII's chapel, Westminster Abbey, according to the practices ordained by *The Directory for Public Worship* of March 1645. As that austere manual prescribed: 'praying, reading and singing, both in going to and at the grave... are in no way beneficial to the dead and have proved many ways hurtful to the living. Therefore let all such things be laid aside.'

It being England, however, a fudge was available, which allowed Cromwell a grand and very unpuritanical state funeral, complete with ostentatious regal effigies. The *Directory*, with an eye on the Puritan grandees who passed it, noted that ritual minimalism did not 'extend to deny civil respects or differences at the burial suitable to the rank and condition of the party deceased while he was still living'. And so a funeral fit for a king was deemed suitable for the Protector, who was not around, in any way, to object. Even in death, puritanism and hypocrisy were natural partners. Richard, too, was absent. According to royal tradition, the new ruler remains hidden until the new ruler is interred, officially. Fleetwood was chief mourner, flanked by viscounts Lisle and Fauconberg, while a riderless horse – Cromwell's – followed, dressed in 'rich trappings' of velvet, 'adorned with white, red and yellow plumes of feathers'. Thousands lined the London streets, though Edward Burrough, the republican, wondered in disgust if Cromwell would have approved:

I knew the man when he was living and had the knowledge of

his spirit and I was persuaded if it had been asked him in his lifetime if such work be acted about him... I say I believe he would have denied it and said it shall not be thus with me when I am dead.[3]

18

Full Circle ·

*Why should they not promise themselves more
advantages from thence, than from anything else
that is likely to fall out?*

EDWARD HYDE

THE AGE-OLD ISSUE of finance forced Richard Cromwell, on the advice of his Council, to call a Parliament, the Protectorate's Third, at the end of 1658. It met for the first time on 27 January 1659.

The Third Protectorate Parliament was summoned on the basis of the electoral system that had been in place before the Instrument of Government of 1653, which meant that a majority of MPs, and there were now 549 of them, represented the more conservative boroughs. Despite this nod to gentry opinion by a Protector and Council ever eager for money, the Parliament became a forum for the fiercer opponents of the regime, centred on the eloquent Vane, to voice their anger and resentments. The atmosphere was febrile; though the Parliament sat for just three months, it ran through as many Speakers.

On 18 February, the regime's republican opponents presented a petition to Parliament explicitly linking their cause to that of the army (though not entirely successfully), with the aim of reducing the Protector's powers. In a chilling reprise of a phrase employed by the beleaguered Charles I, the French ambassador suggested that Richard's opponents were seeking to reduce his powers to those of a 'Doge of Venice' (Charles had feared he was merely a Duke of Venice in his Scottish realm).[1] But again, owing to his opponents' inability to convince Parliament of their cause and Richard's continued command of the army, the petition came to nothing. MPs recognized the legitimacy of the Other House, so precious to the departed Cromwell, returning some of the hereditary peerage to its ranks, and there was no hostility to the presence of the Scottish and Irish members. The Parliament seemed to realize the urgent need for money, especially in light of a developing conflict between Sweden and Denmark, in which the Dutch had become involved. The Baltic, the source of so much of the navy's materiel, had been one of Cromwell's strategic obsessions, a fact of which the new Parliament was well aware. The experienced Admiral Edward Montagu was despatched east with the blessing of MPs. By the beginning of April, the domestic situation looked settled. But then things took a turn for the worse.

The Commonwealthsmen, frustrated by Parliament, had taken their campaign out into the streets, cultivating in particular the junior officers and the rank and file, proffering Vane's *Healing Question* as a blueprint for a republican future. They pointed the finger at those who, in 1653, had brought that brief moment of 'innocency and simplicity' to an end, dismissing the Long Parliament and the hopes of a republic. They insisted that those MPs who spoke admiringly of monarchy and distrusted the army were on the wrong side of history.

In early April, in an act of some courage, Richard had convened a Council of Officers in order to confront army discontents, just as his father might have done. Fleetwood's and Desborough's efforts to neutralize the army's anger appeared to work. On 6 April, the Council of Officers petitioned Parliament to oppose Royalists and sort out their arrears of pay, but made no further demands. By then, however, the army and Parliament were locked in an unblinking, head on struggle because the revenue report, presented before Parliament on 7 April, revealed the catastrophic financial picture. The army was owed almost £900,000 in arrears, the state had debts of £2.5 million and the annual shortfall in revenue was approaching £350,000. It was unsustainable, but the MPs' response was to question the accounts rather than seek long-term solutions to a deteriorating financial situation.

They did so against a logorrhoea of pamphlets and sermons circulating the streets of London, recalling the 'virgin days' when the Good Old Cause was in the ascendant, before the betrayal of the chosen people, and pointing to a new 'confederated triumvirate of republicans, sectaries and soldiers', who claimed they would purify the nation and lead it back to the promised land.[2]

This, in turn, only inflamed the opposition to such radicals in Parliament. MPs voted down the election of two prominent former major generals, the cashiered Packer and Richard Lilburne. Fleetwood and Desborough took notice from their base at Wallingford House, fearful in particular of the renewed presence of the still ambitious John Lambert who had maintained contact with radical junior officers. However, if their aim was to tame the army's most radical elements, they failed in their attempt to do so. Army ultras were ever more fired up as MPs challenged ever more ostentatiously the army's interests. Members impeached the bullish Boteler – in the most provocative manner – for his treatment of Royalists during the rule of the major generals. The army's religious tolerance came under attack, too, when MPs called for a public fast in penance for just the kinds of religious beliefs and 'blasphemies' that many army radicals subscribed to.

Just one day after meeting his senior officers to discuss how best to deal with the crisis, on 18 April, Richard made the move that sealed his fate: he dissolved the Council of Officers and ordered its members to leave the capital. Desborough and Fleetwood publicly signalled their loyalty to Richard, but they, like he, masters of the mixed message, had lost control of events. In desperation, on 21 April some MPs moved a motion to place the army under Parliament's control. The Commonwealthsmen and the junior officers would have no part in any attempt to 'piece and mend up that cracked government'. Fleetwood and Desborough called for the dissolution of Parliament, summoned their charges back from London and engaged in a game of tug of war with Richard for their loyalty. Richard, haemorrhaging the support of his troops, was forced to dissolve the Third Protectorate Parliament on 22 April 1659. It would be the last.

Senior officers met round the clock at Wallingford House in order to seek a solution that would sustain the Protectorate, even if Richard was to be a mere figurehead. None came. The army found itself in the situation it had been in in April 1653, exactly six years before, with no alternative means of governance. More pamphlets spilled from London's printing presses, abusing the army grandees as 'parasites' and 'prostitutes' and 'apostates'.[3] Calls for the restoration of the Long Parliament grew, officers who had been cashiered by Oliver Cromwell, including Packer, returned to take up their commands again, while officers loyal to Richard were dismissed. Lambert, who had sat in the 1659 Parliament for Pontefract, and damned Richard as the 'best man', but a 'man at the best' was back on the scene. Broghill had returned home to Ireland.

The Protectorate, bitterly opposed by the army radicals, collapsed on 7 May 1659. A new/old Parliament, in the form of the Rump, was allowed to assemble again with the proviso that it replace the Council and the Upper House with a Senate, packed with soldiers who would reform the law and the church, granting religious liberty. Richard, who was offered a pension and an estate, resigned.* The rule of the Cromwells was over.

The deposed Protector had been in secret talks with the Scottish and Irish armies. But Monck, knowing the feelings of the men he commanded and preparing to play a longer game, gave his support to Parliament. Richard's brother Henry, though in command of Ireland, could not realistically lead an army to his younger brother's rescue, given the pitiful state of its arrears and its size relative to the army in England. He resigned his post.

The sectarians, republicans and army radicals who stuck the dagger into the body of the Protectorate sought a vision of England's future shared by almost no one else, certainly not the vast majority of the people, nor the men of substance, the 'natural' and preeminent figures in the regions who, sitting in Parliament, had made their opinions of the 'Saints' of the army all too clear. But nor could the Rump, its members alarmed by the renewed presence of the Fifth Monarchists and their call for a new Sanhedrin of seventy godly men – a repeat of the failed Barebones Parliament – get too close to the millenarian minority who were still fighting the struggles of the 1640s. The Rump, with just sixty-five members, soon began to further alienate the powers in the regions by purging the local militia commissioners and seeking reform among the justices of the peace. The rebellious George Booth, the Cheshire grandee whose romantic Royalist rebellion of August 1659 would be crushed by Lambert, described these actions as the work of the 'meanest and fanatic

---

* 'Tumbledown Dick' would return to live in England, after two decades in exile, residing in the Hampshire village of Hursley, dying aged 85 in 1712, the longest lived British head of state until Elizabeth II.

spirits', able to alienate both the nobility and the 'understanding commons'. It was a perception of Parliament shared by much of the nation. Richard's accession had been met with acclaim by the 'natural rulers' of the towns, boroughs and counties – the very people who had opposed the rule of the major generals – but it was the sects and the radicals who were attracted to the Rump.

The more realistic members of the Rump knew that their support base was fatally narrow and, having agreed to sit for no more than a year, set about the task of maintaining a republican government that almost no one wanted. Unsurprisingly they failed, despite the weekly meeting of a Grand Committee at which to discuss such matters. Vane suggested a senate to keep the army's proposal of a Representative of the People in check. Amid the political upheaval, feared by many to be the beginning of a second revolution, Parliament granted a pardon to James Nayler and released the Quaker agitator from prison. The West Country, that old sore, and Wales were now in the hands of Fifth Monarchists, Quakers and other sects. Justices of the Peace withdrew from office in disgust and were replaced by Quaker appointments. The Scottish army was purged by radicals. Similar events took place across the Irish Sea, where Henry Cromwell was replaced by a committee of five 'Saints' as the Baptists re-emerged as a powerful force. If they were revolutionaries, though, they were divided ones. The division, between Parliament and army, was the one that had defined the English polity since the execution of the king in 1649, and the army remained its foundation. Lambert had been restored to his command of the army at the behest of the Council of Officers and was in position when Booth, the Cheshire magnate, formerly loyal to Parliament, made that desperate attempt at a Royalist rising in August 1659, taking control of his county and parts of neighbouring Lancashire and North Wales. Lambert, who had been voted a jewel by Parliament for services rendered, sold it in order to pay his desperate troops, who crushed Booth's forces at Winnington Bridge in Cheshire on 19 August, regaining all the territory lost, including Chester, within a week.

Less romantic and more realistic Royalists sought a constructive alliance with their former enemies in anticipation of Charles's Restoration. They had made entreaties to the Monarchical Party, as they called it, which they identified with the likes of Broghill, St John, Whitelocke and Wolseley, as well as Cromwell's son-in-law John Claypole, Nathaniel Fiennes, John Glynn and Philip Jones: most of them lawyers. Henry Cromwell, whose contemporaries they were, was close to its orbit, as were Thurloe and Monck, the leader of the army in Scotland. The historian Miranda Malins has given them the name 'monarchical Cromwellians', for their loyalty to the Cromwell family and their adherence to a monarchical settlement.[4]

The moderate monarchical settlement in the form sought by the civilian faction was staring at catastrophe. On the other hand, the Royalist court in exile, which had been so despondent on the accession of Cromwell, sensed that the alienation and political chaos wrought by the army and the purged Parliament was playing into its hands. Hyde's patient pragmatism and political nous was paying off and he set his sights on the civilian Cromwellian loyalists as the conduit for the return of a real – Stuart – monarchy, believing that those who had wished to offer Cromwell the crown, in order to legitimize the regime and its succession, were ultimately open to persuasion concerning the most traditional constitutional settlement of all. Was it Richard they wished to restore to power, or Charles Stuart? Who would be most likely to succeed, who would be most viable in the long term? Corresponding with Hyde in June 1659, Lord Culpeper, the future governor of Virginia, expressed his belief that the 'Monarchical party', with its golden calf gone, would, by necessity, realize that 'they cannot possibly set up any other besides the right owner' of the crown.

Those within the band of monarchical Cromwellians saw the issue from different perspectives. While some, like Montagu and Broghill, had distanced themselves from the newly installed republican regime and its restoration of the Rump by heading to their estates, those of less substantial means, such as Whitelocke, St John and Thurloe, continued to work in the capital, dependent still on their income from legal practice for their survival.

Political actors were pulled one way and another by the conflicts of duty and personal interest in this 'age of concience'. A clear conscience was easier to arrive at when one's coffers were full and at a distance from the political centre. Hyde knew that 'conscience and repentance' were unlikely on their own to make men 'lose all they have got'. Any offers of conversion and alliance to those former enemies with whom they might collaborate in order to establish a restoration of monarchy would need to be shielded from retribution for their past deeds and loyalties.[5]

Hyde's first target for conversion had been the deposed Richard, who was contacted by the Royalist agent John Mordaunt, but Thurloe and St John, still loyal to the republican regime, stood in his way, to Hyde's evident frustration: 'Why should they not', he asked of Thurloe and St John, 'promise themselves more advantages from thence, than from anything else that is likely to fall out?'

St John, in particular, became a target for Hyde's advances: 'it should not be impossible', he thought, 'to persuade him that he might find most security and most advance by serving the

King' and re-establish 'the old foundation' he had sought for the Cromwells. Meeting again with little success, Hyde turned his attentions to the other wing of the monarchical Cromwellians, those of financial means or military clout, with a particular focus on the aristocratic Montagu, who was flattered to receive a letter from Charles Stuart himself, in which the exiled monarch promised him his 'entire affection', and requested his help towards the restoration of 'what is my right, and your Country to the happiness it hath been so long deprived of'. Montagu, Charles was informed, had been 'wholly devoted to Old Noll' (Cromwell), but was a 'perfect hater of the men that now rule'. Broghill, though he was not honoured with a personal letter from Charles, was assured by Villiers that he, too, was considered by the king to be a 'person who may be most instrumental to do him service', and that, in return, he would be assured of 'all that he can wish for from the King'.

Heads were not turned by the Royalist advances. Mazarin, in June 1659, pledged French military support to restore Richard, an act he was aware could well lead to the ruin of Richard and his allies – and of the reputation of France. Thurloe, Fiennes reported, rather like his old boss, continued to look for the guidance of a God thought lost: 'as Divine Providence had seen fit thus to dispose of the government of England, no other course remained open but submission'. Their dream of restoring Richard persisted – as Montagu told the diarist Samuel Pepys in March 1660, 'great endeavours' were still being made 'to bring in the Protector again'. But they were great in part because the chances of it happening were so unlikely, and they diminished with time, as the sense that Richard was failing to accept their advice grew. They compared him to the biblical son of Solomon, Rehoboam, who acted against the interests of his counsellors and so lost his kingdom. Monck, with the cold judgement of the military commander, believed Richard had 'forsook himself', for why else would Monck have 'failed my promise to his Father, or regard to his memory'. It was becoming clear, even to the Cromwellian loyalists, what many had always feared and most had known: that the regime had been entirely dependent upon the existence of one man, Oliver Cromwell, and, with him gone, so was its means of long-term survival. Fortunately for them, the pragmatism with which the circle around Broghill had negotiated crises before had not entirely deserted them.

The Rump, or Purged Parliament, continued its quarrel within and without the army, to no effect: each wished to control the other. On 27 October 1659, the army, which had seized power from the Rump in a coup two weeks previously, co-opted some compliant civilians, with which to form a Committee of Safety, of which Lambert was a prominent member. Their plan, if it can be called such, called for around sixty members to form a senate, after which the Rump would be readmitted until some elusive and intangible means of settlement could be agreed upon. In reality, not enough members were willing to serve. Monck, the only one of the Cromwellian officers to have been in support of the civilian interest, offered the support of his army in Scotland, whose radical officer corps he had purged, to the Rump, a decision which put him on a collision course with Lambert's army in the north.

It was with the army's coup against Parliament in October that Monck seems to have decided to take his army in Scotland across the Rubicon. Even though all of the army in England and Ireland, with the exception of neutral Hull, remained loyal to the regime, he declared for Parliament on 3 November. Using political enforcers, reminiscent of Soviet commissars, he imposed rigorous discipline on his men and sought absolute loyalty: more than 100 of his officers were cashiered, a severe loss given that Monck refused to employ Scots troops. The stakes could not be higher, nor Monck's position less precarious. It was Monck versus Lambert: the patient, hard-drinking, jovial commander with Royalist tendencies opposing the flamboyant aesthete who sought rule by an elect.

Lambert marched his men, including many Quakers, a sect Monck abhorred, north to Newcastle. By 15 November, it appeared that the two armies had come to some sort of fragile truce. But the advantage was moving towards Monck. No campaign could be waged in the Borders in winter. The Committee of Safety, in London, engaged with Monck's representatives, were holding Lambert's forces back. His troops were ill shod – some were shoeless – poorly paid and unwilling to attack their comrades who, because of the high tax burden in Scotland, were relatively well paid.

In London the situation was dire. Money was leaving the City, apprentices rioted, a republican plot to seize the Tower was revealed. Fleetwood's army, faced with chaos, was falling apart. Whitelocke advised him to throw in his lot with the king before Monck did. After all, if the king was restored by Monck, would his powers be limited in any way and by whom? Whitelocke, terrified of the implications of a restored Stuart with unrestricted powers, called on Fleetwood to force the king to comply by military means. Broghill spoke of his hope that the 'precious rights' his generation had fought for would be upheld. Fleetwood, having lost control of his men, resigned his authority as commander to the Speaker on Christmas Eve. The Speaker led the Rump's clandestine return, knowing elections would be needed to boost its numbers, despite the promise to dissolve itself by 7 May 1659. Heselrige, with one last throw of the dice, seized Portsmouth with a force of republicans on 3 December 1659. Its garrison mutinied and declared for Parliament. Ten days later the fleet in the Downs signalled its support for the Rump, as did the army in Ireland.

With military authority ceded by Fleetwood and the Council of Officers dissolved, Monck assembled his troops in Scotland, near Coldstream on the River Tweed, his Rubicon, and marched them down the 335 miles to London. Lambert had tried to gather his men to march south in one desperate last act of republican defiance, but, half-starving, they abandoned him. Lambert's former commander, Thomas Fairfax, whom both sides had long sought to turn, led his Yorkshire forces in support of Parliament. Lambert finally submitted, all but abandoned by his troops, having been offered indemnity. He was ordered to retire back to his native county of Yorkshire, but a call for his arrest was made when he was accused of provoking mutiny in London. He addressed the Council of State on 5 March 1660, when he asked permission to serve in the Swedish army. Unable to meet the security, set at a staggering £20,000, he was sent to the Tower, from where he escaped on 10 April. There was still a magic to his name and to that of Edgehill, site of the first great battle of the Civil Wars, where, as the return of the king became all but certain, he assembled six troops of horse for one last defiant stand against the inevitable. He was taken prisoner when his weary troops were confronted near Daventry by a small parliamentary force on 22 April. He was forty-one and would remain in captivity for the rest of his life: the 'army's darling', one of the greatest military commanders in British history, and one of its most tragic figures.

Those soldiers left in the capital ignored their commanders and those MPs excluded by the coup were invited to return to the benches of the Purged Parliament. Following Monck's entry into the capital and the return of those MPs long excluded, many of the monarchical Cromwellians had returned to public life. Thurloe reclaimed his role as secretary of state, Montagu, an MP again, was appointed to the Council of State and a general at sea. Broghill returned as an MP and was appointed commissioner for Ireland. Montagu remained the principal target of the Royalists who sensed the moment. It appears he had distanced himself from Thurloe and St John, who remained suspicious of royalism, in part because they were the generation who had given all to Cromwell's regime, while others were less rooted. Montagu, it was reported, would rather see the nation settled, even if 'my whole family suffer by it, as I know I shall'. But Charles had reassured him, in secret correspondence, that he looked upon Montagu as 'a person to be rewarded'. By April 1660, he had committed to Charles as a 'dutiful and faithful servant'. Having confessed to Pepys his frequent correspondence with the king and his party, he publicly declared for his restoration on 3 May. Others continued to leave their options open, while St John's deep dislike of the Stuarts saw him abandon preferment for principle.

Charles Stuart was restored to the throne on 8 May 1660 with no conditions attached: the Convention Parliament, convened at the instigation of Monck in late April 1660, had proclaimed him king. It was felt that he would not last long, as Montagu, the most well-disposed towards him of the monarchical Cromwellians, observed, unless he behaved 'very soberly and well'. Cromwell had judged Charles Stuart 'so damnably debauched, he would undo us all', though in a more comforting analysis of the new king's ambitions, the Protector believed that the best approach was to 'Give him a shoulder of mutton and a whore, that's all he came for.' Many convinced themselves that Charles's

Declaration of Breda, which he had published on 4 April in anticipation of his return, offered enough assurances on property rights and to those 'tender consciences' who feared a restrictive and narrow religious settlement. However, that is exactly what transpired, with the brutal imposition of the Clarendon Code, which required public officials to take Anglican communion (Catholics and nonconformists were thus effectively barred from public life) and made use of the Prayer Book compulsory in church services. The division between 'Church' and 'Chapel' would become perhaps the most obvious legacy of the Civil Wars to persist in British life.

Cromwell's forced union of the British Isles came to an end, to the rejoicing of many Scots, though weakening Britain as a significant European power, a status it would not regain for half a century. The Cromwellian conquest of Ireland created conditions that would prove permanent: the Irish Catholic elite lost all in the permanent transfer of power and land to Protestant newcomers. The hostility to Cromwell, which has marked Irish political mythology for generations and sees no sign of receding, has parallels in Britain, too, where Cromwell remains, at the least, a divisive figure. This is despite his well-documented personal tolerance, a genuine desire for religious liberty and his remarkable, though perhaps overrated military skills: both Fairfax and Lambert can make claims to superior strategic acumen. Perhaps what is least understood about Cromwell is his conservatism, which often dragged him into conflict with his more radical supporters. Above all, it was Charles I, his head turned by the new ideology of European absolutism, who was the innovator. Cromwell preferred to hold to some form of the Ancient Constitution – though he bowed to 'cruel necessity' on more than one occasion, for none of his parliaments came close to his ideal. Nor, ultimately, did his nation, which he had hoped was rather more saintly than it actually was. In that, he has a more recent historical parallel.

Consider this: an East Anglian, nonconformist, philosemite, suspicious of, though not fundamentally opposed to, monarchy; a unionist uncomprehending of Ireland, a courageous advocate of military action, who left considerable problems of succession to those who came after them? It appears that Margaret Thatcher was cut from similar cloth to the Protector. And it may take just as long for a statue near Parliament to be raised to her.

On 29 May 1660, Charles Stuart's thirtieth birthday, he entered London as King Charles II, the capital 'strewn with flowers, the bells ringing, the streets hung with tapestry, fountains running with wine'. From then on, the day would be celebrated as Oak Apple Day, a reference to Charles' deliverance in the aftermath of the Battle of Worcester nine years before, when he hid in the boughs of an oak tree in the grounds of Boscobel House. Celebrations were suitably ribald, casting off the Puritan yoke of 'that Phanatic Crew' with a chorus courtesy of Rochester's 'Satyr on Charles II':

> Foe breeding the best cunts in Christendom,
> There reigns, and oh! Long may he reign and thrive,
> The easiest King and best-bred man alive.

Such sentiments were never uttered of Cromwell.[6]

On his journey up the Thames the new king was accompanied by William Penn, who along with Robert Venables, had been joint commander of the Western Design, in which divine providence had deserted the regime for the first time. Its failure, and Penn's imprisonment in the Tower on his return, was greeted with glee by Royalists. On his release, in disgrace, Penn had withdrawn to his estates in County Cork, where his son, also William, converted to Quakerism and began the journey that would see him found the American state of Pennsylvania. His father, in favour with the king, became a commissioner of the navy, in which role he became a friend of Pepys and a regular entrant into the diaries, where he was depicted as 'a merry fellow' at first, only to become a 'very villain', a private trajectory at odds with his public life. He died, a substantial figure, in Walthamstow on 24 February 1669.[7]

Another figure accepted the kind hand of providence at the Restoration: Daniel O'Neill, from the time he left the Tower of his own volition, disguised as a woman, had endured much and was to achieve more. The bravest and most brilliant of Charles's Royalist agents had fought for the king's cause for more than a decade. There were no questions over his loyalty. Though he did not enter the Lords – as an O'Neill, he was aristocrat enough – he gathered sinecures almost at will: he had interests in mining, an activity that would be the bedrock of Britain's Industrial Revolution; he gained a monopoly on the country's gunpowder manufacture and distribution; he became the warden of St James's Park and the commissioner for building in London. All helped to make him one of the richest men in the restored realm of a monarch he had served at considerable hardship and danger for so long and in such difficult circumstances, enjoying the fruits provided by a God satisfied with what he saw. O'Neill died in Whitehall, close to the centre of English political power, where a king had been killed, where a new regime of uncertain foundation and full of contradictions had lost the will of God, and where a king was now restored, on 24 October 1664.[8]

General Monck, soon to become the Duke of Albemarle, would be rewarded by the king with vast territories in the Carolinas, in the north of England and ample London estates, which bear his adopted name to this day. Monck had a younger cousin, who was less fortunate, at least at first. Thomas Modyford, who had been a slightly more cautious advocate of a Western Design on the Caribbean than Thomas Gage, had 'abhorred and abjured the interests of the Stuarts' in order to find favour with Cromwell despite a Royalist past. It didn't serve him well at the Restoration, when he was charged with high treason. Monck intervened on behalf of his cousin, who benefitted from His Majesty's Gracious Act of Oblivion. It helped, too, that Monck was head of the king's Committee for Foreign Plantations and able to put Modyford forward for the governorship of Jamaica, not necessarily at that time a dream ticket, but an improvement on a traitor's death. With his experience of and contacts in Barbados and an eye still on the conquest of the Mosquito Coast, in 1664 Modyford headed for Jamaica accompanied by 800 Barbados hands. His wife and his substantial household would join them a few months later. From there he waged a private war on the Dutch, who were officially at war with England from 1665, as well as with the Spanish, in breach of the policy of Monck's Committee. He hoped, as he expressed it in a letter to his king that, like 'the wise Romans', they would 'trust him that was on the place' to come to the right decisions, which cannot always 'be imagined by much wiser men at so great a distance'.[9] Jamaica, which was gained when providence was lost, would become within a century, by the means of men such as Modyford, the profane powerhouse of an industry built on slavery to satisfy a craving for sweetness on the other side of the Atlantic, a place of unimaginable suffering thousands of miles from the island where slaves could not exist, where the very air one breathed blessed freedom upon the individual. A project born of the desire for liberty and framed by an anxious need to fulfil God's providence, would produce misery beyond belief.

Notes

Prologue

1. Philip Bell writing to Nathaniel Rich, March 1629, in Vernon A. Ives (ed.), *The Rich Papers: Letters from Bermuda, 1615–1646* (Toronto, 1984), pp. 319–21, quoted in Karen Ordahl Kupperman, *Providence Island 1630–1641: The Other Puritan Colony* (Cambridge, 1993).
2. For an outstanding account of the role played by Puritan grandees in the outbreak of the Civil Wars see John Adamson, *The Noble Revolt: The Overthrow of Charles I* (London, 2007).
3. Calendar of State Papers: Colonial Series, vol. 1, p. 124.
4. Arthur Young, journal entry for July 30 1787, *Travels* (London, 1794), vol. 1, p. 51.
5. See the discussion on the Second Debate on Policy concerning the Western Design analysed in Timothy Venning, *Cromwellian Foreign Policy* (New York, 1995), pp. 58–61).
6. Lord Brooke, *The Nature of Truth* (London, 1640).
7. Discussed in Kupperman, p. 178.
8. Providence Island Council correspondence to Governor Philip Bell, Kupperman, p. 65.
9. Andrew Foster 'The Clerical Estate Revitalised', in Kenneth Fincham (ed.) *The Early Stuart Church, 1603–1642* (London, 1993), p. 146.
10. Rudyerd writing to Governor Philip Bell 1633, quoted in Kupperman, 'A Puritan Colony in the Tropics: Providence Island, 1630–1641', in Ralph Bennett (ed.), *Settlements in the Americas: Cross-Cultural Perspectives* (Plainsboro, NJ, 1993), p. 240.
11. British Library, Sloane Manuscript 758.
12. John Winthrop, *A Journal of the transactions and occurrences in the Settlement of Massachusetts, and the other New England Colonies, from the year 1630 to 1644* (London, 1790), p. 202.
13. William H. Clark, *The History of Winthrop, Massachusetts 1630–1952* (Winthrop, MA, 1952), p. 78.

14. Description dated 17 June 1640, analysed in Alison Games, 'The Sanctuarye of our Rebell Negroes: The Atlantic Context of Local Resistance on Providence Island 1630–41', in *Slavery and Abolition*, 19/3 (1998), pp. 1–21.
15. Quoted in C. H. Firth (ed.), *The Clarke Papers*, vol. 3, p. 207.

Chapter One

1. Richard L. Greaves, *Glimpses of Glory: John Bunyan and English Dissent* (Stanford, 2002), p. 64.
2. Canne's polemics at this time include *The Discoverer* and *Wherein is set forth* (both 1649).
3. Letter from Cromwell to Speaker William Lenthall, 21 July 1651.
4. Cromwell's speech to the First Protectorate Parliament, 4 September 1654.
5. Cromwell's speech to the First Protectorate Parliament, 12 September 1654.
6. Declaration of the Lord-General and his Council of Officers, 22 April 1653.
7. *Mercurius Elencticus*, no. 58 (26 December 1648–2 January 1649), p. 551.
8. Speech in the Council Chamber 4 July 1653.
9. Clarendon, quoted in Austin Woolrych, *Commonwealth to Protectorate* (Oxford, 1982), p. 165.
10. Blair Worden, 'Cromwell and the Protectorate', collected in Worden, *God's Instruments: Political Conduct in the England of Oliver Cromwell* (Oxford, 2012), p. 230.
11. Cromwell's 'queries' to the Governor of Edinburgh Castle, 12 September 1650.
12. Quoted in Worden, *God's Instruments*, p. 42.
13. Charles Carlton, *Going to the Wars: The Experience of the British Civil Wars 1638–1651* (Abingdon, 2004), p. 191.
14. Edward Hyde, Earl of Clarendon, *The History of the Rebellion and Civil Wars in England*, vol. 2, p. 871.
15. Letter from Cromwell to Speaker William Lenthall, 4 September 1650.
16. W. C. Abbott, *The Writings and Speeches of Oliver Cromwell*, vol. 2 (Oxford, 1989), p. 386.
17. Clarendon Manuscript 47, folio 113.
18. P. A. Chéruel, *Lettres du Cardinal Mazarin* (Paris, 1872–1906), vol. 6, p. 464, quoted in Blair Worden, 'Oliver Cromwell and the Council',

in Patrick Little (ed.), *The Cromwellian Protectorate* (Woodbridge, 2007), p. 94.

19. Peter Gaunt, '"The Single Person's Confidants and Dependents": Oliver Cromwell and his Protectoral Councillors', in *Cromwell and the Interregnum* (Oxford, 2003), p. 96.
20. See David L. Smith, 'English Politics in the 1650s', in Michael Braddick (ed.), *The Oxford Handbook of the English Revolution* (Oxford, 2015), pp. 191–2.

Chapter Two

1. Thomas Gage, *The English-American: A New Survey of the West Indies 1648* (El Patio, Guatemala, 1928).
2. See Allen D. Boyer's entry on Gage in the *Oxford Dictionary of National Biography*.
3. See David Armitage, *The Ideological Origins of the British Empire* (Cambridge, 1996).
4. Thurloe State Papers, vol 3, p. 60.
5. 'The Secret Discovery which Don FENNYN, a Spanish Secretary, made to the Duke of Buckingham, in the year 1623, at Madrid', *Clarendon State Papers*, vol. 1, p. 14.
6. Hugh Trevor-Roper's review of Christopher Hill's *Intellectual Origins of the English Revolution in History and Theory*, 5 (1966), p. 77. I am indebted to Blair Worden for this observation.
7. Quoted in Peter Toon, *God's Statesman: The Life and Work of John Owen: Pastor, Educator, Theologian* (Eugene, OR, 1971), p. 37.
8. S. R. Gardiner, *Oliver Cromwell* (London, 1901), p. 211.

Chapter Three

1. See Firth (ed.), *Clarke Papers*, vol. 3, p. 205.
2. See Gaunt, 'The Single Person's Confidants and Dependents', pp. 107–8.
3. See Firth (ed.), *Clarke Papers*, vol. 3, pp. 207–8.
4. See John Morrill's entry on Venables and C. S. Knighton on William Penn in the *Oxford Dictionary of National Biography*.

Chapter Four

1. J. D. Davis, 'Sir George Ayscue', *Oxford Dictionary of National Biography*.
2. Carla Giardana Pestana, *The English Conquest of Jamaica: Oliver Cromwell's Bid for Empire* (Harvard, 2017), p. 48. Pestana's account of the preparations and expectations of the Hispaniola expedition is essential reading. See also her 'Imperial Designs: Cromwell's Conquest of Jamaica' in *History Today*, vol. 67, no. 5 (May 2017).
3. Hilary Beckles, 'Kalinago (Carib) Resistance to European Colonisation of the Caribbean', in *Caribbean Quarterly*, vol. 54, no. 4 (December 2008).
4. Pestana, *English Conquest of Jamaica*, p. 58.
5. *The Narrative of General Venables*, ed. C. H. Firth (London, 1900), pp. 4–5.
6. See Bernard Capp, 'William Goodson', in the *Oxford Dictionary of National Biography* and the same author's masterly *Cromwell's Navy: The Fleet and the English Revolution, 1648–1660* (Oxford, 1989).
7. Pestana, *English Conquest of Jamaica*, p. 74.
8. Ibid., pp. 78–80.
9. A constant theme of Capp's *Cromwell's Navy*.
10. Firth (ed.), *Narrative*, p. 33.
11. Pestana, *English Conquest of Jamaica*, p. 119.

Chapter Five

1. C. H. Firth, *The Last Years of the Protectorate*, vol. 1 (London, 1909), pp. 24–25.
2. Clarendon State Papers, vol. 3, pp. 135, 181; Nicholas Papers, vol. 2, p. 3.
3. Antony Fletcher, 'The Coming of War', in John Morrill (ed.), *Reactions to the English Civil War, 1642–49* (New York, London, 1982), p. 39.
4. Secretary Hatton to Nicholas, Paris, 1 November 1649, quoted in Geoffrey Smith, *Royalist Agents, Conspirators and Spies: Their Role in the British Civil Wars* (Ashgate, 2012), p. 148.
5. Clarendon, *Rebellion*, vol. 7, p. 299.
6. David Underdown, *Royalist Conspiracy in England 1649–1660* (London, 1960), p. 21.
7. Daniel Defoe, *The Memoirs of a Cavalier* (Edinburgh, 1812), p. 2.
8. Thomas Hobbes, *Leviathan* (1642–51), 21;21.

9. Calendar of State Papers Venice, 1655–6, p. 148.
10. Underdown, *Royalist Conspiracy*, pp. 157–8.
11. See Smith, *Royalist Agents*.
12. Geoffrey Smith, 'Sir Nicholas Armorer', *Oxford Dictionary of National Biography*.
13. Calendar of State Papers Venice, vol. 3, pp. 142–3.
14. Timothy Venning, 'John Thurloe', *Oxford Dictionary of National Biography*. D. L. Hobman, *Cromwell's Master Spy* (Abingdon, 1961).
15. H. N. Brailsford, in Christopher Hill (ed.), *The Levellers and the English Revolution* (Redwood City, CA, 1961), p. 492.
16. Philip Aubrey, *Mr Secretary Thurloe: Cromwell's Secretary of State, 1652–1660* (London, 1990), p. 98.
17. Alan Marshall, 'Joseph Bampfield', *Oxford Dictionary of National Biography*.
18. Smith, *Royalist Agents*, p. 176.
19. Underdown, *Royalist Conspiracy*, p. 106.
20. Ibid. pp. 93, 224–5.
21. B. J. Gibbons, 'Richard Overton', *Oxford Dictionary of National Biography*.
22. See Bernard Capp, *The Fifth Monarchy Men: A Study in Seventeenth Century English Millenarianism* (London, 2011).
23. C. H. Firth, 'Cromwell and the Insurrection of 1655', *The English Historical Review*, 3/10 (April 1888), pp. 323–50.
24. George Fox, *Autobiography* (1694), Chapter 8.

Chapter Six

1. *The Love Letters of Dorothy Osborne to Sir William Temple*, p. 172. See also, Adamson 'Oliver Cromwell and the Long Parliament' in Morrill, *Oliver Cromwell and the English Revolution* (London, 1990), p. 92.
2. James Berry, *A Cromwellian Major General* (Oxford, 1938), p. 78.
3. Smith, *Royalist Agents*, p. 190.
4. Clarendon, *Rebellion*, vol. 6, pp. 2782–3.
5. Ibid.
6. *Diary of Thomas Burton Esq.*, vol. 1, (London, 1828), p. 231.
7. Calendar of State Papers Domestic, 99.
8. Quoted in Austin Woolrych, *Penruddock's Rising 1655* (London, 1955), p. 12. This pamphlet is an outstanding and concise account of the events, as is the section devoted to it in Underdown, *Royalist Conspiracy*, to which I am indebted.

9. Christopher Durston, 'James Berry', *Oxford Dictionary of National Biography*.
10. *Mercurius Politicus*, in *The English Revolution*, vol. III, p. 396.
11. Smith, *Royalist Agents*, p. 195.
12. Alexander Lindsay, 'Abraham Cowley', *Oxford Dictionary of National Biography*.
13. The late Christopher Durston did more than anyone to help us understand the major generals and their rule. His *Cromwell's Major-Generals: Godly Government During the English Revolution* (Manchester, 2001) is essential reading.
14. Thurloe State Papers, vol. 6, p. 20. For more on John Lambert, see David Farr, *John Lambert: Parliamentary Soldier and Cromwellian Major-General 1619–1684* (Woodbridge, 2003).
15. J. P. Kenyon (ed), *The Stuart Constitution: Documents and Commentary* (Cambridge, 1969).

Chapter Seven

1. *The English Revolution III*, Newsbooks 5, vol. 10, p. 274.
2. Quoted in Venning, *Cromwellian Foreign Policy*, p. 56.
3. Edward Winslow to Thurloe, 30 March 1655, Thurloe State Papers, vol. 3, p. 325.
4. Benjamin Wright to Thurloe, 11 May 1655, ibid., p. 420.
5. Cromwell to Fortescue, Jamaica, November 1655.
6. Calendar of State Papers Venice, vol. 30, p. 106. See also James Robertson, 'Cromwell and the Conquest of Jamaica', in *History Today* (May 2005).
7. Benjamin Woodford, *Perceptions of a Monarchy Without a King: Reactions to Oliver Cromwell's Power* (Montreal, 2013), p. 56.
8. Calendar of State Papers Venice, vol. 30, p. 71.
9. Ibid.
10. Nicholas Papers, Works of the Camden Society, 57, p. 65.
11. Thurloe State Papers, vol. 4, p. 153.
12. Cromwell to Goodson, Jamaica, October 1655.
13. Abbott, *Writings and Speeches of Oliver Cromwell*, vol. 4, p. 193.
14. Barry Coward, *The Cromwellian Protectorate* (Manchester, 2002), p. 69.
15. Worden, *God's Instruments*, p. 41.
16. Cromwell to Goodson, Jamaica, October 1655.
17. See Keith Thomas, *Religion and the Decline of Magic: Studies in Popular Beliefs in Sixteenth- and Seventeenth-Century England* (London, 1971).

For a magisterial account of Cromwell's providential world view, see 'Cromwell and the Sin of Achan', in Worden, *God's Instruments*.

18. *The Diaries of Ralph Josselin 1616–1683*, ed. Alan Macfarlane (London, 1976).

19. *Diary of Thomas Burton, Esq.*, vol. III, p. 362.

20. See the discussion of providence in Christopher Hill, *God's Englishman* (London, 1990).

Chapter Eight

1. See Durston, *Cromwell's Major-Generals*.

2. See Farr, *John Lambert* and Paul Hunneyball's groundbreaking account of the aesthetics of the Cromwellian regime in Little, *The Cromwellian Protectorate*.

3. Jerry Brotton, *The Sale of the Late King's Goods: Charles I and his Art Collection* (London, 2005).

4. Andrew Barclay, 'The Lord Protector and his Court', in Patrick Little (ed.), *Oliver Cromwell: New Perspectives* (New York, London, 2009), p. 195.

5. Maurice Ashley, *Cromwell's Generals* (London, 1954), p. 155.

6. Thurloe State Papers, vol. 4, p. 208.

7. Durston, *Cromwell's Major-Generals*, p. 129.

8. Anthony Fletcher, 'Oliver Cromwell and the Localities', in David L. Smith (ed.), *Cromwell and the Interregnum*, p. 127.

9. Calendar of State Papers, vol. 9, p. 236.

10. Durston, *Cromwell's Major-Generals*, p. 67.

11. Ibid. p. 155.

12. Derek Birley, *Sport and the Making of Britain* (Manchester, 1993), p. 87.

13. Clive Holmes, *Why Was Charles I Executed?* (London, 2006), p. 152.

14. Durston, *Cromwell's Major-Generals*, p. 160.

Chapter Nine

1. T. Howell, *A Complete Collection of State Trials* (1816), vol. V, p. 795.

2. Quoted in *British Quarterly Review*, 3 (1846), p. 90.

3. Durston, *Cromwell's Major-Generals*, p. 190.

4. Coward, *Cromwellian Protectorate*, p. 75.

5. Durston, *Cromwell's Major-Generals*, p. 8.

6. Cromwell's speech to Parliament, 17 September 1656.

7. Guibon Goddard's Journal: The Protector's Speech at opening of Parliament (17th September 1656)', in *Diary of Thomas Burton Esq: Volume 1, July 1653–April 1657*, ed. John Towill Rutt (London, 1828), pp. cxlviii–clxxiv. *British History Online* http://www.british-history.ac.uk/burton-diaries/vol1/cxlviii-clxxiv.

8. Burton, vol. 1, p. 281.

9. Barry Coward, *Oliver Cromwell* (London, 2013), p. 145.

10. Calendar of State Papers Venice, vol. 30, p. 276.

11. John Milton, *The Readie & Easie Way to Establish a Free Commonwealth* (1660), quoted in Aylmer, *Interregnum: The Quest for Settlement*, p. 199.

12. On Broghill and his circle, David L. Smith and Patrick Little, *Parliaments and Politics During the Cromwellian Protectorate* (Cambridge, 2007), is invaluable.

Chapter Ten

1. For a detailed study of Nayler, his circle and the early years of Quakerism, Leopold Damrosch, *The Sorrows of the Quaker Jesus: James Nayler and the Puritan Crackdown on the Free Spirit* (Harvard, 1996) is essential.

2. Thomas Hobbes, *Behemoth*, Dialogue 4.

3. Richard Bailey, *New Light on George Fox and Early Quakerism* (Lampeter, 1992), p. 7.

4. Damrosch, *Quaker Jesus*, p. 31.

5. George Fox, *The Works of George Fox*, vol. 2 (New York, 1831), p. 89.

6. Ibid. p. 103.

7. Thomas Fuller, *Church History of Great Britain*, vol. 3 (1665).

8. Rosemary Moore, *Light in their Consciences: the Early Quakers in Britain 1646–1666* (Philadephia, PA, 2000), p. 21.

9. Damrosch, *Quaker Jesus*, p. 66.

10. Henry Reece, *The Army in Cromwellian England 1649–1660* (Oxford, 2013), pp. 133–7.

11. Calendar of State Papers Venice, vol. 30, p. 114.

12. Bernard Capp, *England's Culture Wars: Puritan Reformation and its Enemies in the Interregnum, 1649–1660* (Oxford, 2012), p. 130.

13. Damrosch, *Quaker Jesus*, p. 160.

14. Albert DeWitt Mott, *The Phenomenon of Ranterism in the Puritan*

Revolution: A Historical Study in the Religion of the Spirit, 1640–1660 (Berkeley, CA, 1956), p. 288.

15. Carole Dale Spencer, 'The Man who "Set Himself as a Sign": James Nayler's Incarnational Theology', in Stephen W. Angell and Pink Dandelion (eds), *Early Quakers and their Theological Thought 1647–1723* (Cambridge, 2015).

16. Damrosch, *Quaker Jesus*, p. 137.

17. Ibid. pp. 230–31.

18. 'Of the Erroneous Opinions of the Quakers...', collected in Thomas D. Hamm (ed.), *Quaker Writings: An Anthology* (London, 2010).

Chapter Eleven

1. 'The Bristol Episode', Quaker Heritage Press, 28. www.qhpress.org/texts/nayler/bristol.html.

2. Diary of Thomas Burton, 5 December 1656. Burton diaries are the primary source for the Nayler trial and punishment.

3. Cromwell's speech to the Second Protectorate Parliament, 17 September 1656.

4. Diary of Thomas Burton, 29 May 1657.

5. Cromwell, 'To His Eminency Cardinal Mazarin', 26 December 1656.

6. Damrosch, *Quaker Jesus*, p. 195.

7. Diary of Thomas Burton, 5 December 1656.

8. Ibid., 6 December 1656.

9. Ibid., 11 December 1656.

10. Ibid., 6 December 1656.

11. Ibid., 8 December 1656.

12. Ibid.

13. Ibid., 23 December 1656.

14. Ibid., 11 December 1656.

15. Ibid., 17 December 1656.

16. Damrosch, *Quaker Jesus*, p. 222 and Chapter 4.

17. J. F. Nicholls and J. Taylor, *Bristol Past and Present* (1882).

18. Diary of Thomas Burton, 26 December 1656.

Chapter Twelve

1. Diary of Thomas Burton, 25 December 1656.

2. Ibid.
3. Denton to Sir Ralph Verney, 19 Dec 1656, Buckinghamshire Record Office.
4. Durston, *Cromwell's Major-Generals*, p. 210.
5. Ibid. p. 119.
6. Ibid. p. 211.
7. Farr, *John Lambert*, p. 3.
8. See Fletcher, *Cromwell and the Interregnum*, pp. 135–6.
9. See C. H. First, 'John Claypole', *Oxford Dictionary of National Biography*.
10. Diary of Thomas Burton, 7 January 1657.

Chapter Thirteen

1. Diary of Thomas Burton, 19 January 1657.
2. Discussed in Ann Hughes, *Gender and the English Revolution* (London, 2012), p. 114.
3. Discussed in the introduction to D. E. Kennedy, *The English Revolution 1642–1649* (London, 2000).
4. David Wootton (ed.), *Divine Right and Democracy: An Anthology of Political Writing in Stuart England* (Cambridge, MA, 2003), p. 306.
5. Antonia Southern, *Forlorn Hope: Soldier Radicals of the Seventeenth Century* (Abingdon, 2001), p. 137.
6. Underdown, *Royalist Conspiracy*, p. 180.
7. C. H. Firth, *The Last Years of the Protectorate* (London, 1909, 2 vols), vol. 1, p. 39.
8. Underdown, *Royalist Conspiracy*, p. 180.
9. Alan Marshall, 'Killing No Murder', *History Today*, 53/2 (February 2003).
10. Diary of Thomas Burton, 19 January 1657.
11. Firth, *The Last Years of the Protectorate*, vol. 1, p. 126.

Chapter Fourteen

1. Roy Sherwood, *Oliver Cromwell: King in All But Name, 1653–1658* (Stroud, 1997), p. 71.
2. For a fascinating discussion of the wider scenario, see Jonathan Fitzgibbons, 'Hereditary Succession and the Cromwellian Protec-

torate: The Offer of the Crown Reconsidered', *The English Historical Review*, vol. 128, no. 354.

3.   See Christopher Durston, 'The Fall of Cromwell's Major-Generals', *The English Historical Review*, 113/450.

4.   Diary of Thomas Burton, 7 March 1657.

5.   Calendar of State Papers Venice, 12 January 1657.

6.   Firth, *The Last Years of the Protectorate*, vol. 1, p. 65.

7.   Clarendon Manuscript 53, folio 111v.

8.   Calendar of State Papers Venice, vol. 30, pp. 294–6.

Chapter Fifteen

1.   Little (ed.), *Oliver Cromwell: New Perspectives*, pp. 224–5.

2.   Cromwell's speech to Parliament, 4 September 1654.

3.   Calendar of State Papers Venice, 9 March 1657.

4.   Discussed by David L. Smith in Little (ed.), *Cromwellian Protectorate*, pp. 22–3.

5.   J. P. Kenyon, *The Stuart Constitution*, p. 351.

6.   Ivan Roots (ed.), *Speeches of Oliver Cromwell* (London, 1989), p. 116.

7.   Ibid. pp. 128–38.

8.   Firth, *The Last Years of the Protectorate*, vol. 1, p. 150.

9.   Hobbes, *Behemoth*, Dialogue IV, p. 191.

10.   See Blair Worden, 'Toleration and the Protectorate', in *God's Instruments*, especially pp. 76–85.

Chapter Sixteen

1.   Crawford Gribben, *John Owen and English Puritanism: Experiences of Defeat* (Oxford, 2016), p. 178.

2.   Woodford, *Perceptions of a Monarchy Without a King*, p. 44.

3.   Calendar of State Papers Colonial, vol. 9, p. 123.

Chapter Seventeen

1.   D. L. Hobman, *Cromwell's Master Spy: A Study of John Thurloe* (London, 1961), p. 137.

2.   Andrew Marvell, 'A Poem Upon the Death of O.C.'

3.   Edward Burrough, 'A Testimony Against a Great Idolatory'. The

best description and analysis of Cromwell's funeral is in Sherwood, *King in All But Name*, pp. 155–64.

Chapter Eighteen

1. Adamson, *Noble Revolt*, p. 5.
2. Austin Woolrych, 'Last Quests for a Settlement 1657–1660', in G. E. Aylmer, *Interregnum: The Quest for Settlement, 1646–1660* (Macmillan, 1972), p. 191.
3. Ibid. p. 192.
4. See Dr Malin's excellent 'Monarchical Cromwellians and the Restoration', in *Cromwelliana* 2016 (The Cromwell Association), series III, no. 5.
5. Keith Thomas, 'Cases of Conscience in Seventeenth-Century England', in John Morrill, Paul Slack and Daniel Woolf (eds), *Public Duty and Private Conscience in Seventeenth-Century England* (Oxford, 1993), p. 29 (to which Malins also refers – see note above).
6. Harold M. Weber, *Paper Bullets: Print and Kingship Under Charles II* (Kentucky, 1996), p. 97.
7. C. S. Knighton, 'William Penn', in the *Oxford Dictionary of National Biography*.
8. Jerrold I. Casway, 'Daniel O'Neill', in the *Oxford Dictionary of National Biography*.
9. Calendar of State Papers Colonial, vol. 43, p. 238.

Bibliography

To paraphrase the historian J. G. A. Pocock on the medieval English lawyer Sir John Fortescue, this book is intended to help the reader 'understand an age by coarsening it slightly'. Nothing would make its author happier than that it inspires the reader to search out other books on this period, which has been well served by generations of scholars, but which, for myriad reasons, looms small in public consciousness. The public, generally, has heard of Oliver Cromwell, knows that a king was killed and, possibly, that his son was restored. But little else. This book tries to fill some of those gaps for the general reader.

A synthesis, *Providence Lost* is indebted to numerous scholars and here is a brief bibliographical guide to their work on the events and personalities covered.

The best general history of the entire period, from the origins of the Civil Wars, to their course, through the Protectorate and on to the Restoration is Austin Woolrych's *Britain in Revolution 1625–1660* (Oxford, 2002), which confronts immediately the ambiguity of the term 'Revolution': is it a break or rupture with the past, or a wheel revolving, a return? Perhaps both. Also invaluable is *The Oxford Handbook of the English Revolution* (Oxford, 2015), edited by Michael Braddick, which is the most up to date survey by a stellar line-up of historians of the events, people, institutions and ideas crucial to the period. Clive Holmes' *Why Was Charles I Executed?* (London, 2006) raises and answers many more questions than that and is an accessible, authoritative survey of the period.

Perhaps the most accessible biography of the king is *Charles I: A Political Life* by Richard Cust (London, 2005), though the most entertaining work on the king is Glyn Redworth's *The Prince and the Infanta: The Cultural Politics of the Spanish Match* (London, 2003), which recounts Prince Charles and Buckingham's bizarre journey to Spain in search of a future queen. Kevin Sharpe's *The Personal Rule of Charles I* (London, 1992) is a revisionist, contentious, elegant and massive account of the dominant king.

There are a number of outstanding works on the origins of the Civil Wars: Anne Hughes, *The Causes of the English Civil War* (London, 1991); Conrad Russell, *The Causes of the English Civil War* (Oxford, 1990), which collects his Ford Lectures of 1987–88; and Russell's collection, *The Origins of the English Civil War* (London, 1973), which offers valuable essays by Penelope Corfield and Jack Elliott among others. Derek Hirst, *England in Conflict 1603–1660: Kingdom, Community, Commonwealth* (London, 1999) is a wide-ranging and incisive survey of the 'British problem' from the death of Elizabeth I to the Restoration. John Adamson, *The Noble Revolt: The Overthrow of Charles I* (London, 2007) is a masterly, beautifully written account of, among many other things, the actions of the group of Puritan nobles, who had previously sponsored the Providence Island Company.

The intellectual ideas that fed the conflict are explored in Christopher Hill, *Intellectual Origins of the English Revolution* (Oxford, 1965) and, reaching back further in time, Alan Macfarlane, *The Origins of English Individualism: The Family, Property and Social Transition* (Oxford, 1978). David Wootton's *Divine Right and Democracy: An Anthology of Political Writing in Stuart England* has a brilliantly illuminating introduction by the editor and includes the text of Edward Sexby's justification for

Cromwell's assassination, 'Killing No Murder'. The key texts of the Levellers and other radicals are examined in Philip Baker and Elliot Vernon (eds), *The Agreements of the People, the Levellers and the Constitutional Crisis of the English Revolution* (New York, 2012). John Rees, *The Levellers' Revolution* (London, 2016) is a sympathetic and compendious narrative of the phenomenon. David Como's *Radical Parliamentarians and the English Civil War* (Oxford, 2018) is a valuable recent addition. Another invaluable collection is J. P. Kenyon (ed), *The Stuart Constitution: Documents and Commentary* (Cambridge, 1969), which includes the full text of Lambert's 1653 Instrument of Government.

On the English Civil War itself, John Adamson's outstanding collection, *The English Civil War: Conflicts and Contexts, 1640–49* (London, 2009) includes the editor's brilliant, ground-breaking essay on the historiography of the conflict, and an especially valuable essay on Royalist politics by David Scott, whose *Politics and War in the Three Stuart Kingdoms, 1637–49* (London, 2004) is also essential. Michael Braddick's *God's Fury, England's Fire: A New History of the Civil Wars* (London, 2008) is vivid and exhaustive.

Life for ordinary people during the conflict has been the subject of much scholarship. The following are recommended: David Underdown, *Fire from Heaven: Life in an English Town in the Seventeenth Century* (London, 1992); David Stevenson, *King or Covenant? Voices from Civil War England* (Edinburgh, 1996); Christopher Durston, *The Family in the English Revolution* (Oxford, 1989); and the neglected but brilliant work by Peter Warner, *Bloody Marsh: A Seventeenth-Century Village in Crisis* (Oxford, 2000).

For the soldier's experience of the conflict, try Charles Carlton's *Going to the Wars: The Experience of the English Civil Wars: 1638–1651* (London, 1992); John Kenyon and Jane Ohlmeyer (eds), *The Civil Wars: A Military History of England, Scotland and Ireland 1638–1660* (Oxford, 1998); Keith Roberts, *Cromwell's War Machine: The New Model Army 1645–1660* (Barnsley, 2005); and Henry Reece's long-awaited *The Army in Cromwellian England 1649–1660* (Oxford, 2013), which is outstanding on the Bristol garrison around the time of the Nayler affair.

The collapse of the Rump and the transition to the Protectorate are examined in David Underdown, *Pride's Purge: Politics in the Puritan Revolution* (London, 1971); Blair Worden, *The Rump Parliament* (Cambridge, 1974); and Austin Woolrych, *Commonwealth to Protectorate* (Oxford, 1982).

On the Western Design, the opening chapters of Carla Gardina Pestana, *The English Conquest of Jamaica: Oliver Cromwell's Bid for Empire* (Harvard, 2017) offers a definitive account, which builds on the pioneering work by Karen Ordahl Kupperman, *Providence Island: The Other Puritan Colony, 1629–41* (Cambridge, 1993). Timothy Venning, *Cromwellian Foreign Policy* (London, 1995) offers wider context, while Tom Feiling, *The Island That Disappeared: Old Providence and the Making of the Western World* (London/Brooklyn, NJ, 2017) is an entertaining travelogue-cum-history. David Armitage, *The Ideological Origins of the British Empire* (Cambridge, 2000) is an important study of the ideology at the heart of nascent British imperialism. Thomas Gage, *The English-American: A Survey of the West Indies 1648* (various editions) still manages to transfix the reader more than three and a half centuries later.

There is no better engagement with early modern concepts of Providence than those found in Blair Worden's outstanding collection of essays *God's Instruments: Political Conduct in the England of Oliver Cromwell* (Oxford, 2012). Remarkable in every way. Also highly recommended are: Alexandra Walsham, *Providence in Early Modern England* (Oxford, 1999); William

M. Lamont, *Godly Rule: Politics and Religion, 1603–60* (London, 1969); Christopher Durston and Judith Maltby, *Religion in Revolutionary England* (Manchester, 2006); and the classic Keith Thomas, *Religion and the Decline of Magic* (London, 1971).

On the Protectorate itself, two excellent textbooks take contrasting views: Barry Coward, *The Cromwellian Protectorate* (Manchester, 2002) offers a broadly sympathetic account; Ronald Hutton, *The British Republic 1649–1660* (London, 1990) does not. All remain in the shade of C. H. Firth, *The Last Years of the Protectorate* (London, 1909, 2 vols), his continuation of S. R. Gardiner's history of the period. Patrick Little's collection, *The Cromwellian Protectorate* (Woodbridge, 2007) is essential, not least for Paul Hunneyball's ground-breaking survey of the regime's aesthetics. G. E. Aylmer's collection, *The Interregnum: The Quest for Settlement 1646–1660* (London, 1972) stands up well, especially Austin Woolrych's breathless account of the regime's demise. David L. Smith's collection, *Cromwell and the Interregnum* (Oxford, 2003) is comprehensive in its choice of essays, with a number of seminal offerings. Crudely produced it may be, but Ivan Roots' short collection, *Into Another Mould: Aspects of the Interregnum* (Exeter, 1981) is excellent on the British perspective. Patrick Little and David L. Smith, *Parliaments and Politics During the Cromwellian Protectorate* (Cambridge, 2007) is especially good on Lord Broghill and the kinglings. Jonathan Fitzgibbons, *Cromwell's House of Lords: Politics, Parliaments and Constitutional Revolution, 1642–1660* (Woodbridge, 2018) is an important contribution from a brilliant young historian of the period.

Patrick Little's *Lord Broghill and the Cromwellian Union with Ireland and Scotland* (Woodbridge, 2004) demonstrates the extraordinary influence of this key figure. F. D. Dow, *Cromwellian Scotland 1651–1660* (Edinburgh, 1979) is a definitive account, complemented by Laura A. M. Stewart, *Rethinking the Scottish Revolution: Covenanted Scotland, 1637–1651* (Oxford, 2016) and Kirsteen M. Mackenzie, *The Solemn League and Covenant of the Three Kingdoms and the Cromwellian Union, 1643–1663* (London, 2017). Whether one can have a serious debate about Cromwell and Ireland remains doubtful even after three and a half centuries, but for those willing to try, Tom Reilly, *Cromwell An Honourable Enemy: The Untold Story of the Cromwellian Invasion of Ireland* (Brandon, 1999) is, as the title suggests, sympathetic. Micheál O Siocrú, *God's Executioner: Oliver Cromwell and the Conquest of Ireland* (London, 2008) is more nuanced and convincing than its title suggests. James Scott Wheeler, *Cromwell in Ireland* (Dublin, 1999) is measured and judicious.

For the Rule of the Major-Generals one need look no further than the late Christopher Durston's *Cromwell's Major-Generals: Godly Government During the English Revolution* (Manchester, 2001). The reaction to their rule is examined in Caroline Boswell, *Disaffection and Everyday Life in Interregnum England* (Woodbridge, 2017). The antics of their opponents are surveyed in David Underdown, *Royalist Conspiracy in England 1649–1660* (London, 1960) and Geoffrey Smith, *Royalist Agents, Conspirators and Spies: Their Role in the British Civil Wars* (Abingdon, 2011). Two studies of Cromwell's spy master are less than satisfying: D. L. Hobman, *Cromwell's Master Spy: A Study of John Thurloe* (London, 1959) and Philip Aubrey, *Mr Secretary Thurloe: Cromwell's Secretary of State* (London, 1990). David Farr, *John Lambert, Parliamentary Soldier and Cromwellian Major-General, 1619–1684* (Woodbridge, 2003) is a sound, albeit brief, biography, but this enigmatic figure is surely worthy of something more.

Christopher Hill, *The World Turned Upside Down: Radical Ideas During the English Revolution* (Isleworth, 1972) is an intriguing if somewhat dated survey of the many radical sects that flourished in the 1640s and 1650s. Leo Damrosch, *The Sorrows of the Quaker Jesus: James Nayler and the Puritan Crackdown on the Free Spirit* (Harvard, MA, 1996) is the definitive account of the Nayler affair.

On Cromwell, there is much. For a brief but authoritative life, John Morrill, *Oliver Cromwell* (Oxford, 2007) captures him; it is a version of Morrill's account in the *Oxford Dictionary of National Biography*, which offers many lives of the characters in *Providence Lost*. Among other biographies, the following can be recommended: Christopher Hiil, *God's Englishman: Oliver Cromwell and the English Revolution* (London, 1970) is excellent on the Protector's providential world view; Martyn Bennett, *Oliver Cromwell* (London, 2006); J. C. Davis, *Oliver Cromwell* (London, 2001); Robert S. Paul, *Lord Protector* (London, 1955). To engage with Cromwell's powerful, slippery personality, his speeches reveal much. For an introduction, try Ivan Roots edition of *Speeches of Oliver Cromwell* (London, 1989). If one's appetite is whetted, there is always Thomas Carlyle.

There are a number of excellent collections of essays on Cromwell, including: Ivan Roots (ed), *Cromwell: A Profile* (London, 1973); Patrick Little (ed), *Cromwell: New Perspectives* (New York, London, 2009); John Morrill (ed), *Oliver Cromwell and the English Revolution* (London, 1990). Julian Whitehead, *Cromwell and his Women* (Barnsley, 2019) is a much-needed and revealing study. Roy Sherwood, *Oliver Cromwell: King in All But Name 1653–1658* (Stroud, 1997) is a superb account of the regal Cromwell, complemented by Laura Lunger Knoppers, *Constructing Cromwell: Ceremony, Portrait and Print, 1645–1661* (Cambridge, 2000). Howard Brenton's play *55 Days* (London, 2012) is an incisive and entertaining study of Cromwell's addiction to providence.

Finally, on the continuing and increasingly contentious legacy of the Protectorate, there is: Blair Worden, *Roundhead*

Reputations: The English Civil Wars and the Passions of Posterity (London, 2001), which is as brilliant as one might expect; R. C. Richardson, *The Debate on the English Revolution Revisted* (London, 1977); Jane A. Mills (ed), *Cromwell's Legacy* (Manchester, 2012); Charles W. A. Prior and Glenn Burgess (eds), *England's Wars of Religions, Revisited* (Abingdon, 2011); and Matthew Neufeld, *The Civil Wars after 1660: Public Remembering in Late Stuart England* (Woodbridge, 2013).

Acknowledgments

If this book serves any purpose, it is that it should lead the reader elsewhere, to the works of the generations of remarkable scholars who have shone light on the crises of mid seventeenth-century Britain. This book, which, in John Morrill's memorable phrase, attempts chiefly to answer 'what' rather than 'how' and 'why', is aimed humbly at those who seek an introduction to the aftermath of the Civil Wars that ravaged these islands in the 1640s, when an innovative, if unsuccessful project of 'healing and settling' a nation divided by religion and politics was attempted by a relatively small, but highly motivated, band of men, often at odds with its people, high, low and middling, led and indeed dominated by the extraordinary figure of Oliver Cromwell, perhaps the most contentious and controversial figure in British history, and certainly that of Ireland.

There are too many books – if there can be such a thing – on sixteenth-century England, and too few on the seventeenth, at least for the general reader. But there is a wealth of serious scholarship for those prepared to take the plunge – and I hope readers of *Providence Lost* will wade into these choppy, sometimes challenging waters, to emerge feeling invigorated and refreshed. Consult the Bibliography for an extensive guide to further reading.

The appeal of the Tudors, to readers and, especially, publishers, can be discussed elsewhere, as can the paucity of books for the general reader on the Protectorate; this may be the only one. I am always wary of exaggerating historical analogies – recent years have produced an unwelcome surfeit – but the resonance of the period of Cromwellian rule to Britain's current condition and its relationship to the world is not negligible: the bitter divisions between rulers and ruled, regional divides, the attempts at a comprehensive settlement, the limits of toleration, the notions of English exceptionalism, the relationship between the nations of Britain and Ireland and their role in the world.

This book is indebted to others, on whose shoulders I sit, rather ungainly and precariously. In particular I would like to thank the many early modern scholars I have been privileged to engage with over the years, especially John Adamson, Justin Champion, Jessie Childs, Leanda de Lisle, Michael Hunter, Sean Kelsey, Patrick Little, John Morrill, Sarah Mortimer, Nick Poyntz, John Rees, David Scott, Laura Stewart, Edward Vallance and Filippo de Vivo.

I offer particular thanks to those who read *Providence Lost* in proof form: Jonathan Healey, Tom Holland, Miranda Malins, and the doyen of historians of this period, Blair Worden. It is a better book for their advice, their amendments and corrections, though any mistakes, of both fact and interpretation, are mine alone.

My wife Sue has lived with this book for too long, but enjoyed the results. My son John read the prologue approvingly when I was trying to capture its tone. My parents, Elsie and Albert, made sure our house was always full of books and other stimulations, as well as love. The staff of *History Today*, of which I am honoured to be editor, offer intellect, originality and not a little humour on a daily basis. They are the best of colleagues. I am immensely grateful to my publisher Anthony Cheetham, who has been extraordinarily patient, kind and encouraging, and to Dan Jones, who commissioned the original idea that eventually evolved into *Providence Lost*. Richard Milbank has been a model editor: judicious, questioning and encouraging. It is as much his book as mine. Florence Hare crafted copy with great care. My agent, Charles Walker, took care of business with his usual efficiency and grace.

Providence Lost is dedicated to two teachers, both called Barry, who had a major impact on my life. Barry Dutton, my history teacher, offered the haven of education, erudition and aspiration at a tough Black Country comprehensive during the late 1970s. Years later, Barry Coward, a distinguished scholar of the seventeenth century, nourished and confirmed my love of the period. I am forever in their debt.

Picture credits for the plate section

1. *Portrait of Oliver Cromwell* by Roger Walker, 1649 / Public Domain
2. Oliver Cromwell's signature © Look and Learn / Bridgeman Images
3. *Cromwell at Dunbar* by Andrew Garrick Gow, 1886 / Bridgeman Images
4. *Portrait of John Lambert* after Robert Walker, c.1650 / Public Domain
5. *Portrait of Edward Hyde* after Adriaen Hanneman / Public Domain
6. *Portrait of John Thurloe*, Unknown Artist / Public Domain
7. *Whitehall Palace and St James's Park* by Hendrick Dancherts, c.1670s © Arthur Ackermann Ltd / Bridgeman Images
8. Woodcut depicting Admiral Penn leading the British naval forces in the West Indies, 1665 © British Library Board / Bridgeman Images
9. Nayler's entry into Bristol © British Library Board / Bridgeman Images
10. Gyant Desborough, an illustration from Don Juan Lamberto, 1661 / Public Domain
11. Roger Boyle, Lord Broghill, after an anonymous portrait of 1650 / Bridgeman Images

12. *Portrait of Elizabeth Claypole* by John Michael Wright, 1658 / Public Domain
13. *Portrait of George Monck* after Samuel Cooper, c.1660 / Bridgeman Images
14. *William Penn* by Peter Lely, c.1665 / Public Domain
15. *The Embleme of England's Distractions* © Look and Learn / Bridgeman Images

Index

04643082